SLENDER THREADS
A SADDLEWORTH SHAW

R. O. Shaw

Grosvenor House
Publishing Limited

The right of R. O. Shaw to be identified as the author of this
work has been asserted in accordance with Section 78
of the Copyright, Designs and Patents Act 1988

The book cover is copyright to R. O. Shaw

This book is published by
Grosvenor House Publishing Ltd
Link House
140 The Broadway, Tolworth, Surrey, KT6 7HT.
www.grosvenorhousepublishing.co.uk

A CIP record for this book
is available from the British Library

Hardback ISBN 978-1-83615-262-0

CONTENTS

Illustrations v
Maps vii
Genealogical Tables ix
Preface xx

I: WHAT'S IN A NAME? (1200-1545) 1
   1. Surnames 2
   2. Staley Manor 9
   3. The Manor del Schagh 20
   4. Ramification 28

II: SADDLEWORTH (1545-1815) 41
   5. Tenants at Will 42
   6. Even Such is Time 49
   7. The Old Order Changeth 57

III: BOARSHURST (1590-1770) 69
   8. William and Katrine 70
   9. Five Children 81
   10. The Gyles Shawe Inheritance 94
   11. Lower House 104
   12. The Last Husbandman 115
   13. The Last Shaw of Lower House 123

IV: SHAWHOUSES (1719-1798) 133
   14. William and the Hawkyards 134
   15. Shawhouses Divided 141
   16. Golburnclough 147

V: QUICK MERE (1764-1881)   153
      17. Thornlee   154
      18. A Providential Life   170

V1:   ASHTON-UNDER-LYNE (1860-1960)   187
      19. 'A Conscientious and High-Principled Man'   187
      20. Things Fall Apart   207
      21. A Modern Life   217

      Bibliography   232
      Notes   239
      Index   264

ILLUSTRATIONS

1. Cover Image: The tower of the church of St Chad, Saddleworth, in the shadow of the Pennine moors. Shaws were baptised, married and buried here for six centuries.

2. De Staveley Coat of Arms; from J P Earwaker, *East Cheshire Past and Present, Vol II*, London, 1880, p.167   12

3. Sketch of Staley Manor, reproduced in Michael Nevell and John Walker, *Lands and Lordships in Tameside*, Tameside Metropolitan Borough Council, 1998, p.10: from the original of c.1600 at Lancashire Record Office: DDX 350/21   14

4. View north-east from Lower House Boarshurst towards Saddleworth Moor, with the Pots and Pans stones and war memorial on the hill top   71

5. View northwards from Lower House to Fur Lane   97

6. View southwards from Fur Lane to Boarshurst   106

7. Signatures at the end of the will of 'William Shaw of Lowerhouse in Boarshurst within Sadleworth', 7 June 1701, proved 1702: Lancashire Record Office, WCW/Supra/C275B   119

8. Lower House, Boarshurst as seen today, constructed in periods from early 18th to early 19th centuries. Grade II Listed   129

9. Architect's drawing of Providence Chapel and School in 1855, reproduced in Hartley Bateson: *Providential Lives*, Oldham, 1957, page 19. Original sketch believed to be out of copyright   173

10. Stephen and Mary Shaw and family c.1858   180

11. Johnson Winterbottom and his wife Edna, daughter of Stephen Shaw   181

12. Hugh Winterbottom and his wife Hannah, daughter of Stephen Shaw   182

13. Ashton Town Hall, c.1900, Tameside Local Studies and Archives, t09357   188

14. Prospectus for The Zion British Training Schools, Lees, 1853, Oldham Local Studies and Archives, L32232   191

15. Centenary Medals of the Sunday School Movement, 1880   196

16. Eli Shaw, Richard Shaw and teachers, Ryecroft School c.1896   199

17. Three sons of Eli Shaw, c.1895: George, Richard and Alfred   209

18. Portrait of Charles Shaw, c.1897   217

19. The first Ashton Lacrosse Team, 1896/7   220

20. Charles and Helen Shaw with Madge and Donald, c. 1920   224

21. Manchester Grammar School, 1918   225

22. 'A Picturesque Wedding': Donald Smethurst Shaw and Marion Clarissa Shaw Hewitt, 1933   227

Source of illustrations: Shaw family records, unless otherwise stated above

MAPS

1. The Four Meres of Saddleworth   1

2. Lordsmere   41

3. Boarshurst   69

4. Shawhouses   133

5. Golburnclough   146

6. Quick Mere   153

7. Thornlee   163

Maps are drawn from: Ed. Buckley, Mike; Harrison, David; Khadem, Victor; Petford, Alan; and Widdall, John, *Mapping Saddleworth Volume II: Manuscript Maps of the Parish 1625-1822*, Saddleworth Historical Society, Uppermill, 2010

GENEALOGICAL TABLES

Principal Table

1. Shaws of Lower House, Lees & Ashton:
   1A   x
   1B   xi
   1C   xii

Ancillary Tables

2. Staley Manor   xiii

3. Sub-Manor de la Schagh   xiv

4. Shaws of Boarshurst   xv

5. Shaws of Boarshurst, Fur Lane & Uppermill   xvi

6. Shaws of Boarshurst & Lane   xvii

7. Shaws of Lower House & Grottonhead   xviii

8. Shaws of Lower House, Halls & Arthurs   xix

1A. SHAWS OF LOWER HOUSE, LEES & ASHTON

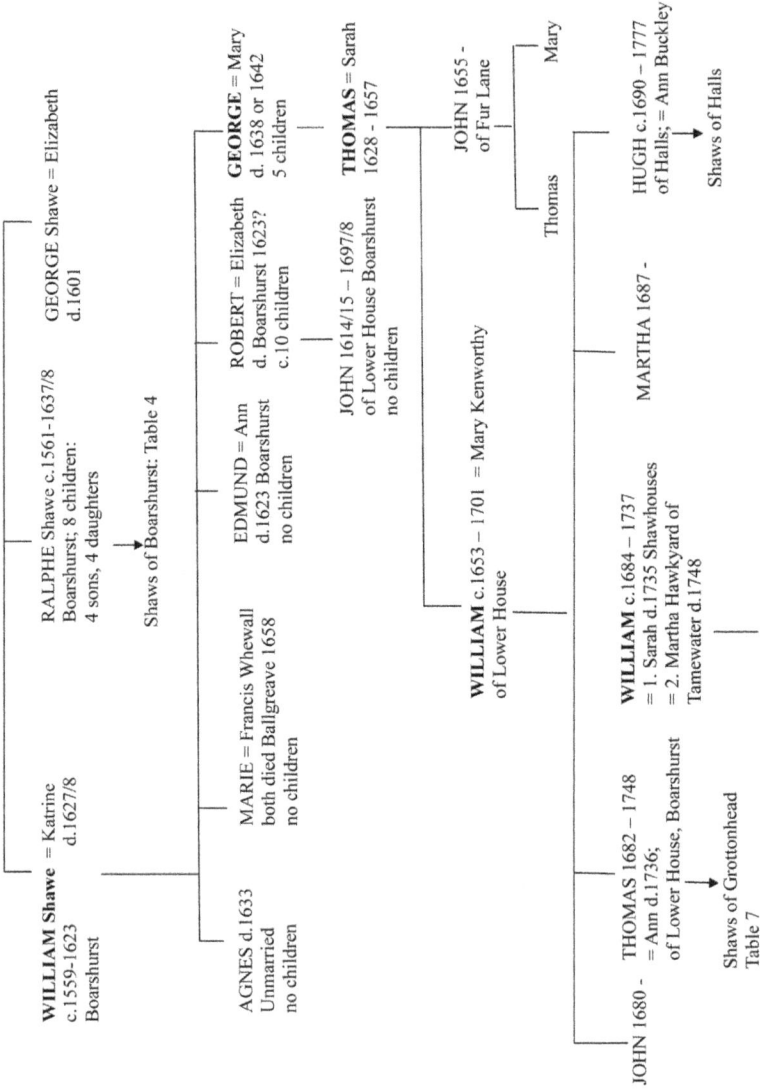

WILLIAM Shawe = Katrine c.1559-1623 d.1627/8 Boarshurst

RALPHE Shawe c.1561-1637/8 Boarshurst; 8 children: 4 sons, 4 daughters

Shaws of Boarshurst: Table 4

GEORGE Shawe = Elizabeth d.1601

AGNES d.1633 Unmarried no children

MARIE = Francis Whewall both died Ballgreave 1658 no children

EDMUND = Ann d.1623 Boarshurst no children

ROBERT = Elizabeth d. Boarshurst 1623? c.10 children

GEORGE = Mary d. 1638 or 1642 5 children

JOHN 1614/15 – 1697/8 of Lower House Boarshurst no children

THOMAS = Sarah 1628 - 1657

WILLIAM c.1653 – 1701 = Mary Kenworthy of Lower House

JOHN 1655 - of Fur Lane

Thomas

Mary

JOHN 1680 -

THOMAS 1682 – 1748 = Ann d.1736; of Lower House, Boarshurst

Shaws of Grottonhead Table 7

WILLIAM c.1684 – 1737 = 1. Sarah d.1735 Shawhouses = 2. Martha Hawkyard of Tamewater d.1748

MARTHA 1687 -

HUGH c.1690 – 1777 of Halls; = Ann Buckley

Shaws of Halls

x

1B. SHAWS OF LOWER HOUSE, LEES & ASHTON

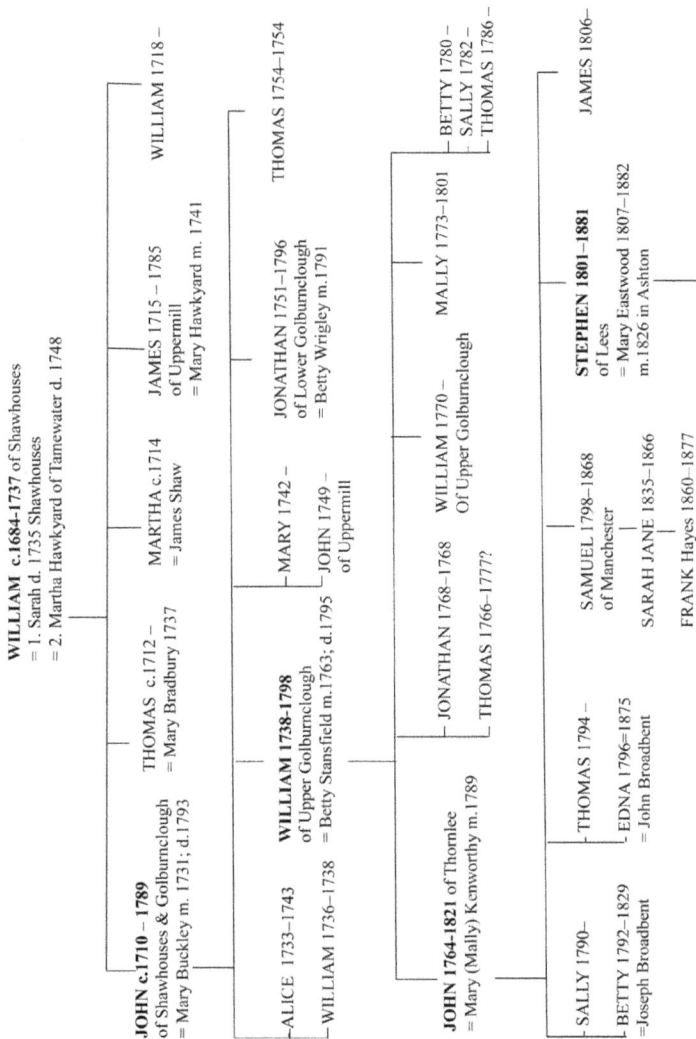

WILLIAM c.1684-1737 of Shawhouses
= 1. Sarah d. 1735 Shawhouses
= 2. Martha Hawkyard of Tamewater d. 1748

JOHN c.1710 – 1789 of Shawhouses & Golburnclough = Mary Buckley m. 1731; d.1793

THOMAS c.1712 – = Mary Bradbury 1737

MARTHA c.1714 = James Shaw

JAMES 1715 – 1785 of Uppermill = Mary Hawkyard m. 1741

WILLIAM 1718 –

ALICE 1733-1743

WILLIAM 1736-1738

WILLIAM 1738-1798 of Upper Golburnclough = Betty Stansfield m.1763; d.1795

MARY 1742 –

JOHN 1749 – of Uppermill

JONATHAN 1751-1796 of Lower Golburnclough = Betty Wrigley m.1791

THOMAS 1754-1754

JOHN 1764-1821 of Thornlee = Mary (Mally) Kenworthy m.1789

JONATHAN 1768-1768

THOMAS 1766-1777?

WILLIAM 1770 – Of Upper Golburnclough

MALLY 1773-1801

BETTY 1780 –

SALLY 1782 –

THOMAS 1786 –

SALLY 1790–

THOMAS 1794 –

BETTY 1792-1829 = Joseph Broadbent

EDNA 1796=1875 = John Broadbent

SAMUEL 1798-1868 of Manchester

STEPHEN 1801-1881 of Lees = Mary Eastwood 1807-1882 m.1826 in Ashton

JAMES 1806–

SARAH JANE 1835-1866

FRANK Hayes 1860-1877

1C. SHAWS OF LOWER HOUSE, LEES & ASHTON

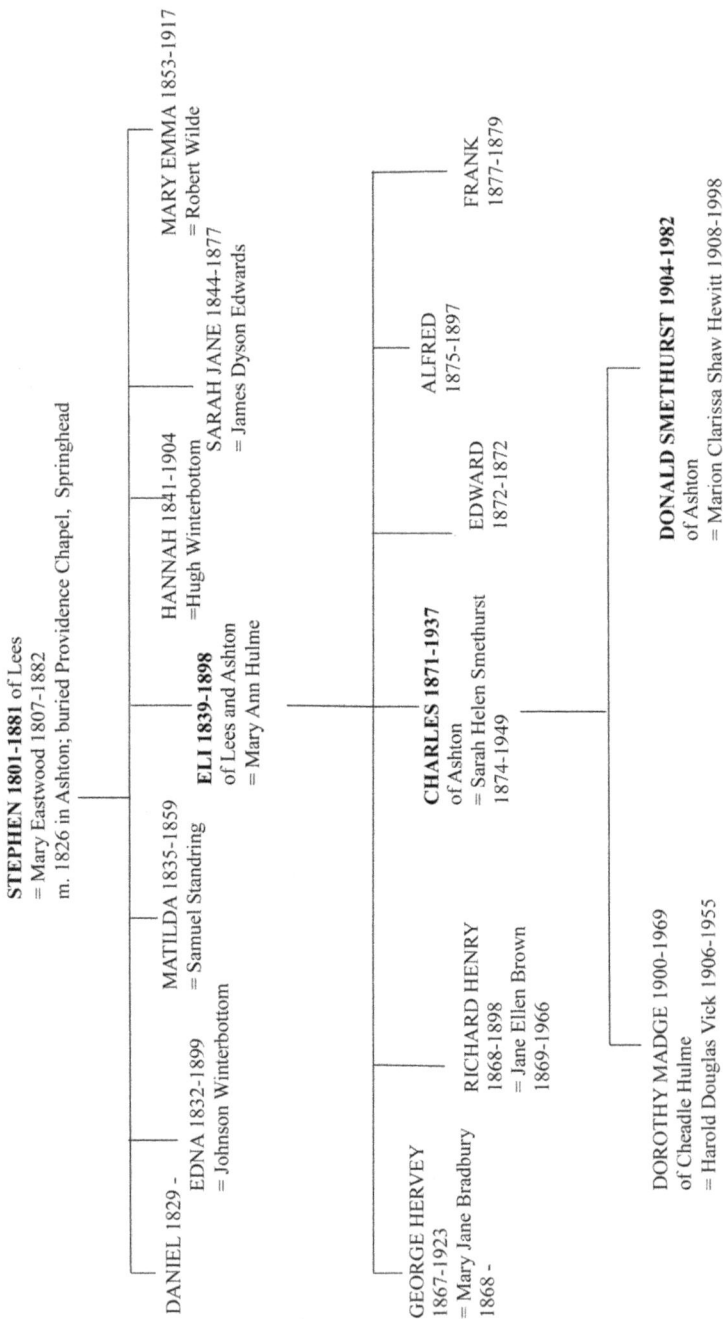

STEPHEN 1801-1881 of Lees
= Mary Eastwood 1807-1882
m. 1826 in Ashton; buried Providence Chapel, Springhead

DANIEL 1829 -

EDNA 1832-1899
= Johnson Winterbottom

MATILDA 1835-1859
= Samuel Standring

ELI 1839-1898
of Lees and Ashton
= Mary Ann Hulme

HANNAH 1841-1904
=Hugh Winterbottom

SARAH JANE 1844-1877
= James Dyson Edwards

MARY EMMA 1853-1917
= Robert Wilde

GEORGE HERVEY
1867-1923
= Mary Jane Bradbury
1868 -

RICHARD HENRY
1868-1898
= Jane Ellen Brown
1869-1966

CHARLES 1871-1937
of Ashton
= Sarah Helen Smethurst
1874-1949

EDWARD
1872-1872

ALFRED
1875-1897

FRANK
1877-1879

DOROTHY MADGE 1900-1969
of Cheadle Hulme
= Harold Douglas Vick 1906-1955

DONALD SMETHURST 1904-1982
of Ashton
= Marion Clarissa Shaw Hewitt 1908-1998

2. STALEY MANOR

SIMON DE STAVELEIA
d. before 1211

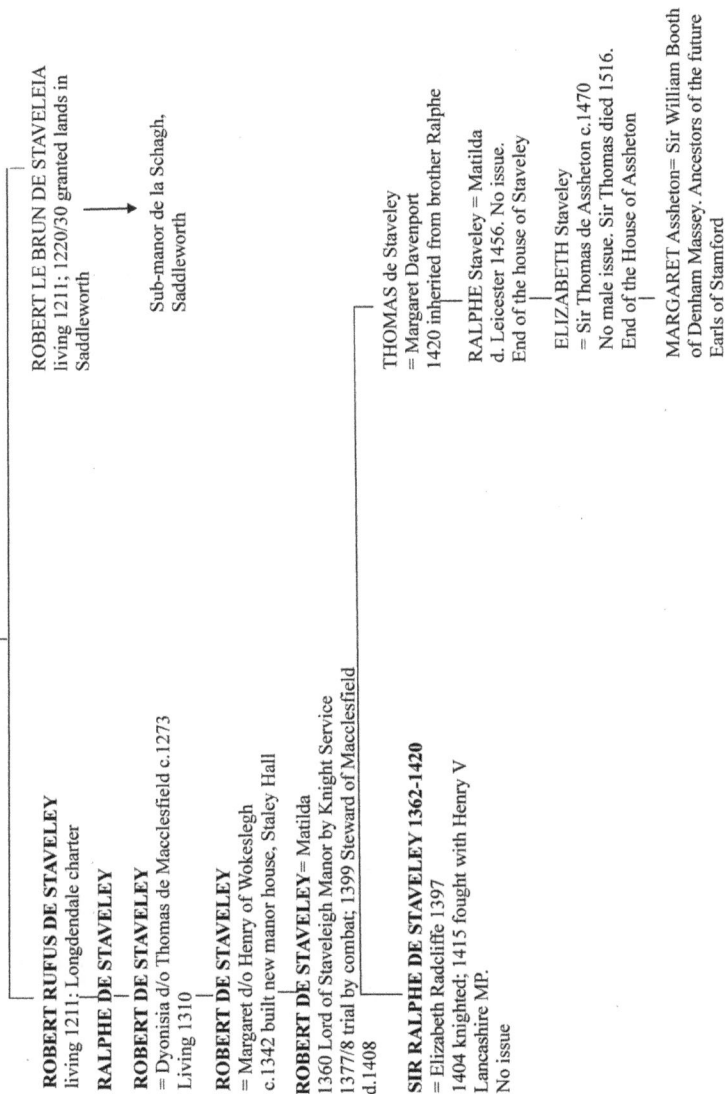

ROBERT RUFUS DE STAVELEY
living 1211; Longdendale charter

RALPHE DE STAVELEY

ROBERT DE STAVELEY
= Dyonisia d/o Thomas de Macclesfield c.1273
Living 1310

ROBERT DE STAVELEY
= Margaret d/o Henry of Wokeslegh
c.1342 built new manor house, Staley Hall

ROBERT DE STAVELEY = Matilda
1360 Lord of Staveleigh Manor by Knight Service
1377/8 trial by combat; 1399 Steward of Macclesfield
d.1408

SIR RALPHE DE STAVELEY 1362-1420
= Elizabeth Radcliffe 1397
1404 knighted; 1415 fought with Henry V
Lancashire MP.
No issue

ROBERT LE BRUN DE STAVELEIA
living 1211; 1220/30 granted lands in
Saddleworth

→

Sub-manor de la Schagh,
Saddleworth

THOMAS de Staveley
= Margaret Davenport
1420 inherited from brother Ralphe

RALPHE Staveley = Matilda
d. Leicester 1456. No issue.
End of the house of Staveley

ELIZABETH Staveley
= Sir Thomas de Assheton c.1470
No male issue. Sir Thomas died 1516.
End of the House of Assheton

MARGARET Assheton= Sir William Booth
of Denham Massey. Ancestors of the future
Earls of Stamford

3. SUB-MANOR DE LA SCHAGH

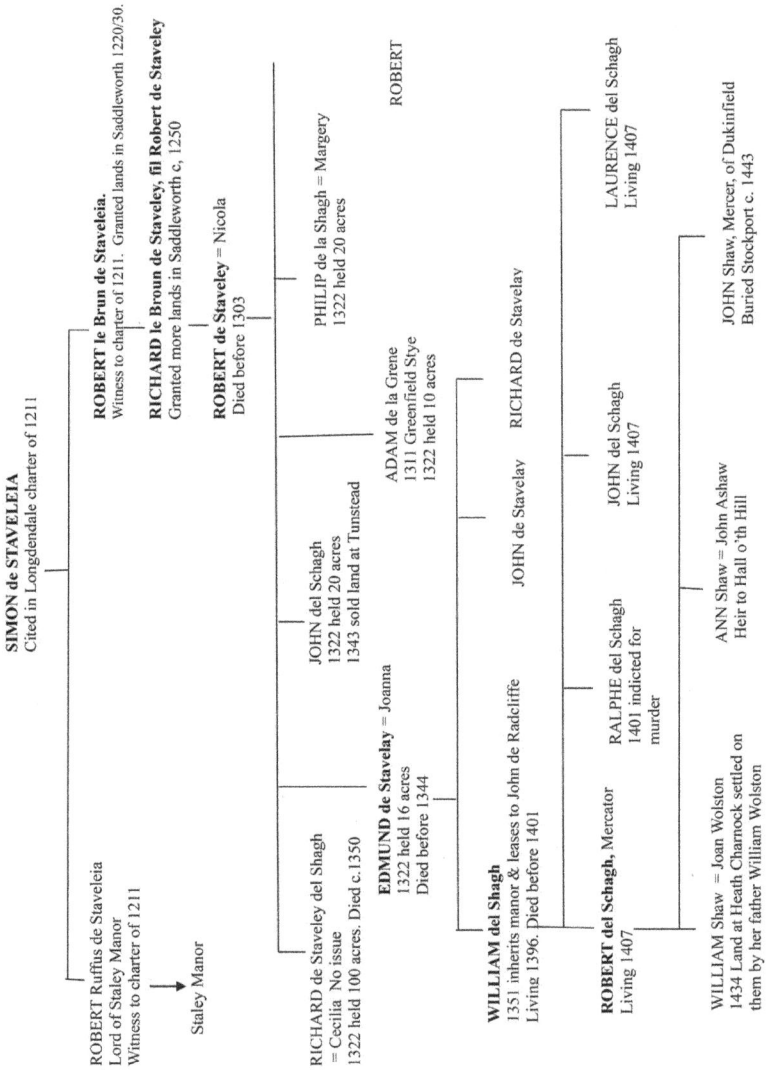

SIMON de STAVELEIA
Cited in Longdendale charter of 1211

ROBERT Ruffus de Staveleia
Lord of Staley Manor
Witness to charter of 1211

Staley Manor

ROBERT le Brun de Staveleia.
Witness to charter of 1211. Granted lands in Saddleworth 1220/30.

RICHARD le Broun de Staveley, fil Robert de Staveley
Granted more lands in Saddleworth c, 1250

ROBERT de Staveley = Nicola
Died before 1303

PHILIP de la Shagh = Margery
1322 held 20 acres

ROBERT

RICHARD de Staveley del Shagh
= Cecilia No issue
1322 held 100 acres. Died c.1350

JOHN del Schagh
1322 held 20 acres
1343 sold land at Tunstead

ADAM de la Grene
1311 Greenfield Stye
1322 held 10 acres

EDMUND de Stavelay = Joanna
1322 held 16 acres
Died before 1344

WILLIAM del Shagh
1351 inherits manor & leases to John de Radcliffe
Living 1396. Died before 1401

JOHN de Stavelay   RICHARD de Stavelay

RALPHE del Schagh
1401 indicted for
murder

JOHN del Schagh
Living 1407

LAURENCE del Schagh
Living 1407

ROBERT del Schagh, Mercator
Living 1407

ANN Shaw = John Ashaw
Heir to Hall o 'th Hill

JOHN Shaw, Mercer, of Dukinfield
Buried Stockport c. 1443

WILLIAM Shaw = Joan Wolston
1434 Land at Heath Charnock settled on
them by her father William Wolston

4. SHAWS OF BOARSHURST

WILLIAM SHAWE c.1559-1623
of Boarshurst

Shaws of Lower House, Boarshurst

RALPHE SHAWE 1561-1637
of Boarshurst

HENRIE
living 1624

THOMAS
living 1624

EDMUND
living 1624

RICHARD
living 1658: named in
will of Marie Whewall
of Boarshurst

Elizabeth Rhodes

Alice Heywood

Margaret

Ellen

HENRY c.1645-1702/3 = Mary Hobson 1673
father's name uncertain   d.1685/6

Daniel
1666/7-1679/80

Ann 1680-1680/1

Mary 1682 -

JOHN 1686-1774
of tenancy137

= Elizabeth Kay m.1714
living 1777

Joseph 1729 -

Jane 1731 --

Joanna 1731 -

JAMES 1734 -1801 = Betty Broadbent 1758; d.1784
of tenancy 137   = Isabella Taylor widow 1786
Boarshurst, Shopkeeper

Sarah 1763 -

James 1765-1765

Mary 1767 -
= Abraham Wood 1788

JOHN 1769 -
of Boarshurst 1809

Alice 1770 -

Ann 1771 -

Hannah 1773 - 1774

Henry1775 -

Joseph 1775 -

5. SHAWS OF BOARSHURST, FUR LANE & UPPERMILL

ADAM SHAWE d.1583 = Alice d.1609
of Boarshurst

GYLES d.1634 = Joan d.1646
of Boarshurst

GILES d.1665/6

HENRY
d.1689
of Lane

→ Shaws of Lane

JOHN d.1665
= Mary
of Boarshurst

SARAH
= Lawrence Kinder

GEORGE
d.1653
of Boarshurst

THOMAS d.1650/1
= Alice
of Uppermill

SARAH

Sarah d.1689/90 =
Ralph Andrew d.1698/99
of Boarshurst

→ Andrews of Boarshurst
& Foulrakes

GILES 1632-1702
of Uppermill

THOMAS 1656-1727
of Uppermill

THOMAS "Junior" 1683-1727

GILES 1681-1748
= Mary Scholefield 1701/2
of Fur Lane

JOHN d.1769

ANN

GILES

GILES 1726-1800
= Hannah Knight d.1789
of Fur Lane

MARY   ALICE

GILES "the Younger"1753-1808
= Jane of Hyde
of Fur Lane

WILLIAM 1766-1838
=Martha Crabtree
of Grasscroft

JOHN
1764-1818

+ 3 children

THOMAS 1751-1818
= 1.Sally Buckley
= 2.Anne of Hyde
of Uppermill

xvi

6. SHAWS OF BOARSHURST & LANE

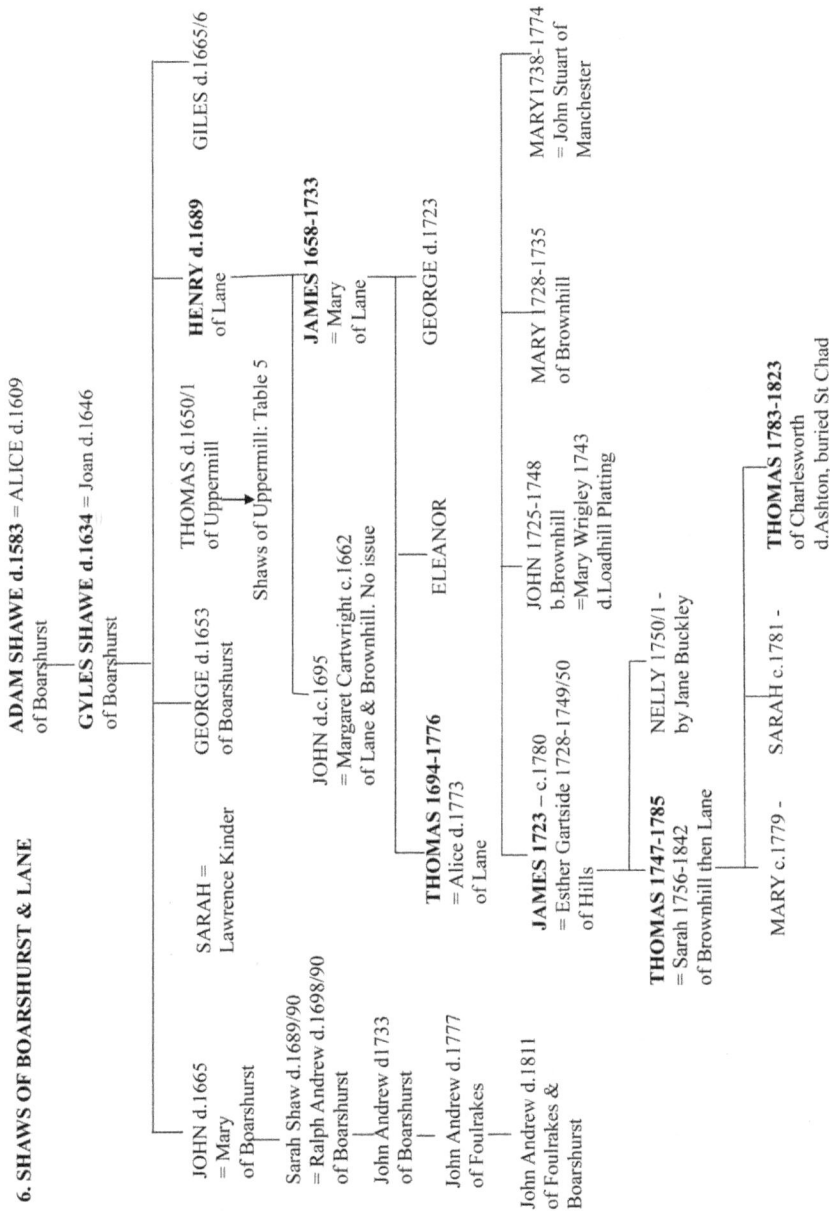

ADAM SHAWE d.1583 = ALICE d.1609
of Boarshurst

GYLES SHAWE d.1634 = Joan d.1646
of Boarshurst

GILES d.1665/6

HENRY d.1689
of Lane

THOMAS d.1650/1
of Uppermill

Shaws of Uppermill: Table 5

JAMES 1658-1733
= Mary
of Lane

GEORGE d.1653
of Boarshurst

JOHN d.c.1695
= Margaret Cartwright c.1662
of Lane & Brownhill. No issue

ELEANOR

GEORGE d.1723

MARY 1728-1735
of Brownhill

MARY 1738-1774
= John Stuart of
Manchester

SARAH =
Lawrence Kinder

THOMAS 1694-1776
= Alice d.1773
of Lane

JOHN 1725-1748
b.Brownhill
=Mary Wrigley 1743
d.Loadhill Platting

JAMES 1723 – c.1780
= Esther Gartside 1728-1749/50
of Hills

NELLY 1750/1 -
by Jane Buckley

SARAH c.1781 -

THOMAS 1783-1823
of Charlesworth
d.Ashton, buried St Chad

JOHN d.1665
= Mary
of Boarshurst

Sarah Shaw d.1689/90
= Ralph Andrew d.1698/90
of Boarshurst

John Andrew d1733
of Boarshurst

John Andrew d.1777
of Foulrakes

THOMAS 1747-1785
= Sarah 1756-1842
of Brownhill then Lane

MARY c.1779 -

John Andrew d.1811
of Foulrakes &
Boarshurst

xvii

7. SHAWS OF LOWER HOUSE & GROTTONHEAD

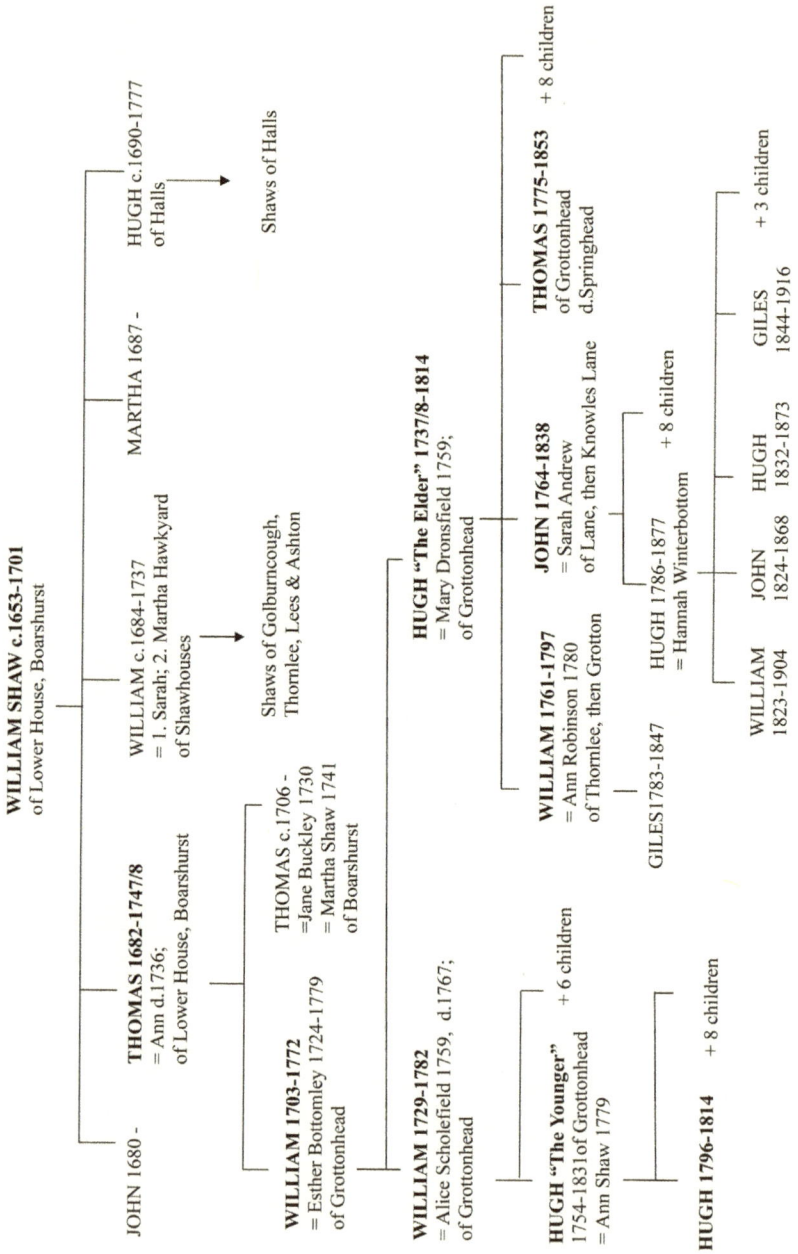

WILLIAM SHAW c.1653-1701
of Lower House, Boarshurst

JOHN 1680 -

THOMAS 1682-1747/8
= Ann d.1736;
of Lower House, Boarshurst

WILLIAM c.1684-1737
= 1. Sarah; 2. Martha Hawkyard
of Shawhouses

→ Shaws of Golburncough,
Thornlee, Lees & Ashton

MARTHA 1687 -

HUGH c.1690-1777
of Halls

→ Shaws of Halls

WILLIAM 1703-1772
= Esther Bottomley 1724-1779
of Grottonhead

THOMAS c.1706 -
=Jane Buckley 1730
= Martha Shaw 1741
of Boarshurst

WILLIAM 1729-1782
= Alice Scholefield 1759, d.1767;
of Grottonhead

HUGH "The Elder" 1737/8-1814
= Mary Dronsfield 1759;
of Grottonhead

HUGH "The Younger"
1754-1831of Grottonhead
= Ann Shaw 1779

+ 6 children

GILES1783-1847

WILLIAM 1761-1797
= Ann Robinson 1780
of Thornlee, then Grotton

HUGH 1786-1877
= Hannah Winterbottom

JOHN 1764-1838
= Sarah Andrew
of Lane, then Knowles Lane

+ 8 children

THOMAS 1775-1853
of Grottonhead
d.Springhead

+ 8 children

HUGH 1796-1814   + 8 children

WILLIAM
1823-1904

JOHN
1824-1868

HUGH
1832-1873

GILES
1844-1916

+ 3 children

8. SHAWS OF LOWER HOUSE, HALLS & ARTHURS

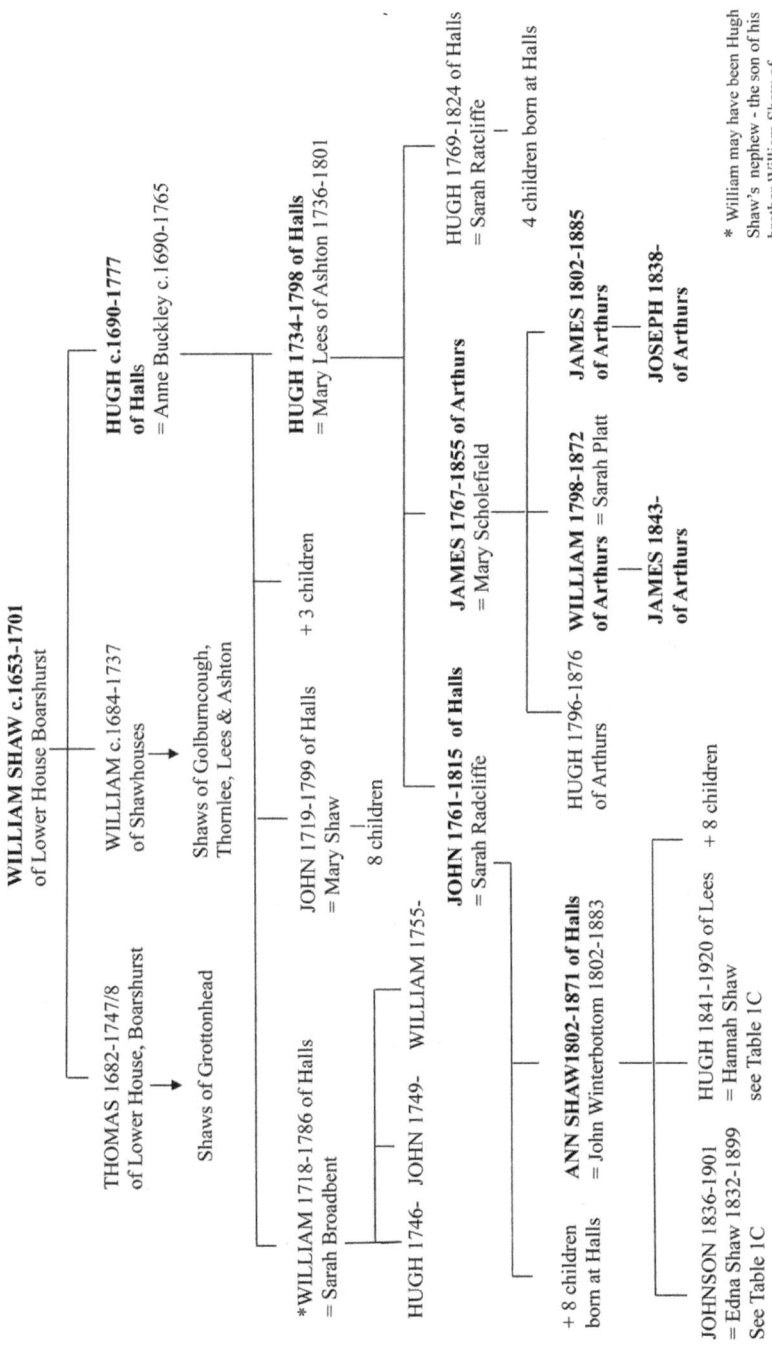

WILLIAM SHAW c.1653-1701
of Lower House Boarshurst

THOMAS 1682-1747/8
of Lower House, Boarshurst

Shaws of Grottonhead

WILLIAM c.1684-1737
of Shawhouses

Shaws of Golburncough,
Thornlee, Lees & Ashton

HUGH c.1690-1777
of Halls
= Anne Buckley c.1690-1765

*WILLIAM 1718-1786 of Halls
= Sarah Broadbent

HUGH 1746-   JOHN 1749-   WILLIAM 1755-

JOHN 1719-1799 of Halls
= Mary Shaw
8 children

+ 3 children

HUGH 1734-1798 of Halls
= Mary Lees of Ashton 1736-1801

HUGH 1769-1824 of Halls
= Sarah Ratcliffe

4 children born at Halls

JOHN 1761-1815 of Halls
= Sarah Radcliffe

+ 8 children born at Halls

HUGH 1796-1876
of Arthurs

JAMES 1767-1855 of Arthurs
= Mary Scholefield

WILLIAM 1798-1872
of Arthurs = Sarah Platt

JAMES 1802-1885
of Arthurs

JOSEPH 1838-
of Arthurs

JAMES 1843-
of Arthurs

ANN SHAW 1802-1871 of Halls
= John Winterbottom 1802-1883

+ 8 children

JOHNSON 1836-1901
= Edna Shaw 1832-1899
See Table 1C

HUGH 1841-1920 of Lees
= Hannah Shaw
see Table 1C

* William may have been Hugh
Shaw's nephew - the son of his
brother William Shaw of
Shawhouses. See Table 1B.

PREFACE

L.P. Hartley's novel 'The Go-Between' famously begins: 'The past is a foreign country: they do things differently there'.

There is of course some truth in this. In researching this book, I had not expected to encounter a Trial By Combat or a medieval legend; or to find that my surname of Shaw had replaced an earlier, different name. I had not expected to enjoy quite so much the carefree approach to spelling and punctuation, and the riot of alliteration, in 17th century documents.; to be moved by the sparse simplicity of possessions in early wills; or to require a good dictionary when presented with items such as swingletrees, nogers and hustlement about the house. For a little while, I was puzzled that a payment was made at St Martin the Bishop in Winter, and that my ancestor Katrine Shawe died in February 1627 but signed her will with an elaborate mark in December 1627.

Yet as we age, the past grows not more distant, but closer, more familiar. We detect fragments of our predecessors' personalities, behaviours and values. We find recognisable acts of selfishness, kindness and expressions of sympathy. Then as now, family disputes broke out over money and neighbourhood disputes over footpaths. Then as now, pandemics swept the land, mortality was a fact of life, and hearts were broken.

Sometimes the past invites us to reflect on the value that previous generations attached to things we may now take for granted: the value of (non-digital) social networks, for example, through extended families, god-parenting, neighbours, or community centres; or their hunger for education and recognition of its transformative power; or their struggles to gain the right to vote or to choose how they worshipped.

Sometimes it seems that the past reaches out to touch us, unexpectedly, as it were through a gap in the fabric of time, or a moment like a 'madeleine de Proust'. It touched me when I stumbled across an apparently stern Victorian ancestor's pet names for his children; or the single word written on a card on his funeral wreath; or when, as a child, I met a man in his nineties, who had been his pupil.

This book traces the male line of a Saddleworth Shaw, from the reign of King John to the present day. It tells a story in broadly chronological sequence, though the flow of chronology tends to meander. After all, it is not so very interesting to learn that an ancestor was called William or John (as a lot of them were); nor especially to know the dates of their birth and death. Of greater interest is who they were, how they lived and worked, the relatives and neighbours with whom they interacted, and the external events beyond their control that were the context for their lives.

Most of our ancestors did not aspire to shape history, rather just to survive it. For some eight centuries, they lived within an area of north-west England just five miles in diameter, one of many Shaws to emerge from the same source. They were, however, shaped by history: by primogeniture, by pestilence, by politics, by social and religious movements, by economic change, by education. This is not a story about kings and queens, presidents and prime ministers, but about an ordinary family who experienced great change. In that sense, it could be the story of any number of families.

*****

A word on conventions. When quoting from documents in English, I mostly retain the original spelling, punctuation and grammar unedited.

This shares an echo of how people expressed themselves in another time and place, although it may pose challenges and certainly gives rise to variation and inconsistency. The name Katherine, for example, was spelt in no fewer than three different ways in Katrine Shawe's will: Katrine, Katirene and Kattereene. The place name Golburn Clough had numerous variations, of which Goldburn, Golbrun and Gowburn are just three, while the surname Shaw evolved over time through Shaghe, Shag, Shay and Shawe.

Until the 18th century brought increased standardisation of written English, capital letters tended to indicate random emphasis, while abbreviations of nouns require palaeographical skills to decipher. First names too were sometimes abbreviated, as in Willm, Ed, Jno, or occasionally latinised, as in Guiliamus, Edmundus or Johannes. Many of the terms for household goods or farming tools are no longer in use today, while spelling often reflected local accent: thus, 'gear' may be written 'gayre', rhyming with 'chayre' or 'a payre of loombes'.

In 1752, England adopted the Gregorian Calendar that we use today, in which New Year's Day falls on 1 January. For some six centuries before that, England used the Julian Calendar, in which New Year's Day fell on 25 March, also known as Lady Day. In the Julian calendar, the day following 31 December 1700 was 1 January 1700; and the day after 24 March 1700 was 25 March 1701. This of course explains the timing of Katrine Shawe's will and death in 1627. To avoid confusion, while acknowledging the customs of the time, I use the convention of combining of Julian and Gregorian calendars for dates between 1 January and 24 March in the years before 1752, for example Katrine's death in February 1627/8.

The Julian Calendar divided the year by Quarter and Cross Quarter days on:

25 March: New Year/Lady Day	1 May: May Day
24 June: Midsummer;	1 August: Lammas
29 September: Michaelmas;	1 November: All Hallows
25 December: Christmas.	2 February: Candlemas

These were commonly cited in loan repayments or rental contracts, even long after the Reformation, as were the important lunar dates of Easter and Pentecost, and certain popular saints' days, such as Martinmas (the mass for St Martin of Tours on 11 November, by which date the sowing of winter grain was completed and landless labourers needed to look for new work). I refer to several of these in the narrative.

Finally, this book owes much to the help of others, in the local archive centres of Ashton and Oldham, the Lancashire Records Office in Preston, the National Archives in Kew, and in particular to the Saddleworth Historical Society, whose extensive collection of records and skilful research has helped inform and motivate the writing of this story.

I WHAT'S IN A NAME? (1200-1545)

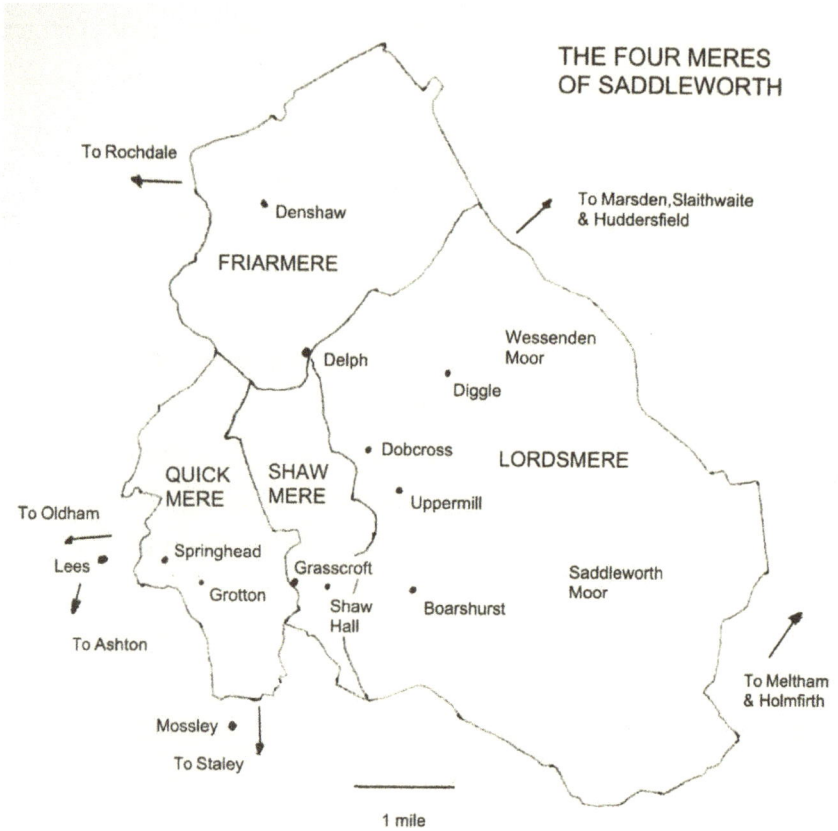

THE FOUR MERES OF SADDLEWORTH

To Rochdale

Denshaw

FRIARMERE

To Marsden, Slaithwaite & Huddersfield

Wessenden Moor

Delph

Diggle

Dobcross

LORDSMERE

QUICK MERE

SHAW MERE

Uppermill

To Oldham

Springhead

Lees

Grasscroft

Grotton

Saddleworth Moor

Shaw Hall

Boarshurst

To Ashton

To Meltham & Holmfirth

Mossley

To Staley

1 mile

1 : SURNAMES

In Lewis Carroll's book *Through the Looking* Glass, Humpty Dumpty takes Alice to task for not knowing the meaning of her own name, adding for good measure: 'My name means the shape I am – and a good handsome shape it is too.' So in deference to Humpty Dumpty, we had better begin by reflecting on names: why, when and how surnames were adopted in England, and the origins of our own family surname of Shaw, in Saddleworth. And the subject is more interesting than we might think. There are four principal categories of English surname (and multiple sub-categories).

Locational Names derive either from the names of old settlements or, more frequently, from the names of very small, local places or topographical features, such as a field, a wood, a woodland clearing, a valley or a hill side. The distinction between place names and topographical names is often blurred, as many hamlets and farmsteads were themselves named after topographical features. Almost all early Saddleworth surnames fall into the topographical category, for example: Briarley, Broadbent, Haslegreave, Hawkyard, Lees, Marsland, Platt, Rhodes - and Shaw, which means a wood. For Norman land-owning classes, the surname usually identified the place where the head of a family held lands, for example the name of his manor.

Patronymic names derive from the father, for example: Robertson (or Roberts), Williamson (Williams), Richardson (Richards). Although baptismal and other records generally identified the parentage of a child, as in 'John fil de Robert', hereditary patronymic names do not occur at all among early Saddleworth names.

Occupational names reflect a trade, profession or office held. A small number of early Saddleworth names fall into this category, including Prestson, Milner, Tayler, Whewall and, in 1401, Robertus le Clerke. National examples are much more plentiful, for example among office holders: Abbot, Constable and Reeve; or among trades: Butcher, Carter, Dyer, Mason, Smith, Thatcher.

Nicknames reflect a person's physical appearance or character trait and were sometimes complimentary, sometimes less so. There are hardly any early Saddleworth names in this category, Whitehead being one notable exception. Nationally, names such as Armstrong, Broad, Short, and Wise fall into this category. Quite a few fictional names occur as well, including Humpty Dumpty.

In Anglo-Saxon England, and after the Norman Conquest, most people had just one name, which was not hereditary. Second names, usually patronymic or nicknames, were sometimes used to distinguish two people with the same first name, for example: King Edward the (apparently pious) Confessor, King Harold's (allegedly elegant) wife Edith Swan-neck, and the (undoubtedly fearsome) Danish king Sweyn Forkbeard. William, known as the Bastard due to the circumstances of his birth, but more commonly now as the Conqueror, had sons who went by the nicknames Robert Curthose and William Rufus. But many of these second names were applied retrospectively, and none were hereditary.

In continental Europe too, non-hereditary nicknames were prevalent, at least in historical records of powerful men. After Charles the Great (Charlemagne), his less charismatic Carolingian descendants were granted less flattering nicknames, such as Charles the Bald, Charles the Fat and Charles the Simple.

It was the Norman barons who introduced the notion of hereditary surnames to England, after the Conquest of 1066. Most of these names were locational, deriving from the place-names of their estates, in France or in England, and were often prefaced by de, du, des or de la. Surnames served to show continuity of property ownership, and right of inheritance, through the eldest son. The barons were accompanied by knights and other supporters, who were rewarded with lands at the expense of the native English landowners, and it became more widespread practice for these smaller landowning classes also to adopt the names of their estates as surnames. By the 13th century, second names were increasingly applied by the manorial classes to all their children, and possession of a second name became an indicator of gentle birth. As the Elizabethan author William Camden explained, 'it seemed a disgrace for a Gentleman to have but one single name, as the meaner sorte and bastards had.'[1]

However, surnames could still change, for instance as land ownership changed hands. As William Camden illustrates, 'Roger de Mortimer was the son of Walterus de Sancto Martino, who in turn had a brother who took the surname of Warren'. Similarly, Roger de Mowbray was the son of Nigel de Albani, 'which Nigel was brother to William de Albani, Progenitor to the ancient Earls of Arundel'.[2]

For 'the common people', as Camden calls them, a single name sufficed for many generations after the Conquest, and the spread of surnames across the general population was slow and uneven: more rapid in the south of England than the north, more rapid among the better off than the poor. The main formation of fixed, hereditary surnames thus took place in England over two centuries, between about 1200 and 1400, and by the time of the poll tax of 1379, the development of surnames in West Riding settlements appears to have largely, if not entirely, concluded.[3] Saddleworth lagged somewhat, compared to its Yorkshire neighbours, but even here only 13, out of a total of 56 taxpayers, had no recorded surname. These were identified in the older manner by their relationship to a father, master or husband,

4

as in: 'Johannes filius Adam', 'Elena filia Adam', 'Johannes seruiens Johannis', or 'Magota relicta Rogeri'.

Why then were surnames adopted? The point of a surname is to help distinguish one individual from another. In small rural settlements, where everyone knew each other, there was little need for a second name. If necessary, a non-hereditary nickname or reference to a person's father or husband would suffice.

There were, however, two main drivers for change. The first was the spread of Norman first names. Old English names typically combined two qualities in a compound name and were capable of almost endless diversity. 'Aethel', for example, meaning noble or wise, was a common part of names such as Aethelstan (noble stone), Aethelwin (noble friend), Aethelfrith (noble peace), Aethelflaed (noble beauty), Aethelric (noble rule) and of course King Aethelraed (noble counsel), whose disastrous rule earned the ironic nickname 'the Unraedy'. Among names beginning with 'Ed' (prosperity), we find Edmund (prosperity and protection), Edward (prosperity and guard), and Edgar (prosperity and spear). The placid 10th century King Edgar's nickname 'Edgar the Peaceful' is a pun on his name's meaning.

After the Conquest, Norman names began to replace traditional English ones, as the native English copied the customs of their new rulers, and stigma may have attached to old English names. But these new names were notably lacking in variety. The 1379 poll tax returns for Saddleworth identify 46 men as heads of household. Just six names account for 85% of them: John (13), Robert (9), William (7), Adam (5) and Thomas (5). A study of poll tax returns for the Sheffield area finds just 20 names distributed amongst 715 men, over half of whom were called John or William.[4] A wider survey, of poll tax returns across ten counties of England, finds that 78% of men were named John, William, Thomas, Richard or Robert.[5] First names alone could no longer be relied on to distinguish one person from another.

A second major driver for the adoption of surnames was feudalism. From the Domesday Book forward, the Crown had always sought to be clear who held which lands, in exchange for defined services and fiscal payments, at least as regards the landowning classes. As the base of taxation broadened, however, through the poll tax and lay subsidies, it became necessary to distinguish individuals among more humble citizens too. Manorial estates also needed to keep records of their tenants, the duration of the leases, the rental or other payments made and the services due to the Lord of the Manor. Thus, manorial clerks and tax collectors hastened the adoption of surnames.

The word 'shaw' has its origins in the Old English word 'sceaga', and the Middle English word 'schaghe', meaning a wood, a copse or a stand of trees. It may also be related to the Old Norse word 'skagr' meaning wood or forest, Yorkshire having formed part of 10th century Danelaw.[6] The surname Shaw thus derives from a topographical feature or a local place name, and it originally identified a person who lived near to a wood.

A shaw is a common enough landscape feature, and local places that contain the name are found in many parts of England. So it is not surprising that the surname Shaw originated separately in different regions. The Oxford Dictionary of English Surnames, for example, notes records of the surname Shaw, in the period 1195-1333, in Berkshire, Essex, Somerset, Wiltshire, Worcestershire and Yorkshire. In 1853, the surname Shaw featured among the fifty most common in England and Wales, listed at number 46.[7] Today, excluding Shaws with a prefix or suffix, such as Ollerenshaw or Shawcross, the number of people named Shaw in the UK is reckoned to be just over 100,000 – fewer than the three commonest names of Smith (700,000+), Jones (450,000+) or Williams (400,000+), but still among the top 70.

However, by far the most populous concentrations of Shaws were found in northern regions, and most especially in south-east Lancashire and the West Riding of Yorkshire. An analysis of the 1881 census finds that the English counties with the greatest number of people named Shaw were Yorkshire (13,698) and Lancashire (11,616), followed by Staffordshire with just 3,065.[8] The same census shows that the three parishes with the highest percentage of the population named Shaw, and also the greatest number of individuals named Shaw, were: Saddleworth (3.139% & 701 people); Ashton-under-Lyne (1.004% & 761 people); and Oldham (0.812% & 909 people).

What then are the origins of the surname Shaw in Saddleworth? Several local place names include the word shaw, such as Denshaw, Crowshaw Bent, Hathershaw and Castleshaw. A prefix descriptor typically identifies the individual wood. However, in medieval times, one local place in Saddleworth was named simply 'la Schaghe. This was a large wooded hill-side. It lent its name to a hunting lodge, which became Shaw Hall; to a field called 'le Schaghefeld' or 'Great Shaw Field'; to the manor of 'la Schaghe'; and, later, to 'Shaw Mere', one of the four administrative areas of Saddleworth. It was also taken as the surname of a family who, in the 14th century, discarded their previous family name in order to adopt that of their new manor.

While the name has arisen in many different locations across England, there is strong evidence that the origin of the surname Shaw in Saddleworth lies with this single family. The Lancashire historian R. Cunliffe Shaw, for example, identifies five distinct family groups living in the north-west of England from the mid 13th century and known by the name Shaw, or 'of the Shaw'. Four groups lived in Lancashire, near Rivington (between Bolton and Preston), Scarisbrick (in Ormskirk parish), Flixton (near Warrington) and Cartmel (in Furness, now part of Cumbria). The fifth family group lived in Saddleworth, and 'gave rise to many branches inhabiting the valleys of this district and the eastern parts of Rochdale parish, where their descendants remain to this day.'[9]

The first use of 'Shaw' as a surname in Saddleworth appears in the early 14th century, when a branch of a family called de Staveley were granted lands and a sub-manor at a place known as la Schaghe, and began, in the Anglo-Norman fashion, to style themselves 'del Schaghe'. So to understand our earliest origins as Shaws of Saddleworth, we have to go back before the 14th century, to the de Staveley family.

2 : STALEY MANOR

Late in the reign of King John, in 1211 or soon after, Thomas de Burgh, Lord of Longdendale in Cheshire, summoned the lords of his manors and other senior figures to act as formal witnesses to a charter. The purpose of the charter was to create the new manor of Godley, and to grant the manor to Adam son of Reginald, who would thereafter, in the Norman custom, adopt the name of his lands and be called Adam de Godley.[1]

Among the dozen or so witnesses were two brothers, sons of Simon de Staveleia, the recently deceased Lord of nearby Staley Manor. Both brothers were named Robert, distinguished by the colour of their hair and beards and by their nicknames, Rufus and le Brun. A younger son with the same name as an older one was often born of a different mother. The two Roberts, therefore, may have been step-brothers, their distinct hair colour reflecting different maternal genes. The eldest, Robert Rufus de Staveley, had recently inherited the manor of Staley from his father. The younger brother, our ancestor Robert le Brun de Staveley, had not. The Norman practice of primogeniture did not favour younger siblings.

This chapter follows the fortunes of the descendants of Robert Rufus, who formed the house of Staley until the expiry of the male line in the 16th century.[2] (Genealogical Table 2) Chapters 3 and 4 follow the fortunes of the descendants of Robert le Brun de Staveley, who were granted lands at a place called la Schaghe in Saddleworth and who adopted this place name as their surname. (Genealogical Table 3)

The name of Staveley (also spelt Stavelegh and Staveleiea), and the shortened version of Staley, derive from two Old English words:

'staef' (meaning stave) and *'leah'* (meaning a lightly wooded area, or a woodland clearing) – thus a woodland clearing where staves are cut or brought.[3] In the 13th century, four contiguous manors in the Lordship of Longdendale, running from north to south, ended with the word 'leah' or 'ley' (Staley, Matley, Godley and Hattersley), indicating a landscape that was lightly wooded or partly cleared of woodland. The modern settlement of Stalybridge acquired its suffix after the medieval bridge across the river Tame was replaced in 1707.

In Norman England, the Manor of Staley[4] was held under the Lordship of Longdendale, which in turn was held from the Earl of Chester. William de Neville was granted Longdendale by the Earl of Chester in about 1181, and on de Neville's death in 1211 the Lordship passed to his son-in-law Thomas de Burgh. There is no mention of Staley in the Domesday Book of 1086, but the large manor of 'Motre' (Mottram) is recorded. Between 1086 and 1220, the population of England had more than doubled and, with the climatic warming of western Europe at this time (the 'Medieval Climate Optimum'), much woodland and waste land was cleared and brought into cultivation. There was a need therefore to create additional manors to help feed a growing population, as well as to meet the aspirations of the landowning classes. Thus, a century or so after the Domesday Book, probably during the time of William de Neville, the central part of Mottram Manor was retained as the demesne manor of the Lord of Longdendale, but other parts were gradually split off into some eight separate, smaller manors. One of the earlier manors to be created was the Manor of Staley, whose Lord was Simon de Staveleia. One of the later to be created, as we have seen, was the Manor of Godley.

Vast tracts of land previously held by the Anglo-Saxon English were transferred to Norman ownership after the Conquest. William the Conqueror had numerous followers who expected to be rewarded with land for aiding his success, while in the turbulent years after the

Conquest he also needed men of reliable loyalty to govern the villages and countryside on his behalf. The suppression of repeated rebellions created opportunities for the widespread confiscation and redistribution of lands held by native English; and, where lands were not formally transferred by the new king to his followers, they were often taken by violence and intimidation. Twenty years after the Conquest, there was a need to clarify land tenure, while confirming the King's ultimate control over land distribution, and the tax and services to be rendered to him. This was the task of the Domesday Book of 1086, and it shows that by then only a tiny minority of manors were still held by the native English.

The Earldom of Chester was held by the Norman Hugh d'Avranches from soon after 1066. The Domesday Book records that the earldom contained over 300 manors, one of which was Mottram, unusually retained in 1086 by a native English lord named Gamel. However, a century later, the name of the Lord of Longdendale, William de Neville, was strongly suggestive of Norman descent. The manorial lords within Longdendale also styled themselves in the Norman fashion, with no trace of old English names, for example, among nearby manorial lords: Hugh de Godlegh, Robert de Bredbury, Ralph de Hatterslegh, Henry de Matttelegh, Thomas de Hollinworth. Only the place names reflect English origins.[5]

It is therefore reasonable to assume, though we cannot be certain, that the de Staveley family adopted their surname, in the Anglo-Norman manner, after being granted a manor of that place name – just as 'Adam son of Reginald' became 'Adam de Godlegh'. There is further evidence to suggest that they were descended from Norman or other followers of William at, or in the century or so after, the Norman Conquest.

Over many generations, the de Staveleys chose first names that were Norman in origin. After Simon of Staveleia, the next six generations of the eldest de Staveley sons were named either Robert (4) or Ralph (2). Other names to occur regularly were Richard, William, Henry and John. These names, in the Norman custom, were passed on from one generation to another.

The de Staveleys also had a coat of arms in the Norman style, with an azure blue engrailed chevron on a silver shield.[6] Their immediate neighbours, the de Asshetons, with whom the family merged in marriage in the 15th century, explicitly claimed Norman descent. A rent roll of 1422 records that: 'at the ffeast of Martyn in winter' in the first year of 'the King Henry (the sixth after the conquest) ... All the Tenants of the Lordship of Assheton-under-Lyne, taking their tenements to ffarm for twenty winter term, at John of Assheton, Knight, *the which came out of Normandy*.'[7]

For the Normans, land conferred power, prosperity and status. In addition to naming themselves by their lands, they also introduced to

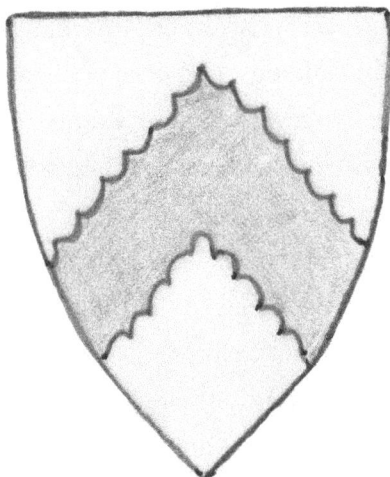

The coat of arms of the Staveley family:
'Argent a chevron engrailed azur'.

England the custom of primogeniture, whereby the eldest son inherited his father's lands exclusively. The purpose of primogeniture was to protect estates against sub-division between siblings. It was an arrangement that most clearly benefited the eldest son: younger male siblings faced downward social mobility, obtaining much smaller landholdings or becoming tenants, rather than owners, of land. A 16th century Elizabethan spy named Catlyn, who worked for Henry Walsingham, attributed his 'poor living' to the adverse consequences of primogeniture: 'for being the youngest son of a younger brother, my position was only seven feet of inheritance, which has constrained me to seek my living hic et ubique.'[8]

In the late 13th century, the younger offspring of Robert Rufus de Staveley appear in charters that granted them lands in Ashton Manor. Thomas de Assheton, Lord of the Manor of Ashton, granted to Ralph son of William Rufus de Staley all his lands of Souracre; he also granted to William Rufus lands within the bounds of Luzley, close to the border with Saddleworth.[9] Meanwhile Richard Rufus de Staveley granted his brother Ralph de Staveley half his land at Fernlee, in Saddleworth, and one and a half acres at "Sadulworthirst".[10] However, these were small landholdings, certainly in comparison with a typical manor. Most of the 'youngest sons of younger brothers' were living modestly as small farmers and tenants of larger landowners.

By contrast, a sketch map of Staley Manor shows some 26 tenant farmsteads cultivating lower lying fields, near the River Tame. Two thirds of the estate, to the north and east, was higher ground, uncultivated and unenclosed, on which stood Buckden Castle, thought to have been built by William de Neville.[11] The future manor of the Schaghe in Saddleworth would be of similar size.[12]

Simon's eldest son Robert de Stavelegh, who witnessed the first Godley Charter, soon after 1211, also witnessed a second Godley Charter, in the period 1225-1249.[13] Relations between the manors of

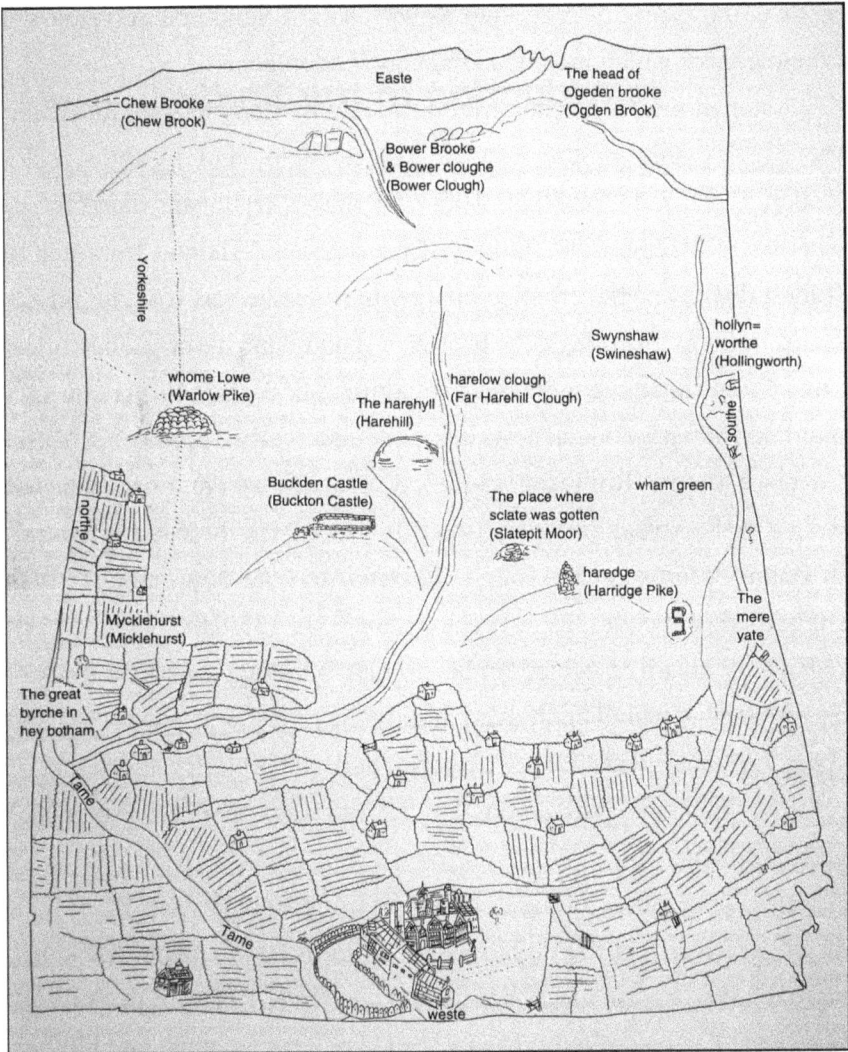

A sketch map of Staley Manor, c.1600, drawn for the Booth family who inherited the Staley estates. The manor hall overlooks the river Tame at the bottom, with the ruins of Buckden Castle on higher ground.

Staley and Assheton, which bordered opposite banks of the river Tame, remained close, and it is also recorded that 'Orm de Eston II granted lands in the manor of Ashton to Robert, son of Simon de Staveley, the boundaries of which included Hurst and Greenlache'.[14]

Later in the 13th century, the Lordship of Longdendale fell under the overlordship of the Earl of Macclesfield, and in about 1273 Robert's grandson (another Robert) married Dyonisia, daughter of Thomas of Macclesfield. As part of the marriage, Thomas 'remitted to Robert de Stavelegh certain annual rents which he was wont to pay for lands held in Stavelegh'.[15] It was a good match for Robert. The family's fortunes were on the rise, and soon after 1340 his son (yet another Robert) built a new manor house, called Staley Hall. The Cheshire Puture Rolls for 1342-3 record this as 'le Chaumbur' of Robert de Stavelegh of Staley, and fifty years later, there is a reference, in rental records of Sir Ralph Staveley, to 'the new halle', which suggests recent additions or replacement.[16] By 1580, the hall had been replaced with a five-gabled timber-framed building, described in 1823 as 'situated on a high knoll overhanding the river Tame ... a roomy and spacious house with extensive barns and stable'.[17] By the late 20th century, that house was largely derelict and was converted into houses and apartments.

In 1360 a survey of the Lordship of Longdendale sheds more light on the services that the de Staveleys, as lords of the manor of Staley, were required to provide to their feudal overlords. Robertus de Staveley is recorded as one of ten names sworn as a juror (juratus) and holding 'the manor of Stavelegh from the Lord of Longdendale by knight service' (per servicium militare).[18] The Hundred Years War with France had begun 20 years earlier, while the Peasants' Revolt lay 20 years ahead, and conflict with Scotland was never far away. The largest landowners still held their lands by feudal tenure, which involved providing military service to the king; and they in turn could require military service from their lords of manor.

A court case of 1377/8, in the reign of Richard II, reflects the violent times, in which might was often held to be right.[19] Robert de Staveley submitted a plea that three of his free tenants in the manor of Staveley, John de Oldum (a priest) and two other men, were claiming part of his lands as their own and 'withholding it from him'. These included 'forty acres of land, 20 acres of meadow and 30 acres of woodland with appurtenances in Staveley'.

The Lord of Longdendale appointed his steward Henry de Mareschal to hear the case at his manor of Mottram, and Henry ruled that the trial should be determined by combat. The two parties, or their appointed champions, should fight in formal single combat, and the victor would be deemed to be successful in the case. The three tenants appointed a champion on their joint behalf, a Robert de Longdene, while Robert de Staveley named his son and heir Ralph as his champion. The prospect of facing young Ralph in trial by battle was clearly not an attractive one, and Robert de Longdene did not show up on the appointed day. Robert de Staveley was therefore adjudged to have won his quit claim.

By now the Staveley family was well-connected, and Ralph was a member of the household of Henry Bolingbroke, son of the Duke of Lancaster John of Gaunt. In 1390, as Henry's Steward, Ralph accompanied him on crusade to Lithuania and in 1393 as far as Venice on his pilgrimage to Jerusalem. But these were febrile and dangerous times. In 1398, Henry was exiled from England by King Richard II, who soon afterwards confiscated the hereditary lands and titles that Henry stood to inherit from his father. Henry returned the next year with an army at his back, to reclaim his inheritance and forcibly replace Richard as king. The Staveleys supported Henry and were generously rewarded when he was crowned King Henry IV. Ralph's father Robert was appointed Steward of Macclesfield, while in 1403 Ralph was knighted at the bloody Battle of Shrewsbury, where King Henry suppressed a large armed rebellion. Sir Ralph was also appointed Steward, Bailiff and Master Forester of the High Peak, as well as High Sherriff and Member of Parliament for Lancashire.[20]

More locally, Ralph also provided services for William Lovell, who at the beginning of the 15th century was the Lord of both Longdendale and Saddleworth, while also owning some lands in Ashton, Matley, Newton and Quick. In a record of Lovell's tenants in 1407/8, known as the Staley Rental, Ralph is named as his 'seneschal', that is his bailiff or rent-collector.[21] The freehold tenants listed for Saddleworth include: Robertus de Staveley (Ralph's father and Lord of Staley, who died a year later); and Robertus del Schagh (descended from Robert Le Brun), who by then had adopted the name of his manor of the Schaghe.

The rental record shows that in 1407 the Staveley family of Staley Manor had expanded their landholdings to include 58½ acres in Quickmere, Saddleworth, probably acquired from the Grotton family earlier in the 14th century. This included land at: Grotton, above Thornlee ('the Thornleghe'), Crowshaw ('Grueschagh'), Stonebreaks, Shelderslow ('Schelderlowe'), Austerlands ('Alstonlonds') and Carr ('Kar').[22]

As we can see from Sir Ralph's life, knights were increasingly given a variety of public roles, for example acting as sheriffs, tax collectors or members of the lower house of parliament. But they still retained military duties. In 1415 Ralph was called on to support Henry V's plans for an invasion of France, which culminated in the Battle of Agincourt. He joined the English army with a personal retinue of four men-at-arms and 12 archers, as well as a contingent of 50 archers raised by the Crown for which he was later paid £113.15s in wages.

By 1420 Ralph had died, and effigies of him in a suit of armour, alongside his wife Elizabeth, can be found in the Staley Chapel, in the parish church of Mottram-in-Longdendale.[23] He died childless, and his younger brother Thomas briefly inherited his estates, while also holding smaller lands in Ashton, at 'the Bastal, the Hyrst and three houses'.[24] However, Thomas too soon died, in 1422, and his son, another Ralph, proved to be the last of the male line. Ralph lived away from the area, drawing up his will in Leicester in 1456. He bequeathed his estates to his daughter Elizabeth, and willed that she should marry Thomas Assheton, heir to the Manor of Ashton. His wish was carried out, and the manors of Ashton and Staley were thus briefly joined together. However, Thomas and Elizabeth also died without issue, ending the male lines of the houses of both Staley and Assheton. Their estates in Ashton, Staley and Quick Mere were acquired by the Booth family of Dunham Massey.

*****

A legend tells of a member of the Staveley family of Staley Manor named 'Sir Roo'.[25] The story goes that Sir Roo set off for the crusades, some say with Richard I. As he left, he broke his wedding ring in two: he gave one part to his wife and swore to keep the other part to his breast until he returned. He fought in the Holy Land but was captured there and imprisoned in Syria. Meanwhile, back in England, it was reported that he had been killed. At last he managed to escape, and he made his way back to England in disguise.

On arriving at Staley Manor he was not recognised by anyone, except, of course, for his faithful old dog, who knew him instantly. He asked to see the lady of the manor, but was informed that she was preparing to be married the very next day, and could not see anyone. Needless to say, she was re-marrying under pressure from a powerful neighbouring landowner. So Roo asked for a cup of water, and, having drunk it, placed his half wedding ring in the bottom of the cup and requested that it be given to the lady. On seeing the half ring, she thought that the person must have news of her husband's death, and she invited him in. Sir Roo entered and shed his disguise, to great relief and rejoicing.

Who was Sir Roo, if indeed the story is based on fact? The name appears to be a shortened form of Rufus, the nickname of the Lords of Staley Manor and their descendants. Was he perhaps, as V. M. Bowman suggests, the Richard Ruffus de Staveley, who had held lands in Ashton, and who, she claims, went by the nickname Roo? This would place him in the early part of the 13th century, when Thomas de Assheton granted lands previously held by Richard Ruffus to 'Ralph son of William Ruffus de Staley'.

The local historian James Butterworth, writing in 1827, claims that the story was handed down through the Knights of St John of Jerusalem, who named Roo as 'Sir Ralph Staveleigh in the time of Richard the First' (whose crusade took place in 1189/92, two decades before the charter witnessed by the two Robert de Staveleys.)

The story may be difficult to reconcile with known historical facts. But we can appreciate it as romantic medieval legend.

3 : THE MANOR DEL SCHAGHE

While Robert Rufus de Staveley was enjoying his inheritance at the Manor of Staley, his younger brother Robert le Brun de Staveley (our ancestor) was obliged to leave the ancestral home to seek a new living. Such was the implication of the law of primogeniture. The younger Robert must have known something about estate management, however, and this stood him in good stead, as he secured employment from Sir Robert Stapleton in the neighbouring manor of Saddleworth. (Genealogical Table 3)

In the 12th century, the Stapleton family, based at Stapleton near Pontefract, held the Lordship of some ten manors across the West Riding of Yorkshire.[1] The Saddleworth area, often called 'Saddleworth Fryth' (forest), was largely wooded and used as hunting land for the Stapletons, as the place names Boarshurst and Hawkyard testify. As absentee landlords, they would have needed someone to keep an eye on things, to preserve their hunting rights, to protect the forest from poaching and woodcutting, and perhaps to provide hospitality for their visits to the hunting lodge of Shaw Hall or to look after their hawks for hunting parties.

Parts of Saddleworth were also settled, and a growing population brought increasing pressure to accommodate more settlements and agriculture. The 13th century saw some forest land make way for enclosures (or 'intakes'), while the following centuries also saw sub-division of larger land-holdings to cater for increased demand.[2] This presented an opportunity for the landowner to generate more rental income, but he needed a bailiff to collect the rents. Here was a role for a younger son of Staley Manor.

Robert de Stapleton had inherited the Honor of Pontefract from his father William in about 1220, and died in about 1260. During that period he is thought to have made four grants of land to the de Staveley family. The earliest charter, not yet found, is assumed to have granted the property of Shaw Hall and nearby lands. The second charter, in about 1230, was to 'Robert, son of Simon de Staveleia', 'for homage and service'. The third, about a decade later, was to 'Robert le Brun de Staveleia'. And the fourth charter was to Robert's son, Richard. All the charters granted land in what later became known as the Shawmere division of Saddleworth.[3] Through these grants the de Staveleys created a large estate based on Shaw Hall. Technically, this Manor of the Schagh was a sub-manor within the pre-existing manor of Saddleworth, but it had its own manorial rights, including a mill and its own manorial court.[4]

The de Staveleys served the Stapletons in other ways too, as a reliable local witness to legal agreements and transactions. This is evident from six charters settling a land dispute, thought to date from the 1240s. Each of these charters is witnessed by Richard le Brun de Staveley, who by then had succeeded his father Robert le Brun. Richard also witnessed a further charter agreement between Robert de Stapleton and the Abbot of Stanlow confirming a grant of land for the glebe.[5]

Richard le Brun's son was named Robert, and he in turn had six sons. In 1293, this Robert made preparations for the inheritance of his estate after his death. A deed of feoffment confirms to himself, 'Robert son of Richard le Brun of Stavelegh of all his messuages, land and tenements in Sadilworthefrith in the Vill of Quicke'.[6] The deed then goes on to name Robert's six sons: Richard, Edmund, John, Adam, Philip and Robert. It determines that on his death the lands would pass to his eldest son Richard and his heirs. If his eldest son Richard died without issue, the lands would pass on his death to the second son,

Edmund, and his heirs. If Edmund in turn died without issue the lands would pass to the third son, John, and his heirs, and so forth in the order listed. In the event, Robert's eldest son Richard did indeed die without issue in about 1350. The Manor of the Schaghe thus passed through the second son, Edmund, to his son William. This William would be known as William del Schagh.

The deed helpfully supplies us with the names of Robert's six sons, some of whom we meet again, three decades later, in the Contrariants Roll of 1322. Five have clearly Norman names, but Edmund, though not unknown in France, is more typically an old English name, held by Anglo-Saxon kings in the 9th and 10th centuries, including the popular Edmund the Martyr. Though not a common name, it recurs regularly among Saddleworth Shaws for the next 200 years. This was the reign of Edward I, the first king since the Conquest to have an English name, to speak English and to promote written English. More than two centuries after 1066, in a small way, the name Edmund may be indicative of eroding social and ethnic divisions between Normans and English.

Robert's prodigious fertility would have important repercussions. In 1348/50, the Black Death swept the country, almost halving the population, and extinguishing many family lines for ever. While some of Robert's children and grandchildren may have perished in the pandemic, others survived to continue the family name.

There are three other points of interest here. First, the deed sets out in meticulous detail how the law of primogeniture was applied. By 1305, Robert's eldest son Richard had inherited the Schaghe, and we learn from a financial transaction (a probable mortgage) that the estate included: 'three messuages, 19 tofts, a mill, 152 acres of land, 102 acres of meadow, 100 acres of woodland and a rent of 7s. 3d. in Quick'.[7] By contrast, Richard's younger siblings occupied much smaller tenancies in Saddleworth. The Contrariants Roll of 1322, drawn up by Edward II following abortive attempts to overthrow him, records that Richard's brother Edmund held 1 messuage and 16 acres of land; John and Phillip each held 1 messuage and 20 acres of land; while Adam de la Grene held 1 messuage and 10 acres at Greenfield Stye, later known as Fur Lane.[8]

Primogeniture protected the integrity of the estate through the inheritance of the eldest son, but was not designed to protect the social and economic status of younger sons. As R. Cunliffe Shaw puts it, 'The operation of the laws of primogeniture have produced in nearly all [manorial] families the material decadence of younger sons and their remote descents.'[9] The Contrariants Roll illustrates how the fortunes of the younger sons were small in comparison to those of the eldest, and already we can see a pattern and scale of tenancy emerging that is replicated in manorial records two centuries later. Family wealth and entitlement passed to the eldest son: younger sons fared more modestly, and appear to have held smaller tenancies in Saddleworth Manor, outside the family estate of la Schaghe.

A second point of interest is that the commercial interests of Richard, Lord of the Manor of the Schaghe, were diversifying far beyond estate management. The likely reason for mortgaging the estate was to raise funds for investment in more profitable business activities, notably wool trading. This was a time when international trade was booming, and ships plied between Hull and Flanders, where Yorkshire wool was spun into cloth and marketed across Europe. In 1307 a legal case was brought against him by Nicholas, son of James le Flemyng, a citizen of York, for failure to pay for a sack of wool ('good, clean and saleable'), valued at 10 marks. In another case, in January 1307/8, he accepted that he owed £20 to Sir John de Barton and agreed to pay it by the Feast of St Peter ad Vincula.[10] Land was now seen not only in terms of family heritage, social status or as an income source from rentals, but increasingly as an asset to provide security against loans that could be invested in trade.

Thirdly, in the early 14th century the family name of the Saddleworth de Staveleys was evolving. By now this branch of the de Staveley family had lived in Saddleworth for almost a century, during which time they had become Lords of the Manor of the Schaghe. Legal documents could not allow any ambiguity about a person's identity, and the family now had as many as three ways of identifying themselves: first, by their ancestral origins at the manor of Staley Hall; second, by their residence in Saddleworth; and third, by the lands granted to them at la Schaghe. At the start of the 14th century all three locative names are used to identify members of the de Staveley family at la Schaghe. In the mortgage document of 1305, Richard is identified as 'Ricus fil Robert de Stavelay'. In the two documents of 1307 relating to a debt of 10 marks, he is named as 'Ricus fil Robert de Staveley del Schaghe', while his brother, who stands as a witness, is named as 'John del Schagh'. In the 1307 case of a £20 debt, Richard is named as 'Ricus fil Robert de Staveley de Sadelworth'. In the Contrariants Roll of 1322, Richard and his brother Edmund are both named as 'de Stavelay'; but two younger brothers are named as 'John del Schagh' and 'Phillip de la Schagh'. Here we see the clear need for fixed, hereditary surnames, and we witness the birth of the surname Shaw in Saddleworth, the family name that would be borne by many future generations of Saddleworth Shaws.

While doubtless proud of their Staveley heritage and the status this conferred, it was time to identify themselves by their own land-holdings – if for no other reason than to avoid confusion with their cousins from Staley Manor, the Lord of which also held lands in Ashton and Saddleworth. Surnames were about to become fixed and hereditary; records needed clarity of identity and inter-generational consistency. By the time Edmund's son William inherited the manor of la Schaghe in 1350, the ambivalence had been resolved: he is named consistently as 'William del Shagh', and his children and grandchildren carried the same surname, until the spelling evolved into the name Shaw.

In about 1350, William del Shagh, son of Edmund de Staveley and nephew of Richard de Staveley del Schagh, inherited the Manor of the Schagh.[11] He was not, however, resident in the area, and he immediately leased the estate to John de Radclyffe of Ordsall for life. The lease of the estate would become the subject of a long legal dispute that would not be resolved until after William's death.[12] After John de Radclyffe died, his son Richard continued the lease; but when he too died in 1380, William moved to restore his right to the estate. In this, he met staunch resistance from Richard Radclyffe's widow, Sybilla, who argued that the lease had in fact been a full transfer of ownership, and that she therefore had dower rights to a third of her late husband's estate. She brought a successful suit against William in 1382, but claim followed counter-claim for nearly thirty years. Just a few years earlier, a similar dispute over land ownership had been resolved decisively in Longdendale, through a trial by combat. But such trials were becoming less common, and Sybilla's status as a widow gave her extra leverage.

For much of this period, Sybilla, now re-married and named Sybille de Fulthorpe, retained her hold of one third share of the estate (her dower entitlement), while William del Shagh held the other two thirds. A series of records between 1388 and 1393 confirm that Sybilla's part share of la Schaghe comprised 80 acres of arable and meadow and six messuages worth £4 per annum, corresponding to one third of the whole estate, as itemised in 1305.[13] The situation was unchanged in 1397, when William and Sybilla both paid chief rents to the Lord of Saddleworth, as we see in the rental document known as the Staley Rental (thus known because it was recorded by the heir to Staley Manor, Ralph de Staveley, acting as seneschal for Lord Lovell, the then overlord of both Saddleworth and Longdendale).[14]

By 1401, William del Shagh had died, and his son Robert del Shagh had inherited his two thirds portion of the estate. Robert was already quite a wealthy man as a result of his trading interests: 'Robert del Shagh, Mercator' (merchant) had topped the list of poll tax returns for Saddleworth in 1379, paying 12d in tax compared to a rate of 4d for everyone else.[15] However, by the turn of the century he was not resident in the area either, and his interest in the estate lay primarily in the security it offered against loans that he could invest elsewhere. On 14 August 1401, using the land to raise a mortgage, he 'sold' his two thirds share of the Schagh estate to three men: John de Assheton (Lord of the Manor of Ashton), John de Doconfeld (Dukinfield) and a John de Wood.[16] The transaction involved a peppercorn rent, followed by a lump sum payment of 40lb of silver after 18 years.

The following year, Robert reclaimed Sybilla's lands, an action which enabled him to extend the term of his loan against the estate from 18 to 24 years.[17] The Staley Rental of 1407 records 'Robtus del Schagh' and his son William in possession of the entire estate. However, Sybilla was dogged, and in 1410 the dispute was finally resolved through arbitration. Robert agreed to sell the entire estate for 270 marks (£180).[18] This paved the way for Sybilla's great-grandson, Alexander Radcliffe, to become the new Lord of the Manor of the Shagh. The Radcliffe family continued to own the Shaw estate and Shaw Hall, until they sold them to William Ramsden in 1604 and 1611 respectively, when the hall and lands were re-united with Saddleworth Manor.

Robert del Shagh was still alive in 1410 but had not lived in Saddleworth for several years. He had now achieved wealth and social standing. His eldest son William married Joan Wolston, who brought to the marriage her family's lands at Wolston Place, Heath Charnock in Lancashire. His daughter Ann married John Ashaw, heir to Hall o' the Hill at Heath Charnock, who was from one of the unrelated Shaw families in Lancashire identified by R. Cunliffe Shaw. Robert's younger son John became a successful mercer and wool stapler in Dukinfield. Even greater fortune awaited the next generation. John's son Edmund moved to London where he became Master of the Goldsmiths Company, Royal Jeweller to Edward IV, Richard III and Henry VII and in 1482 Lord Mayor of London. He is even mentioned in Shakespeare's play Richard III. For all this fame he did not forget his roots: on his death in 1487 he left £17 to found a school in Stockport and clothes to be distributed to 200 poor persons in Stockport, Mottram, Ashton and Saddleworth.[19]

What, though, were the prospects of Robert del Shagh's less immediate relatives, his brothers, cousins and nephews, who formed a network of Shaws in Saddleworth, and whose descendants would ramify in Saddleworth and the surrounding area? We must now leave behind the drama and high politics of the de Staveleys, and the wealth and fame of the del Schaghs, to explore the more modest lives of their Saddleworth descendants.

4 : RAMIFICATION

By 1410, Robert, the head of the del Shagh family, and his three children, had all left Saddleworth for good and were successfully pursuing fame and fortune elsewhere. But they left behind a network of extended family members. Back in Saddleworth, cousins and nephews were living a more modest lifestyle: they may have had security of tenure on their farmsteads, but they enjoyed more limited disposable income, prospects and mobility. It is this family network that provides the link to the Saddleworth Shaws of later years.

We saw in chapter 3 that, as early as 1322, the Contrariants Roll identified not only Richard de Staveley, then Lord of the Manor of the Schaghe, but also several of his five younger brothers, who were farming smaller tenancies in Saddleworth. These included: Edmund de Stavelay (16 acres), whose son William del Schaghe would later inherit the manor of the Schaghe; John del Shagh (20 acres), who purchased land at Tunstead from Edmund; and Philip de la Shagh (20 acres). Adam de la Grene, who held a ten-acre tenancy at Greenfield Stye, later known as Fur Lane, also appears to have been Richard's brother. Tunstead and Greenfield Stye were in Saddleworth Manor, the area later known as Lordsmere. (A Robert de Staveley, holding 40 acres, could have been Richard's youngest brother of that name, but was more probably the Lord of Staley Manor.)

The Great Mortality of 1348/50, later known as the Black Death, temporarily reversed the ramification of Shaws in Saddleworth. The poll tax records of 1379 show that only two (out of 34) married couples were named Shaw, and only one (out of 26) unmarried individuals. Head of the list for Saddleworth, as we have seen, was 'Robertus del

Schag Mercator, & uxor', heir to the manor of la Schaghe and now a successful merchant. However, two other names suggest a wider family network.

'Willelmus de Schagh & uxor', in 12th position on the list, and paying 4d in tax, could not have been Robert's father, who would surely have preceded his son on the poll tax record, had he been resident in Saddleworth at the time. In fact, it appears Robert's father William was living away from Saddleworth in 1379, returning only in the 1380s in an attempt to repossess Sybilla's part of the estate. Nor could this William have been Robert's son of the same name, who was too young to pay tax in 1379. We have to conclude that William de Schagh was a less immediate relative of Robert.

A third Shaw, 'Johannes del Schagh', appeared later on the list among the unmarried men and women. This could be Robert's younger brother named John or, like Willelmus de Schagh, a more distant relative. Both William and John paid tax of 4d, compared to Robert's 12d, indicating a more modest level of income and assets.

We find further evidence of a network of Shaws in 1401. Four days after agreeing a loan with Robert del Schagh against the Schagh estate, the new mortgage lenders convened a Halmote del Schagh.[1] This served two purposes. First, it confirmed the roll of estate tenants and the terms by which they held their lands. The tenants paid rents and also had to contribute their labour to the Lord of the Manor, typically: three days reaping, one day mowing, one day harrowing and one day ploughing. Seven tenants were also appointed as jurors for the manorial court. In all, twelve tenants farmed the land, while another was tenant of Shaw Hall. However, none of these tenants were named Shaw. Sybilla's 80 acres of land and meadow would have been occupied by a further six tenants, but these are not listed.

Secondly, the Halmote introduced stricter management of the estate, replacing what had clearly been a lax regime under absentee landlords. Three tenants were charged with failing to maintain their houses on the estate, while an inquiry was launched into the tenant occupying Shaw Hall, William Harrison, who had allegedly failed to maintain the building, 'that is, thatching the house, repairing the walls and saving the timber from rot, from the time of the death of William del Schaghe to the present day.'

The court also imposed 20 fines on 17 individuals for cutting down trees on the estate without the right to do so. Of those fined, four were Schagh Manor estate tenants. However, the remaining 13 were not, and three of these were named Shaw. John del Schaghe was fined 3d for cutting down an ash tree, decimating an oak tree and taking three loads of wood; Henry del Schaghe was fined 4d for cutting down two ash trees; and Lawrence del Scaghe was fined 2d for cutting down an aspen tree.

Who were these three Shaws? At this time, Robert and his children had left Saddleworth. So too had his first brother Ralph (indicted for murdering the Earl of Macclesfield's bailiff in Disley). However, John and Lawrence may have been Robert's younger brothers, the same who were named with him as defendants in an assize case brought by Sybilla in 1402.[2] John may also be the same John del Schaghe recorded in the poll tax returns of 1379, while Henry may have been another younger brother or cousin. All three had stayed on in Saddleworth after Robert's departure, providing a bridge to later generations of Shaws. They were not, however, tenants of the Manor del Schagh, but appear to have lived in Saddleworth Manor, the area later known as Lordsmere.

There follows a wide gap in Saddleworth records, but there is compelling evidence of the continuity of Shaws. After 1379 the most comprehensive record of Saddleworth taxpayers is to be found in the Lay Subsidy of 1543-1545. Parliament had agreed to levy a subsidy for Henry VIII to pay for an invasion of Scotland and 'for his other great and urgent occasions', which included a planned invasion of France in

1544. The subsidy was raised on lay people (not clerics) with movable goods or real estate valued above £1. Movable goods included household utensils, furniture and corn in more humble households, as well as jewellery, silverware or wall hangings in more prosperous households. In this, the lay subsidy differed from the 1379 poll tax, which had no financial threshold for tax exemption and was therefore more universal in its coverage. A study of Richmond in Yorkshire estimates that 54% of the population were required to pay the lay subsidy, while 46% were exempt.[3]

Records for 'Qwyk' (Saddleworth), dated 1545, list 43 taxpayers, 38 male and 5 female, with no distinction between those married or single.[4] All the returns are for movable goods rather than lands. Out of 43 returns, 17 people are assessed for goods valued at 20s, that is £1, incurring a tax payment of 1d.; 19 are assessed at 40s or £2., incurring tax of 2d; five are assessed at £3, incurring tax of 3d and two are assessed at £4 incurring tax of 4d.. Six of these tax-payers (13.9%) are named Shaw (or 'Shay', as then commonly spelt, and pronounced, in Yorkshire). Americ Shay had goods valued at £3, Laurence at £2 and the remainder, William, Edmund, James and Robert at £1. The record does not include place names, but a cluster of of six names is associated with the Tunstead and Boarshurst area, where the same surnames occur 45 years later: 'George Whewall, 'uxor Johis Whewall and Willms Knyght' (at Tunstead) and 'Amer Shay, laur Shay and Willms Shay' (at Boarshurst).

We might also note here that in 1519 a Lawrence Shaw was a witness to a deed of feoffment from John Fernele, involving 'all his land and tenements in the Parish of Sadilworth frythe called Grenefeld Stye'.[5] This is the same Greenfield Stye mentioned in the Contrariants Roll of 1322, and later known as Fur Lane, in Boarshurst.[6]

In the winter of 1590/1, two days after Candlemas (i.e. 4th February), John Ramsden, who had just bought Saddleworth Manor, commissioned a record of all his tenants in Lordsmere, the rents they owned and the payments they made.[7] Of about 70 tenants at will (allowing for double entries) the most common surnames were: Broadbent (12), Platt (11) and Shaw (9).

The recurrence of surnames in Saddleworth is indicative of continuity of residence. While some new names appear in the records of 1545 and 1590, others have much earlier Saddleworth origins. Over time the spelling changed, and the prefix 'de' or 'del' was dropped during the 15th century. However, the following surnames appear in the main records for Saddleworth between 1322 and 1590 and indicate the longest established Saddleworth families:[8]

1322	1379	1397/8	1401/10	1545	1590
del Shagh	del Schaghe	del Schagh	del Schag	Shay	Shawe
de Merslande	de Mescheland	de Merslond	....	Marsland	Marslande
de Haukeserde	Hawred	de haukyard	Hawkeherd	....	Haukeyearde
del Plat	del Platte	de Plat	del Platte	....	Platt
de Hasilgref*	....	....	de Hasulgreve	Hesilgreve	Hasselgreave
(* 1297 lay	de Queuwall	de Qweywall	de Cwewalle	Whewall	Wheawall
subsidy)	Wryglegh	Wrygley	Wrigley	Wrigley	Wriggleye
		Qwytehered	Cwythed	Whithed	Whitehead

There is also a striking continuity of first names within the Shaw families of Saddleworth over the same period. Some of these were in common use of course. We saw in chapter 1 that, in 1379, 85% of male Saddleworth taxpayers shared just five first names, so a recurrence of these names amongst Shaws is scarcely surprising. However, other names are much less common. A survey of ten English counties finds that the names Edmund and Lawrence, for example, are very uncommon in 1377/81 and in the 16th century.[9] Yet these names, in particular Edmund, recur in Saddleworth Shaw families across several generations, and are therefore another indicator of continuity. The following first names of Shaws are recorded in two or more of these time periods.

1322	1379	1401/1410	1545	1590/1612
Robert	Robert	Robert	Robert	Robert
Richard	William	William	William	Richard
John	John	John	Lawrence*	William
Edmund		Ralph	Edmund	John
		Laurence		Ralphe
		Edmund	* also 1519	Edmund

The continuity of Shaws in Saddleworth is mirrored in comparative analysis of trends in neighbouring settlements. A survey of the poll tax returns from 1379 in twelve West Riding settlements in the near vicinity of Saddleworth shows a striking diversity of surnames.[10] Excluding 26 taxpayers who clearly do not yet have a recorded surname, the records for these twelve settlements contain a total of 437 entries, each naming either a married couple, or a single individual aged 16+. The entries comprise no fewer than 282 distinct surnames, or a ratio of 1 surname to 1.5 taxpayers.

This diversity of names is striking, but not surprising. In these early days of surname formation, names had been adopted to distinguish one individual or family from another. So in most cases, a surname is unique within the settlement, and there is very limited commonality of names between different settlements. Out of the 282 distinct surnames, only 23 are recorded in more than one settlement; and only six in more than two settlements.

In Saddleworth, just six surnames occur more than once in the 1379 poll tax returns: the names Shaw, Hawkyard, Fernlee, Whewall, Sykes and Preston are each borne by two married couples, while the first four of these names are also held by six unmarried individuals. This does not imply unrelated families that happen to bear the same name. Rather, the pattern illustrates the normal ramification of families whose surnames have been established for longer: the first three of these surnames (Shaw, Hawkyard and Fernlee) are already recorded in

Saddleworth in the much shorter list of names in 1322. If anything, these records illustrate how dramatically the Black Death must have curtailed the ramification of Shaws in Saddleworth, after Robert de Staveley del Schaghe, the great grandfather of Robert del Schagh Mercator, had fathered six sons earlier in the century.

By comparison, the 1545 lay subsidy records contain a very similar number of taxpayers, but a greatly reduced diversity of surnames. In 1379, 282 distinct names were shared between 437 taxpayers: a ratio of 1:1.5. In 1545, just 152 surnames were shared between 457 taxpayers: a ratio of 1:3. Many surnames had been lost for ever. Within Saddleworth, the names Tasker, Lyggard, Kirkyarde, Nuttehirst, de Oranden, de Grotton, del Den and Bakestoman appear in 1379, but had disappeared for ever by 1545. Many names must have been lost through failure to produce a surviving male heir, as the population continued to decline for at least a century after the Black Death.

But as the population recovered and began to increase, certain well-established surnames became more populous. Our survey of twelve neighbouring settlements in the West Riding finds that of the 282 distinct surnames recorded in 1379, only 66 survived within these twelve communities to appear in the lay subsidy of 1545, while as many as 86 new names were recorded in 1545, indicating significant inward migration. However, the surviving names, belonging to families long established in the area, were much more populous. The 66 surviving names were held by 272 taxpayers (59% of the taxpaying population), while 86 new names were held by just 185 taxpayers (41% of the tax-paying population). The older, established surnames had ramified more in their ancestral communities than those of more recent arrivals.

Saddleworth witnessed a similar pattern. Compared with 1379, the 1545 lay subsidy shows a greatly reduced diversity of surnames in

Saddleworth, but the surviving names are more populous: of of the 43 taxpayers listed, as many as 33 shared just eight surnames. The name Shaw had survived, and the number of Shaw families was increasing too. The Shaws lived mainly in Lordsmere, rather than other parts of Saddleworth, and they were mostly taxpayers, rather than the exempt poor.

Year	Saddleworth Records	Total Recorded	Total Shaws
1379	Poll Tax payers: all aged 16+	56	3
1545	Lay Subsidy payers: income of £1+	43	6
1590	Saddleworth Manor Tenants	70	9
1641	Protestation Returns: all males aged 18+	383	30
1664	Hearth Tax payers all Saddleworth (exemptions)	242 (78)	19 (3)
1664	Hearth Tax Payers Lordsmere only (exemptions)	85 (36)	13 (2)

*****

Migration also played a part in the ramification of Shaws. In Medieval times migration was limited. Family members typically remained in their home settlement, occupying hereditary lands or indeed tied to a feudal estate; but others, perhaps failing to inherit lands, or in search of new opportunities, may have looked outside, Where migration did occur, it generally involved movement to an immediately neighbouring settlement within the same parish, or more occasionally to an adjacent parish. Migration over longer distances was unusual, except for the wealthy. This was due in part to limited means of mobility, but also to constrained cultural horizons in an agrarian economy. An identification with a dialect, a type of work, a church, an extended family or social networks nurtured a reluctance to move beyond one's own 'country'.[11]

Nevertheless, migration is evident in new names that appear in Saddleworth in the 1545 lay subsidy. Some of these evidently migrated into the area from adjacent settlements in the east of Lancashire. Of the

43 taxpayers listed for Saddleworth (or "Qwyk") in 1545, as many as 12 were named either Scolefield (6), Buckley (2) or Gartside (4). None of these names had been present in Saddleworth in 1379, but all three derive from local place names in Rochdale and Oldham, indicating an eastward migration of members of these families into Saddleworth. In 1379, three Scolefields and two Buckleys had been recorded in Butterworth, the division of Rochdale that borders Saddleworth, while two more Buckleys had been recorded in the Hundersfield division of Rochdale and in Ashton-under-Lyne. The name Gartside appears in the 1524 lay subsidy for Rochdale, identified as being 'of Gartside in Butterworth', as distinct from the same place name in Oldham.[12] These new arrivals did not have to move far to settle in Saddleworth.

There is also some limited evidence of migration from Saddleworth eastwards, further into Yorkshire. For example, two married couples named Sykes were recorded in Saddleworth in 1379: by 1545, the name had disappeared from Saddleworth, but five Sykes were recorded to the east: four in nearby Slaithwaite, and one in Huddersfield.[13]

Was there any migration of Shaws in this period? There is no evidence to indicate migration of Shaws from east Lancashire into Saddleworth. The Salford Hundred returns for the poll tax of 1379 contain not a single Shaw in Saddleworth's immediate neighbours to the west, namely Rochdale, Oldham and Ashton. Further afield in Lancashire, we find evidence of the Lancashire Shaw families identified by R Cunliffe Shaw (see chapter 1), but these are too distant to offer a plausible migration pattern into Saddleworth.[14] Nor is there evidence to suggest any migration of Shaws from other parts of Yorkshire into Saddleworth. Such few Shaws as are recorded in the West Riding of Yorkshire in 1379 are far distant from Saddleworth, in the vicinity of Sheffield, Halifax and beyond. The ramification of Shaw families within Saddleworth was due to the internal growth, not migration from elsewhere.

Nor do we find evidence of any westerly migration of Shaws from Saddleworth into Lancashire. The lay subsidy records of 1524 and 1545 show no Shaws in Oldham, Rochdale or Ashton. The later, and much more numerous, Protestation Returns of 1641, recorded all adult males, regardless of wealth or status, who took the oath 'to live and die for the true Protestant religion, the liberties and rights of subjects and the privilege of Parliaments'. Most records confirm that every adult male in the community took the oath, without exception. Even at this later date, the name Shaw is still found only very rarely in neighbouring Lancashire settlements: 0 out of 221 names in Oldham; 1 out of 371 in the Rochdale division of Butterworth; 4 out of 615 in Ashton-under-Lyne. Migration on any scale from Saddleworth into east Lancashire would not occur until the industrial revolution.[15]

There is, however, evidence of some eastward migration. While Shaws clearly multiplied strongly within Saddleworth, some branches of the family also migrated along the Colne Valley, to the nearby settlements of Marsden, Slaithwaite and Huddersfield. While they may have been attracted by new opportunities to farm on recently enclosed lands, the pattern certainly reflected Saddleworth's identity as a settlement in the West Riding of Yorkshire since before the Conquest, and its strong historical links with the manors of Almondbury and Huddersfield. In 1322, and again in 1584, Almondbury manor was responsible for courts leet and tax collection in a number of satellite townships, including Saddleworth. Sir John Ramsden of Longley, whose family had acquired the manor of Saddleworth in 1590, also took possession of Huddersfield Manor (in 1599) and Almondbury Manor in 1627, reflecting and further strengthening cross-Pennine links with Saddleworth.[16]

The number of Shaws recorded, out of the total returns in 1379, 1545, 1641 and 1664, shows a steady increase therefore, both within Saddleworth and in these neighbouring West Riding settlements:

Shaw Entries	1379:Poll Tax (all adults aged 16+)	1545: Lay Subsidy (£1+ income)	1641: Protestation Returns (all males aged 18+)	1664: Hearth Tax returns (incl. exempts)
Saddleworth	3/56	6/43	30/381	22/320
Marsden	-*	3/29	25/198	13/83
Slaithwaite	0/13	1/14	9/269	6/95
Huddersfield	0/35	2/31	13/303	6/141
Almondbury	0/30	0/60	8/274	0/184

* *(There are no separate records for Marsden in 1379: these were probably included in returns for Huddersfield and/or Almondbury)*

Ramification of Shaws, from 1379 to 1545, follows a similar pattern to that of several other surnames that became prominent in this part of the West Riding. By 1545, across 12 neighbouring West Riding settlements, just nine surnames were held by more than ten taxpayers. But each of these nine names, from small beginnings in 1379, had both multiplied within its ancestral community and also spread to immediately neighbouring settlements (or 'vills').

Surnames with 10+ entries recorded in 1545

	1379		1545	
Name	Vills	Taxpayers	Vills	Taxpayers
Armitage	Crosland	1	Crosland + 6 other vills	21
Beaumont*	Crosland	-	Crosland +3 other vills	20
Brook	Huddersfield	5	Huddersfield +1 other vill	17
Dyson	Crosland +1 other vill	2	Crosland +2 other vills	13
Haigh	Wharmby	1	Wharmby +4 other vills	16
Hirst	Wharmby	1	Wharmby +6 other vills	20
Key	Farnlay Tias	1	Farnlay Tias +5 other vills	16
Ramsden	Holmfirth	1	Eland +1 other vill	18
Shaw	Qwyke	3	Qwyke +3 other vills	12

* *(The Beaumont family is not named in the poll tax of 1379 but had been granted lands in South Crosland earlier in the century.)*

In 1658, Marie Whewall, of Ballgreave in Lordsmere in Saddleworth, the daughter of our ancestor William Shawe, wrote an informative will, bestowing small legacies on numerous relatives. These included relatives on the eastern slopes of the Pennines: Elizabeth, wife of Abraham Shawe of Marsden, and Mary, wife of James Bottomley of Longland in Slaithwaite.[17] Both husbands' names appear in the Protestation Returns of 1641 for Marsden and Slaithwaite respectively. They appear to have formed part of a wider pattern of migration, eastwards from Saddleworth.

The surname of Shaw had originally been adopted, in the 14th century, as a means of distinguishing one family from another. Now, in the 17th century, it signalled membership of an extended family network, based on a common ancestry. Later we will trace the fortunes of one branch of this family, who, in the late 16th century, held a manorial tenancy in Boarshurst, Saddleworth. But before then we should pause the chronological narrative of the Shaws, to reflect on the social, political and religious context which shaped their lives.

II SADDLEWORTH (1545-1815)

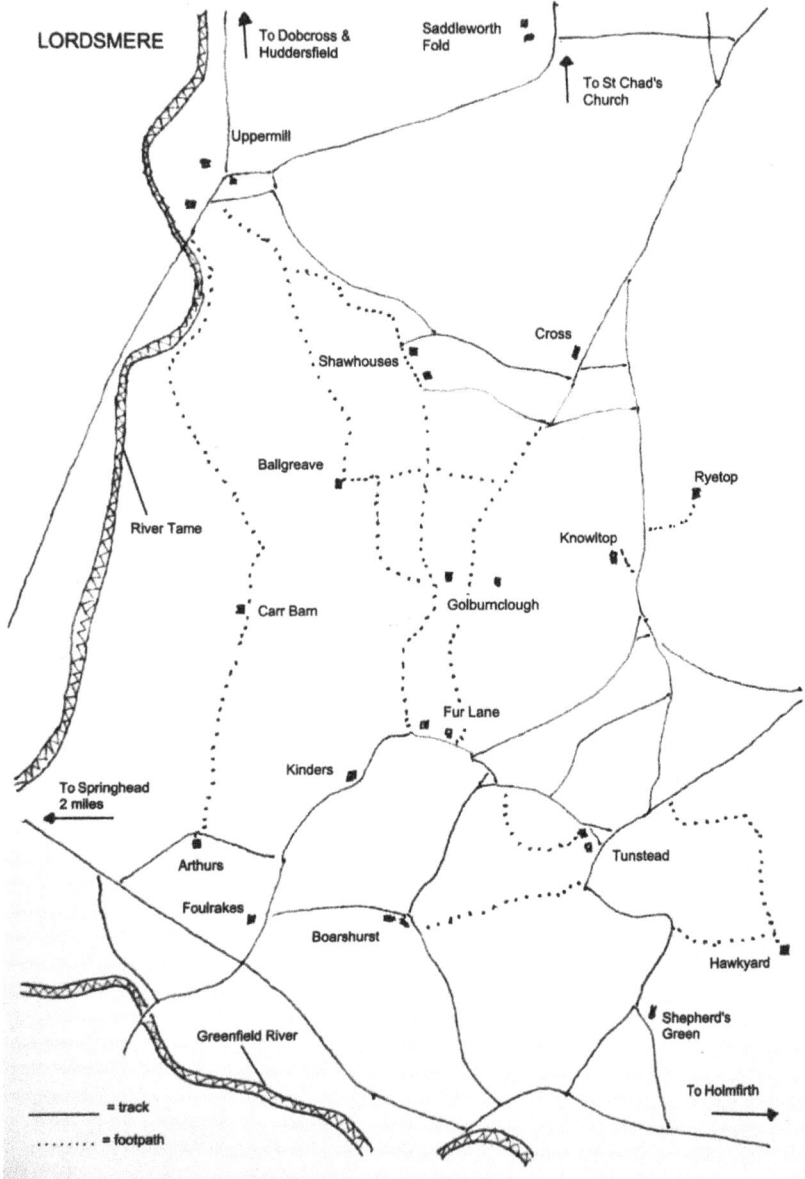

LORDSMERE

To Dobcross & Huddersfield

Saddleworth Fold

To St Chad's Church

Uppermill

Cross

Shawhouses

Ballgreave

Ryetop

River Tame

Knowltop

Carr Barn

Golburnclough

Fur Lane

Kinders

To Springhead 2 miles

Tunstead

Arthurs

Foulrakes

Boarshurst

Hawkyard

Greenfield River

Shepherd's Green

To Holmfirth

——— = track

.... = footpath

5 : TENANTS AT WILL

The origins of the name Saddleworth are obscure but are thought to derive from the Old English word 'scead', meaning a boundary, and 'worth', a common name in the western Pennines meaning enclosure or summer pasture.[1] Saddleworth (also known as Qwyk or Quick) was located in the West Riding of Yorkshire, although on the western side of the Pennine watershed, and until 1866 was a chapelry within the Lancashire parish of Rochdale. Today, with a population of around 25,000, the area comprises a collection of villages and suburban settlements, such as Dobcross, Delph, Uppermill, Grasscroft, Greenfield, Grotton, Austerlands and Springhead; but before the industrial revolution, Saddleworth was characterised by tiny hamlets and scattered farmsteads. James Butterworth, in 1828, described 72 hamlets, and could have included more.[2]

In pre-industrial times (see map on page 1), Saddleworth was divided into four 'meres' (administrative boundaries or 'constablericks'):

- Lords Mere, to the east, was much the largest area geographically, covering lands to the east of the River Tame. It included the modern-day villages of Digglee, Dobcross and Uppermill and areas to the south and east of them. The name reflects the estate of the Lord of the Manor of Saddleworth.
- Shaw Mere in the central area was carved out of Lordsmere to create a sub-manor for the junior branch of the de Staveley family, who subsequently changed their family name to 'del Schaghe'. The area included the settlements of Wharmton and Grasscroft, as well as Shaw Hall and the medieval estate of the Schaghe.

- Friar Mere, to the north of Delph, was named after a Black Friars house and estate that existed until the dissolution of the monasteries in 1536.
- Quick Mere, in the south west, was named after the 14th century de Quick family, and included Lydgate, Grotton, Lane, Thornlee, Austerlands and Springhead. To the west it bordered the settlements of Rochdale, Oldham, Lees and Ashton Parish, while to the south it bordered Stalybridge and Mossley. In medieval times Quick appears to have been a separate 'vill' from Saddleworth Frith, but later the whole of Saddleworth was often referred to as 'Quick' or 'Saddleworth-cum-Quick'.

We saw in earlier chapters that the manor of Saddleworth initially covered the areas of both Lordsmere and Shaw Mere, and that the Shaw estate was granted to the del Schaghe family, descendants of the de Staveleys of Staley Manor, becoming a sub-manor within Saddleworth Manor. By 1410, leading members of the del Schaghes having left the area, ownership of the Shaw estate transferred to the Radcliffes. Saddleworth Manor meanwhile changed hands several times after the male line of the Stapletons ended, until it was bought by William Ramsden of Longley in 1590. Subsequently the Ramsdens also bought the Shaw Estate from the Radcliffes in 1604 and Shaw Hall in 1611, re-uniting them with the manor of Saddleworth,

After the English Civil War, in which the then Lord of the Manor, Sir John Ramsden, died on the losing side, his family would have been required to pay reparations during the Commonwealth, through forced land sales or the Decimation Tax, and the Saddleworth Manor was sold to William Farrer of Ewood for £2,950 in 1654. When his great-grandson, James Farrer, died in 1791, the estate was sold in lots, mostly to the principal tenants, who overnight cast off their status of tenants and husbandmen to become landowners and yeomen.

In the late 16th century our Shaw ancestors were husbandmen, tenants of the Lord of the Manor of Saddleworth, whose estate expanded to comprise over 3,000 acres by the mid-18th century. Our ancestors farmed in Lordsmere. For about three centuries they lived in Boarshurst, and later close by within a triangular area south-east of modern-day Uppermill, about a mile from north to south, and a mile at the base of the triangle from east to west. They lived in farmsteads or hamlets whose names have changed little over the years: Boarshurst, Lower House, Shawhouses, Golburn Clough, Fur Lane, Carr Barn and Ryetop. Although modern development has expanded along the valley of the River Tame and immediately to the south of Boarhurst, the area to the north and east of Boarshurst remains rural, crossed by narrow lanes that were farm tracks in earlier centuries.

We saw in the last chapter how Shaws ramified in Saddleworth, and always constituted a sizeable proportion of the local population, almost 14% of tax-payers in the 1545 lay subsidy, for example,[3] and about 12% of the manorial tenants in Lordsmere.[4] Hearth Tax Returns of 1664-1674 also show a heavy concentration of Shaws in Lordsmere, some 15% of all tax-payers there.

Exemptions from the Hearth Tax were made for those occupying a house, tenement or lands with a yearly value of less than 20 shillings, those whose assets were worth less than £10 and those who did not pay poor rates. About a quarter of Saddleworth families were exempted from paying the Hearth Tax, but of the 22 Shaw families listed across Saddleworth, only three were exempted.[5] Shaws were well-established in the area.

Trade directories compiled for the whole of Saddleworth in 1818, 1822, 1829 and 1834 show that around 6% to 8% of the trading population were named Shaw.[6] Applying this percentage to the overall population suggests that over 350 people named Shaw lived in

Saddleworth in the late 18th century and over 600 by the 1820s. The 1881 census records 701 Shaws.

The Shaws living in Lordsmere in the 16th, 17th and 18th centuries shared a common ancestry. In 1658, Marie Whewall, daughter of William Shawe of Boarshurst, provided numerous small legacies to nephews, nieces and cousins, their children and grandchildren and more distant relations, who were almost all living in this area. Such an extended family network, bolstered by the custom of god-parenting and operating in parallel to neighbourhood networks, continued deep into the 18th century. It was often of practical value. For instance, a younger son, newly married and looking for a cottage or land to rent, might be helped out by a member of his extended family network.

In terms of social hierarchy, husbandmen sat between yeomen (who owned the land they farmed) and labourers (who were paid wages). Husbandmen were tenant farmers.[7] In the 16th century, husbandmen in Lordsmere were not freemen, but 'tenants at will'. They held their tenures according to the good will of the Lord of the Manor and on his terms and conditions. However, they had developed significant customary rights, in particular the right to retain the tenancy in the family across generations. This continuity was useful for the landlord too, as it gave tenants a greater motivation to maintain the fabric of buildings and lands. Many of these tenancies comprised 20-25 acres of land, although population growth led to the sub-division of farms. The tenant could also, with the agreement with the Lord of the Manor, sub-let parts of the land for income; so while leading a simple life they generally enjoyed financial stability.

At the end of the 16th century most leases were for a fixed duration, but could be renewed at the end of the term, subject to payment of a one-off 'garsome' or entry fine.[8] A lease could also, by custom, be passed on to the leaseholder's heirs at his death. Most leases agreed in

1594/5 appear to have lasted for 18 years, as they were renewed in 1612/13, but later leases could last 21 years or longer still. Gyles Shawe of Boarshurst held two leases at his death in 1634: one of these was said to have thirty years left before expiry.[9]

By now, the old custom of contributing several days of work to the Lord of the Manor had largely fallen away, to be replaced by rent and garsomes. Garsomes were cash payments to renew the term of a lease, although they could be made partly in kind, with oxen, cattle or sheep. The rent was by custom held at a low level, but the garsome or entry fine could increase markedly, becoming the principal element of the payment to the landowner. Most will inventories of the period record the value of the 'reversion of the lease', which reflected the years remaining on the lease and the cost of the garsome. This could account for up to 50% of the value of a husbandman's estate at his death.

The Lord of the Manor also held two courts that tenants may be asked to support, as part of collective community responsibility for ensuring zgood conduct. These were named the Court Baron and the Court Leet. The Court Baron dealt with offences against the customs of the manor and regulated agricultural affairs. It typically issued warnings to tenants, or 'amercements' (fines), for misdemeanours such as: failing to maintain their buildings; letting their animals graze on the Lord's land; felling wood or digging turf where they had no right; diverting the path of a stream or blocking a pathway. Tenants could be asked to serve as jurors on the court, and those who neglected to attend the court were liable to be fined.

The Court Leet was concerned with the maintenance of law and order, and for Saddleworth it fell under the manor of Almondbury, on the eastern side of the Pennines. The community was required to elect five tenants annually: one to act as Constable and four to act as his Bylawmen. Essentially their role was to report crimes to the court – 'to present misdemeanours within the view of Frankpledge'. Most of these misdemeanours involved affray: more serious cases of 'affray drawing blood' would incur a larger amercement. The roles were unpaid and burdensome, so not very popular. It is unclear how individuals were 'elected', but one record suggests that a roll of the dice might have played a part.[10]

An indenture of 1629, for a 24 year lease, illustrates the sort of terms and obligations that applied to manorial tenants. It stated that:

'Sir John Ramsden of Longley in the Countie of yorke knight... doth demise lease grant and to Ferme lett unto the said Giles Shaw All that his Messuage and Tenemente beinge parcell of the Boareshurste ... and all other houses edifices buildinges, Cottages barnes outshutts gardens Landes Closes Meadowes pastures and Turbarye thereunto belonginge ...'

Giles was principally required to:

'...[paye] the yearly Rent or Ferme of Eighteen shillinges of good & lawfull money of England att the Feastes of Penticost and St Martin the Bishopp in Winter by even porcions , And one Fatt Capon at Easter yearly duringe the said terme';
'...bringe or cause to be brought All the Corne and graynes of Corne that shalbe within the said term upon the premisses growinge his corn' to one of Sir John Ramsden's mills 'to be grinded and moultered at such Rate and quantitye as other like Tenantes Corne is';
'...make and doe suit and servisse unto the Court of the said Sir John Ramsden and his heires';
'...sufficiently Repaire uphold mainetaine and defend all the said Messuage and Tenemente and all the houses and buildinges apppertaineinge the same with all needfull and necessarie

Repaireacons And all the landes Closes and groundes hereby demised with hedges walles ditches wayres pilerow and other defens';

'... not Fell or Cut downe any ashe or oake in and upon the predemised premises growinge';

'And also shall ayde and beare parte of the Charge with the said Sir John Ramsden and his heires when and as often as he or they shalbe Called uppon and charged to serve in the warres with the kinges most excellent majestie his heires and Successors or to make forthe any man or men, horse or horses or any parte of Armor belongeinge thereunto like as other Tenantes of the said Sir John Ramsden in Saddleworth afforesaid shall doe.'[11]

The last (feudal) requirement here, to support the Lord of the Manor in wars on behalf of the King, was still a common condition in manorial leases at this time, as the text of the lease implies. A lease to James Whewall of Ballgreave in 1612, for example, contains almost identical wording.[12] It was perhaps primarily intended for wars against foreign powers, but was it enforced just a few years later, in 1642, in the English Civil War? And what impact did this have on the tenants of Saddleworth Manor?

There is limited evidence, but one record in the Saddleworth Archives suggests that the condition in the lease was activated. It relates to Edmund Shawe, son of Edmund Shawe Senior, who had inherited the family lease at Overmylne (Uppermill) in 1632: 'Edmund Shawe, leasee, being called out by the Ramsdens of Langley to follow in their train during the Civil Wars of Charles the 1st reign, according to tradition, most probably met his death at the time when even the noblest of the land could not escape.'[13] The condition was dropped from leases after the civil war, as we can see from a lease to a Robert Shay, dated 1 March 1648/9, six weeks after the execution of Charles I.[14]

6 : EVEN SUCH IS TIME

Life in pre-industrial Saddleworth was hard, and more often than not short. All the more important was it therefore to bequeath possessions and money to later generations in an orderly manner. A surprising number of wills survive from this period and they reflect a determination to manage an orderly death, and a degree of confidence and self-esteem, underpinned by faith. Joseph Scolefeild of Arthurs reflected this in his will of 1713, which used common phraseology: 'being sicke or weak in Body but of Sound and perfect Memory, Thankes be given to Almighty God for the same, And knowing the Uncertainty of this life on Earth and being desirous to Settle things in Order...' Great care was taken to distribute assets fairly, to ensure continuation of the family tenancy, to protect the livelihood of the widow, and (not always successfully, as we shall see in chapters 10 and 11) to avoid family disputes over inheritance.

Surviving wills from this pre-industrial period illustrate that, even for the better off husbandman, possessions were sparse and functional. Some 17th century wills contain bequests of clothing – a hat, a cloake, even a used 'payre of breeches'. The inventories attached to wills, 'prized' or assessed for their value, are touching for the meticulous detail they provide. Inventories from the first half of the 17th century generally itemise around 10-15 items, without sub-dividing 'husbandrie geere' or 'hustlement about the house'; but by the start of the 18th century inventories often run to 35 items.

Inside the house of an 18th century testator, possessions may have included: 'the bed on which I now lye' (usually bequeathed to the testator's wife), beddinge, apparel, an arke, an earthen pott, a chayre, a stoole, ffyre Irons, a payre of Bellowes, a skillett, ffrying pans, laders, Hacking knives, Fackenhooks, tresles, a hopper, a lantherne, a Wiskitt, a Baskitt, a smoothing Iron, butter, cheese, a cheese presse, meale, a garner, a grindle stone...or even 'a straw hamper with somewhat in it'. In a small nod to personal comfort, 'Chushions' or 'Cushins' were now sometimes itemised.

A huge assortment of husbandry gear is listed in inventories of the period – wheelbarrows and trindles, a turf sledge and turves, a ground sledge, a hay sledge, sythes, sickles, ploughs, forks, shovels, spades, saws, sives, chizels, pincers, axes, hamers, mattocks, rakes, muckforkes, ridels, scuttels, nogers, a stone trough... There were often animals, young and old, productive, barren or lame: sheep, cows, a meere (mare), a swine, as well as the gear that went with them, such as a pack sadle, a hackney sadle, a swingletree...

Several wills refer to bee-keeping, no doubt exploiting moorland heather. At Boarshurst in 1634, Gyles Shawe kept 'Bees, pollen and a swine' valued at £1.10s. At neighbouring Tunstead in 1641, in addition to oxen and sheep, John Whewall kept bees valued at £1. At Arthurs in 1715, Joseph Scolefeild owned 'Stockes of Bees at home and Abroad', valued at £1.10s., while at Uppermill in 1727, Thomas Shaw Senior (a descendant of Gyles of Boarshurst) had 'one ould Stock of Bees & A swarme of Bees, valued at £1'.[1]

As time passes, there is evidence of a gradual increase in the sophistication of household possessions: we find pewter, brass pots, occasionally an Houre Glasse or even a Clocke or a gun. There is increasing evidence of wool weaving, supplementing, if never completely replacing, husbandry: 'loombes, combestocks, sackes of woll' appear in most 18th century inventories. Later again, in the more urbanised 19th century, we find items of decoration and personal comfort, such as china, glassware and even pictures.

For the duration of the 17th and 18th centuries, life expectancy from birth in England averaged under 40 years, with no upward trend. Mortality was particularly high amongst children: in the period 1550-1800: some 18% of children died in their first year of life, and around 30% before the age of 15. For those who survived beyond the age of 15, life expectancy increased to over 50 years, and we see a few cases of people living into their 60s, 70s and beyond. There was little difference in life expectancy between rich and poor, but rural areas tended to have better life expectancy than crowded and unsanitary towns. From the mid 16th century onwards, however, high mortality rates were offset by even higher birth rates, leading to population growth that has largely continued to the present day.[2]

Death usually arrived, not as the culmination of a slow decline into old age, but as the result of disease. Life was vulnerable to sudden shocks. Bad harvests, such as occurred in England in 1621-23, 1629-31, 1646-51, 1673-74, and 1693-98, could lead to steep increases in the price of bread, acute hardship and death through 'famine fever'. Waves of pestilence periodically swept the land, affecting rich and poor alike. As John Taylor, the water poet, wrote in the fever year of 1623:

'Thou see'st the fearful plague, the flux, the fever,
Which many a soul doth from the body sever.'

The spotted fever (probably typhoid), the flux (dysentery) and the pox (smallpox) were all widespread in the 17th century; so too were malaria and pulmonary infections such as influenza, pneumonia and tuberculosis. Fever seasons were recorded across rural England in 1612-13, 1623-1625, 1638, 1643-1644, 1651, 1657-9 and 1661-1665. Not only children but also the elderly were especially vulnerable. As the contemporary physician Thomas Willis put it, 'Yea old men, and men of ripe age, it ordinarily took away.'

Fevers could not always be identified. In 1625 Abraham Holland described the latest malignant fever as 'the ague with a hundred names'. Between 1643 and 1685 at least five epidemics were named 'new disease'. The fevers could linger for several months. It was as well to prepare a will early in the onset of symptoms: while some recovered, 'those who died passed away in a stupor without consciousness to dispose of their goods'.[3]

Bubonic plagues re-appeared in successive waves. After the Black Death, it is thought that there were thirty further outbreaks of bubonic plague in the period 1351-1485, while there were four major outbreaks between 1603 and the last epidemic in 1665.[4] In one of these, in 1604, the city of York lost a quarter of its population in a single year due to an outbreak of plague.[5]

We cannot precisely track the impact of these episodes in Saddleworth: church registers tend not to record the causes of death and are too patchy to enable comparison of baptism and burial numbers for relevant years. However, we can see sudden and shocking mortality affecting individual families. In the fever year of 1623, William Shawe watched two adult sons die before he also succumbed – all within the space of a month. His brother Ralph, on the other hand, survived to the age of 76. In the spring of 1658 there was an outbreak of influenza. According to the physician Willis, 'suddenly a distemper arose as if sent by some blast of the stars'. It was followed in the summer and autumn by a malignant fever epidemic that claimed many lives, including possibly, on 3 September, that of Oliver Cromwell, who is thought to have suffered from malaria.[6] Perhaps these epidemics carried off our ancestor Marie Whewall (nee Shawe) and her husband Francis Whewall, who died within three months of each other in the spring and summer of that year.

Life expectancy rates altered little in the 18th century, but there were two significant changes in the causes of mortality: the disappearance of bubonic plague after 1666 and the rapid spread of phthisis, commonly known as 'consumption' and later as tuberculosis. In 1689 a leading physician described how the symptoms were especially acute in young adults: 'The Consumption of young Men, that are in the Flower of their Age, when the Heat of the Blood is yet brisk… is for the most part acute. But in old Men, where the natural Heat is decayed, it is more Chronical.'[7] The number one killer in the eighteenth century, consumption was called 'the Robber of Youth', because so many of its victims were young; and the 'Great White Plague' or the 'White Death', because of the pallor of TB sufferers. By its peak, in about 1780, 1.25% of the country's population died of consumption each year, and it accounted for a quarter of all deaths in England.[8]

Death from consumption came slowly. When George, the 11 year old son of Thomas and Ann Shaw of Uppermill, and a descendant of Gyles Shawe of Boarshurst, died of consumption in 1799, his parents had a verse inscribed on the gravestone:

'A pale Consumption gave the fatal Blow
The Stroke was certain but the effect was slow
With waisting Pain death found Him long opprest
Pitty'd his Sighs and kindly gave him rest.' [9]

Another inscription, on the gravestone of a 17 year old girl in 1770, cautions that youth is no guarantor of a long life:

'Take care, ye young and Gay;
Your sun may set at Noon,
Like me be clad in Clay
Before another Moon.'[10]

For just 17 months, between January 1772 and May 1773, the new curate of St Chad's church, Saddleworth, recorded age and cause of death for entries in the parish burial register.[11] His local records were broadly consistent with national trends, consumption, smallpox and fever being particularly virulent. Incidence of child mortality was dreadful: out of 152 burials in the 17 month period, 46 (30%) were of children aged 0-4 years old, while only 18 people (about 12%) were older than 64. The curate thought it superfluous to attribute a cause of death to infants (the 24 children who died before their first birthday) or to the elderly (the 18 people aged 64-94), while a few cases were uncertain. But he recorded cause of death for 100 other burials:

Causes of Death in 100 Burials: 1772-1773			
35	Consumption	2	Cholic
23	Smallpox	2	Drowned
18	Fever	2	Childbed or Overlain
10	Convulsions	2	Sore Throat or Teeth
5	Dropsy	1	Palsy

In the period 1791-1796, a later curate took to recording accidental deaths, perhaps for curiosity or rarity value. They included: 'Died on Hown Moss accidently'; 'Drowned at Gatehead Bridge'; 'Killed by a horse'; 'shot by accident'; 'killed in the colepit'; and 'Killed by lightning'. Other references are to a death 'in the poorhouse' and the death of 'a poor boy', which again required no further explanation.

For all the rapid increase in population in 18th century Saddleworth, there remained waves of especially high mortality. In the 1790s, war with revolutionary France and resultant food shortages increased vulnerability to disease, and in six of the last ten years of the century burials exceeded baptisms in the registers of St Chad's. In 1793, the year war was declared, John Bentley of Boarshurst lost three of his children in the space of four months.

The church of St Chad had been founded in about 1205 as a chapel of ease within the parish of Rochdale, and built beside a trans-Pennine pack-horse route. Until the later 18th century it remained the only church in Saddleworth, so all baptisms, marriages and burials took place there. From Elizabethan times through to the 19th century, except for a brief interlude during the Commonwealth, church attendance was compulsory (in theory at least). The church of St Chad was, therefore, a vital social hub that brought together all of the scattered rural communities of Saddleworth.

Its surviving registers start from 1612, but for the next century they are ill-preserved and punctuated by wide gaps, while the surviving loose sheets record very little detail. From 1720 onwards, however, they provide a rich source of information. Baptism registers, for example, record the names of the mother as well as the father, his occupation and the place where they lived. We find other social detail too. Of 18th century baptisms, around 3%-5% annually were to 'single women' or 'spinsters', though the father is usually mentioned too. In 1731, for reasons unknown, the proportion was a remarkable 14%.

The curate of St Chad's for 50 years, from 1721-1771, was the colourful John Heginbottom. A regular customer at the Cross Keys Inn, it was said of him that 'his manner of living was lax, which lost him the esteem of the devout portion of his flock'. He nevertheless prided himself on raising the morals of the community and was known for his 'pungent' sermons.[12] While his church registers generally record the facts without embellishment, the curate is occasionally moved to add local detail or a dry comment, for example:

Burial 1724: Mary Bradbury: Single Woman, de Dig-lee (Vulgo, Mall o'th Coblers)

Marriage 1737: Robert Tomins an Irishman Sojourner in Saddleworth and Catherine his pretended wife

Baptism 1742: Thomas son of Ann Shaw of Wall Hill Spinster, by No Man (as She Saith)

By the 18th century, very few people gave their occupation as husbandman, and more than 80% were described as 'clothier'. However, the registers do record a wide range of additional occupations that illustrate community life at the time, for example those mentioned in the baptism register between 1726 and 1736:

badger, blacksmith, carpenter, carrier, clogger, cloth dresser, collier, cropper, fuller, fustian weaver, hostler, inn-keeper, labourer, linen webster, mason, miller, plaisterer, scribler, shoemaker, slater, soldier, tailor, webster, yeoman.

The registers now show younger people moving frequently from one location to another. William Shaw, a grandson of our ancestor William who had died in 1701, lived at Wharmton Brow, Boarshurst and Wellihole, before inheriting his tenancy at Boarshurst; he subsequently moved to Grottonhead in Quick Mere for his later years. His younger brother Thomas lived at five different locations in the space of 20 years: Boarshurst, Knarr, Uppermill, Dobcross and Dodlecroft.

The registers also show increasing interaction not just between different parts of Saddleworth, such as Lords Mere and Quick Mere, but with neighbouring parishes in Ashton, Mossley, Oldham, Mottram and Manchester. Horizons were broadening. Times were changing.

7 : THE OLD ORDER CHANGETH

There were periods of social, religious, economic and political upheaval. In the English Civil War, the Lord of Saddleworth Manor, Sir John Ramsden, like other larger landowners and merchants, championed the Royalist cause. Even though he appears to have raised troops from his tenants, local opinion may not have been supportive. In 1642, as the country lurched towards civil war, a Protestation Return for 'Quick-cum-Sadleworth' lists males over the age of 18 who took the oath 'to live and die for the true Protestant religion, the liberties and rights of subjects and the privilege of Parliaments'. Some 383 Saddleworth men took the oath, of whom 30 were named Shaw.[1] Of course, Parliament's invitation to take the oath may have felt more like an instruction, and the returns are thought to represent the entire adult male population of Saddleworth at the time. In 1654, during the Commonwealth, Sir John Ramsden's son William would be obliged to sell Saddleworth manor, a cost of being on the losing side.

The English Civil War left fault lines in English social life that would persist for centuries, between Anglicanism and Puritanism, Church and Chapel, and in politics between Tory and Liberal parties. By the late 16th and early 17th centuries, Puritanism was strong in the Pennines, and several curates at St Chad's had been of non-conformist outlook.[2] We know that our ancestors were non-conformist from the early 19th century, but their sympathies probably began earlier. There is evidence that families read the bible for themselves in English, or, as the Puritan Reverend Richard Baxter put it: 'Yea, some few that cannot read get others to read to them, and get a good measure of saving knowledge'.[3]

Following the restoration of monarchy in 1660, however, Anglicanism received strong royal support. The Corporation Act (1661) restricted municipal leaders to those who received the Anglican communion; and the Act of Uniformity (1662) restricted the ministry to those who had been ordained by a bishop, thus disqualifying Puritan clergy. The Lord Lieutenant of the North Riding of Yorkshire, Lord Fauconberg, commented that in Lancashire, 'not one man in the whole county intends to conform', and similar comments were made of Yorkshire.[4] In 1661 the curate of St Chad's in Saddleworth, Ralph Wood, resigned rather than take the oath of conformity.[5] By the 18th century, St Chad's was firmly episcopal in outlook, sufficiently so to turn away John Wesley on a visit to Delph in 1788. But his attempted visit was a sign that the non-conformism was on the rise again.

The Black Death in 1348-1350 had reduced England's population by over 40%, and it took around 200 years for the population to recover to pre-pandemic levels. However, by the 17th century, despite high rates of child mortality and largely static life expectancy, population growth was rapid in Saddleworth, as elsewhere in England. For the period of 1612-1750, the St Chad church registers contain almost twice as many baptisms (3,007) as burials (1,568), while between 1720 and 1790 there were more baptisms than burials in all but three years. The industrial revolution gave yet further stimulus to population growth, as we see below.[6]

The growth in population led to important changes. First, it constrained the availability of land to rent. Younger sons had to move away from the family farm in search of other land, as a tenant or sub-tenant, while increased demand fuelled higher rental prices. Tenancies were often reduced in size – as happened at Boarshurst, where the Shaw's Lower House tenancy was divided in 1713/14.[7]

Estimated Population of Saddleworth

1379 - 180/200

1545 - 220/260

1641 - 1,070

1665 - 1,200/1,400

1750 - 4,000

1782 - 6,918

1801 - 10,665

1821 - 13,902

1841 - 16,829

Second, a shortage of land gave impetus to the domestic weaving industry, initially as a supplement to farming income, but soon as the principal income. Our earlier ancestors were tenant farmers, but by the early 18th century, in common with the majority of Saddleworth residents, they called themselves clothiers. Before long, Saddleworth had developed a reputation for fine broad cloths that were more popular than the older, heavier, woollen cloth. Production increased from 8,640 pieces of woollen cloth in 1740 to 36,637 in 1792 and 60,820 in 1820.[8] By 1822 there were 3,500 woollen looms being operated in Saddleworth, while cotton looms numbered just 300-400.[9] Water-powered mills ('engines' in land tax records) were introduced, and in the early 19th century industrialisation was rapid in both woollen and cotton manufacture, with cotton mills particularly prevalent in western Saddleworth, as well as in the neighbouring towns of Oldham and Ashton.

Domestic manufacture was eventually squeezed out by the more efficient larger mills, and patterns of employment changed again. In the 18th century, all of our male Shaw ancestors in Saddleworth were clothiers who married clothiers' daughters. However, they still farmed land, working in a dual economy that spread risk. After the death of

John Shaw, in 1821, they moved away completely from the land to work in a recognisably industrial economy.

The face of Saddleworth was changing rapidly. James Butterworth, writing in 1828, was struck by the geography of the area, describing Saddleworth as 'a mountainous though in some parts pleasant and romantic country ... interesting though uninviting ... interspersed with high and barren hills and fertile valleys.' He describes the agrarian economy and the common practice of carrying cut corn and hay from the field 'on the shoulders of men, on account of the difficulties of carriages moving up and down the steep declivities of the mountains, and... the scarcity of draft horses, those which are kept being so employed about trade that they can seldom be spared for husbandry.' He also notes the rapid economic and demographic changes: 'The population of Saddleworth has been amazingly on the increase since the introduction of manufactures and trade, these being a stimulus to population and improvements.'[10]

In the same year James Pigot's Commercial Directory was struck by the speed and scale of industrialisation: 'It would be difficult to find a portion of Britain in which industry appears more predominant than this; from a barren and almost uninhabited spot it has become well inhabited, highly cultivated, and abounding with woollen and cotton manufactures, and has gained considerable celebrity from the excellent quality of the articles produced in the district as being equal to any made in the county. The trade of Saddleworth has increased in a very rapid degree.'[11]

The period after 1791 saw political change too. The last Lord of the Manor of Saddleworth died in that year, and his estate was broken up and sold in lots to sitting tenants and entrepreneurs, leading to a more fluid pattern of land ownership and tenancy. The French Revolution had sent shock waves through Europe and increased political tensions, while prompting a vigorous domestic intolerance of dissent. Britain's wars with revolutionary and Napoleonic France led to steep price rises (especially of bread), disruption of trade (including in wool), increased taxation and dramatic reductions in wages (down from 18s per week in 1800 to 5s per week in 1818). There were food riots in 1795-1819, and in 1817 over 3,000 of the 13,000 population of Saddleworth were receiving parish relief.[12] Weavers from the north west of England were active in many of the radical movements of the late 18th and early 19th centuries, demanding universal suffrage and an end to the corn laws (which protected landowners' interests but increased the price of bread).

On 16 August 1819, there was a large protest meeting on St Peter's Field in Manchester to demand reform of parliamentary representation. Five hundred men were said to have practised drilling on Saddleworth Moor, before marching to Manchester with black banners. Many were accompanied by wives and children. They were joined by others from Lees, Mossley, Oldham, Middleton, Ashton-under-Lyne and other Lancashire towns, perhaps as many as 60,000 people. It was a peaceful gathering, but it was dispersed by the local militia with shocking violence, in what became known as the Peterloo Massacre (an ironic echo of the victory over Napoleon at Waterloo in 1815). It is thought that 14-18 people were killed on the day, while some 400-500 were injured, many trampled by horses and some wounded by sabre or bayonet. Subsequent petitions for an inquiry into the violence were dismissed.

At this time, our ancestors, John Shaw and his 18 year-old son Stephen, were living at Thornlee in the far west of Saddleworth, bordering Ashton. They would have known all about the demonstrations, even if they did not take part. It was always told in our family that one of our ancestors had to flee the country to America in the crack-down following Peterloo, but we do not know who, how close a relative or how true that was. An oil-on-wood painting of the Peterloo Massacre, of no great artistic merit, was among family possessions in my childhood. Peterloo was recalled as a significant moment, and one that helped shape the family's social and political outlook.

The Chartist movement in the 1830s and 1840s drew strong support from weavers. The weavers of Ashton-under-Lyne gained a reputation for radical protest more inclined to violence. However, the more peaceable wing of Chartism promoted education, temperance, religious adherence and self-improvement as ways of gaining the right to vote. These were values promoted by the non-conformist movement, which became a strong force in early 19th century Saddleworth, with charismatic preachers at chapels such as Providence Chapel in Springhead and Zion Methodist Chapel in Lees. Our ancestors turned to non-conformism in this period, retaining their commitment deep into the 20th century. Stephen Shaw's first child, Daniel, was baptised at Providence Chapel in 1829, while Stephen and his wife Mary were buried there in 1881 and 1882 respectively. Their surviving son, Eli, became a Member of Ryecroft Independent Church in Ashton-under-Lyne in 1863, and later a Deacon, as well as Headmaster of the Ryecroft Day School and Sunday School.

*****

Increasing literacy was key to many of these changes in society and the economy. There is much academic debate about how to measure literacy, and estimates of historical literacy rates vary. For example, one study estimates that in 17th century England around 30% of adult males and 10% of adult females were fully literate, but that almost 100% of the gentry were literate, some 60% of yeomen and only 15-20% of husbandmen and labourers. A further study suggests literacy rates in the north of England of 35% for men and 9% for women in

1640, rising to 70% for men and 32% for women in 1740.[13] It is clear that literacy skills increased in the 17th and 18th centuries, and that there was some correlation with gender and with social standing. However, in Saddleworth, and no doubt elsewhere too, it is evident that reading skills were more widely developed than writing skills.

In 1543 Henry VIII had called a parliament in an attempt to quell religious discord by passing an Act 'for the advancement of true religion, and abolishment of the contrary'. This banned reading of the bible in public. It allowed merchants and gentlemen to study the bible in the privacy of their own homes. As for 'the lower sort', however, it was considered that bible reading only caused them to fall into error and dispute, so: 'no women, nor artificers, apprentices, journey-men, serving-men under the degree of yeomen; nor no husbandmen, or labourers' were permitted to read the bible, either in public or in private.[14] One implication of this measure is that significant numbers of people under the degree of yeoman were already literate enough to read the bible: why else would a ban be necessary?

Henry's son Edward VI, an unambiguous protestant, soon revoked the Act, and the combination of Protestantism and the printing press ensured the rapid spread of literacy in general, and of bible reading in particular. The 17th century Reverend Richard Baxter, a campaigning Puritan minister and profuse author of sermons and other treatises, was a strong advocate for literacy. Two months before his death in 1691, with an unsteady hand, he wrote his final treatise, *The Poor Husbandman's Advocate to Rich Racking Landlords.* Husbandmen, he lamented, 'are usually so poor that they cannot have time to read a chapter in the bible or to pray in their families. They come in weary from their labours so that they are fitter to sleep than to read or pray.' Once again, the implication is that many husbandmen knew how to read – all the more so since Baxter's focus is on the poorer kind of husbandman who was subject to exploitative rack rents, and who lacked supplementary income from domestic craft or manufacture.[15]

For Saddleworth husbandmen and clothiers, the main purpose of literacy, as Baxter suggests, was to read the Bible, as this was key to understanding the word of God. Several wills from the time provide evidence of bible reading. In 1658, Marie Whewall (daughter of William Shawe of Boarshurst) left 'a great Bible' to two nieces. In 1703, Michael Shaw of Ryetop left 'a Bible and a Sermon Booke', while in 1759 his son, another Michael, bequeathed to his wife Mary: 'four Books (to witt) my largest Bible, Practice of Piety, Companion to the Alter and Common Prayer Book'. He also gave to his grandson 'other a Bible or money to buy one'.[16] These latter bequests in particular suggest some sophistication of reading skills, beyond memorising and repetition, at least in relation to bible reading and church worship.

But there are indications too of reading skills being applied beyond religious teaching to other forms of knowledge and documentation. A striking illustration of reading ability appears in evidence to a Court of Chancery hearing in 1666. In the case of Shawe v Broadbent (see chapter 11), a husbandman named 'Francis Wood of Boareshurst' gave evidence that he had been shown a deed, which granted the disputed lands to the defendant William Broadbent in exchange for a payment of £16. This much he had grasped after 'he did read a little at the beginning of the said Deed.' Even allowing for exaggeration, he would surely not have testified to have understood the gist of a legal document had he been entirely illiterate.[17]

Writing was a more advanced art, of less practical use in a predominantly agrarian economy, and seemingly less widespread. Marie Whewall's husband Francis was an exception. He appeared as a witness or appraiser in many wills of the time, and was clearly skilled in writing as well as reading. In the same court case of Shawe v

Broadbent, he is reported to have witnessed and signed an indenture in 1653. By the time of the second court hearing of 1680 he had been dead for over twenty years, and the authenticity of his signature was called into question. The matter was settled by John Whitehead of Lidyate, who held a recognised legal role on behalf of the Manor: he assured the court that the signature was genuine, as 'he was very well acquainted with the handwritings of ffrancis Whewall'.[18] Francis did indeed have an ornate and accomplished signature.

Many others, however, could read but were little practised in writing. The yeoman, Henry Shaw of Lane, who owned 'Bookes' valued at £1.2s., marked his will with a cross in 1689. This was not just because he was 'Aged and weake in body': he had similarly witnessed his father's will with a wobbly letter 'H' in 1634. Ralphe Shawe of Boarshurst, the other witness to the will, signed with a more accomplished letter 'S'. John Whitehead of Kinders also owned books valued at 4 shillings in his inventory of 1708, but did not sign his name, though his son of the same name did so confidently.

The same went for Joseph Scolefeild of Arthurs, son of a Master weaver of the same name. In 1713, 'sicke or weak of Body', Joseph marked his will with a cross despite leaving 'Bookes belonging to the deceased' valued at 5 shillings. His inability to sign his name was not due to his state of health. In 1702, when prizing the estates of his neighbours William Shaw of Lower House and Henry Shaw of Boarshurst (great-grandson of Ralph Shaw), he marked his name with a cross on both documents, despite his robust good health at the time. By contrast, another Boarshurst neighbour, John Bentley, signed the same Henry Shaw's inventory with a confident flourish.[19]

As the 18th century dawned, signatures became more commonplace, and it was soon apparent who could and could not wield a pen. Our ancestor William Shaw of Lower House in Boarshurst signed his will in a handsome script in 1701, despite his wasting illness; so too did his brother John, who signed as a witness. However, we know from other documents, in 1674 and 1696, that their uncle John Shaw of Lower House could not sign his name.

Skills in both reading and writing were now advancing apace, fuelled by the distribution of printed reading material, both religious, such as bibles and prayer books, and secular, such as newspapers, broadsheets, handbills and almanacs. The growing sophistication of the economy also required more literacy and numeracy skills, for communication, record keeping and accounting.

In 1731, Thomas Hawkyard, a husbandman of Tamewater, who we shall meet in chapter 14, signed his will with assurance, despite 'being Aged and decayed in Body', using the older variant spelling of 'Hawkyeard'.[20] He also left to his infant son 'all my Bookes and Accounts'. Fifty years later, William Shaw of Grottonhead, descended from the Shaws of Lower House, Boarshurst, maintained a book in which he kept important records. Expressing the intention, in his will of 1782, to distribute a part of his estate equally amongst his six children, he noted that he had already given five of them 'such and such different sums of money in part of their portions or legacies, as I have set down in my book.' (The sixth child was in the West Indies, and it was not known if he would return.)[21]

In earlier times, the church curate alone had recorded marriages, but from the mid-18th century onwards, the bride, groom and two witnesses were offered the opportunity to sign the register. A majority of men signed their names: all the males of our Shaw family did so with some confidence and style, including both John Shaw and his father William in John's marriage certificate of 1789. Being able to write one's name may have become an article of male fashion or self-esteem, but it surely also reflected the practical need for enhanced literacy skills in daily social and economic activity. Most women, however, still marked the marriage register with a cross.

Until the mid 18th century, schools had been scarce, and formal education the preserve of more affluent families. Rochdale Grammar School had been founded in 1561, but for most Saddleworth residents, the best they could hope for was some basic teaching by the chapel curate in the chancel of St Chad's, home visits by tutors, or help from a literate parent.[22] However, the 18th century saw a drive in Saddleworth to educate poorer children, at least in the basics of reading and writing. The first such day school in Saddleworth was founded as an endowed school, thanks to Ralph Hawkyard, brother of Thomas above (see chapter 14).[23]

Other endowed schools followed. In 1755, John Walker of Ashton left £600 in his will to support education in Ashton, Oldham and Saddleworth. A day school was founded at Lydgate in 1763, with two schoolrooms (one on the ground floor and the other above), a piece of waste land used as a playground and three acres of land attached. It taught English reading and writing, arithmetic and Latin. A school at Delph was also founded at about the same time, while in the first years of the 19th century, a curate of Heys chapel was said to have 'kept a respectable day and boarding school at Springhead'.

Resurgent non-conformism laid strong emphasis on the importance of education, and the Sunday School movement provided classes for both children and adults. In 1785, a Methodist Sunday School started in Oldham. At Springhead, the Independent Providence Chapel Sunday School grew to become the best attended in the whole township of Saddleworth. By 1815, over 1300 children attended eight Sunday Schools in Saddleworth, comprising over 10% of the township's entire population.[24] Education had become a gateway to self-improvement and enhanced prosperity, as it would prove for our Shaw family.

III BOARSHURST (1590-1770)

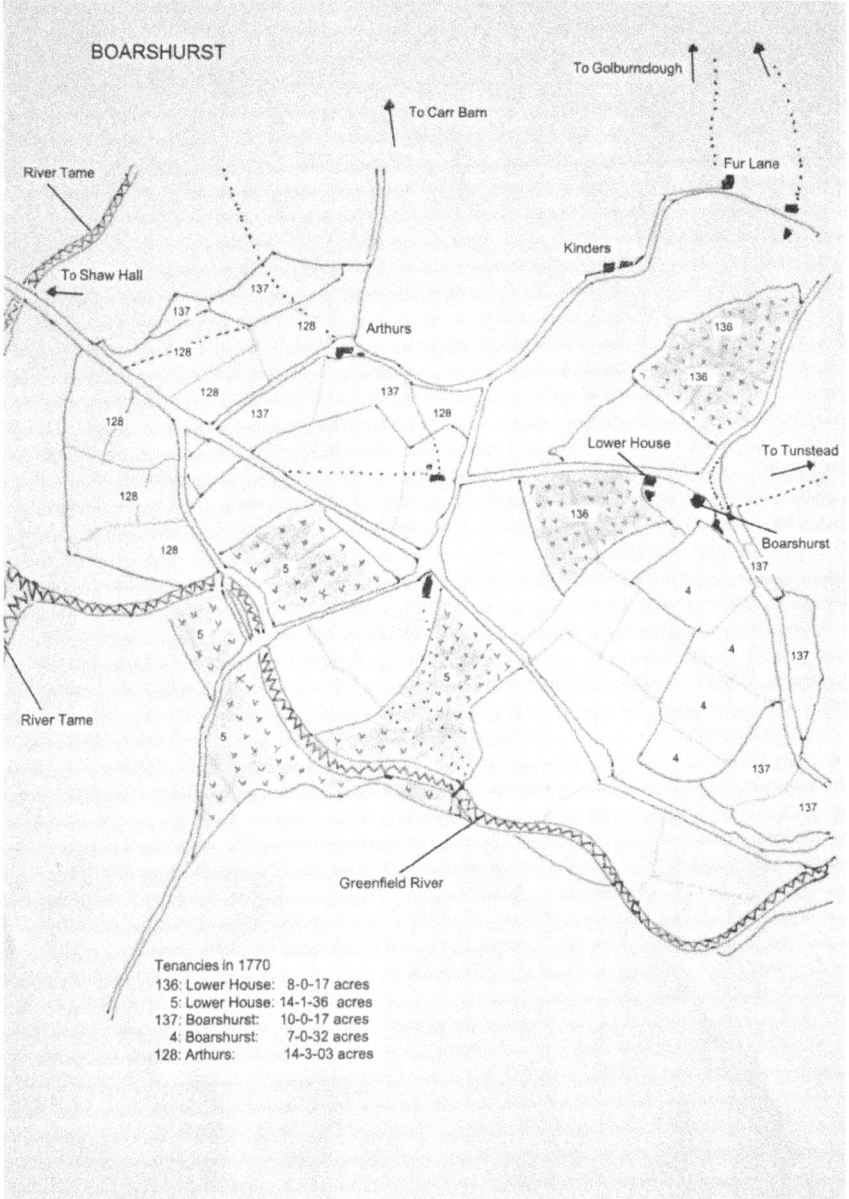

BOARSHURST

To Golburnclough

To Carr Barn

River Tame

Fur Lane

To Shaw Hall

Kinders

137

137

128

Arthurs

136

128

136

128

137

128

128

137

137

128

Lower House

To Tunstead

128

136

128

Boarshurst

137

5

4

5

4

137

5

River Tame

4

5

137

4

Greenfield River

137

4

137

Tenancies in 1770
136: Lower House: 8-0-17 acres
  5: Lower House: 14-1-36 acres
137: Boarshurst: 10-0-17 acres
  4: Boarshurst: 7-0-32 acres
128: Arthurs: 14-3-03 acres

69

8 : WILLIAM AND KATRINE

It was almost Christmas when, on 20 December 1590, John Ramsden of Longley, gent (1512-1591) and William, his son and heir apparent (1558-1623), bought the Manor of Saddleworth from Francis Tunstall of Thurseland. With the freehold of the manor came ownership of about 70 tenant farms and lands that covered most of Lordsmere in Saddleworth. Seven weeks later, on 'the iiij[th] daye of februarye 1590' (ie 1590/1), they commissioned accounts listing their manorial tenants and the annual rents they paid. The terms of the tenants' leases, carried over from the previous owners, came up for renewal four years later, in 1594/5, when the accounts record payments of garsomes, or entry fines.[1] At Boarshurst, five tenant farmers occupied lands that together extended to about 90 acres. Three of these tenant farmers were named Shawe, and one was our direct ancestor, William Shawe (Genealogical Table 1A).

Boarshurst sits high in the shadow of the Pennines, whose moorland looms over the farmsteads. The land slopes from the north east to the south west, from the glowering hill marked by the 'Pots and Pans' rock structures, with Saddleworth Moor behind, down to the Tame Valley, an important trans-Pennine route to Huddersfield, which today includes road (A670), rail and canal links. To the south, the land falls to the Greenfield River, now called Chew Brook, and another trans-Pennine road route (A635) eastwards to Holmfirth.

James Butterworth, in his romanticised account of Saddleworth in the 1820s, describes an area 'agreeably situated amongst some rich pasture ground, which though surrounded by fences of stone (which are the general mode of inclosing the lands here) render it upon the whole not at all an unpleasant situation.' [2] It is indeed an area of great beauty, but one that must have offered a hard living in a pre-industrial, predominantly agricultural economy.

Here, our ancestor William Shawe and his descendants held a tenancy of over 20 acres of land to the north and south west of Boarshurst. Their fields to the north remain in light agricultural use today, populated by a scattering of sheep. To the south-west their fields are now covered by development, but used to extend alongside Kinders Lane and Ladhill Lane, as far as Chew Brook, adjacent to the modern-day Greenfield Cricket Ground.

View North Eastwards from the 'Upper Meadow' at Lower House,
Boarshurst, towards the Pots and Pans rocks and
the more recent war memorial.

What do we know for certain of the origins this William? We know that his brother Ralph was born in about 1561 and lived in Boarshurst all his life, or at least from the age of 15.[3] William too must have been born in Boarshurst, in about 1559, and his family would have lived there for several generations before that. The lay subsidy of 1545 lists three tax-payers named Shaw, who appear to be from Boarshurst: Americ, Laurence and William. One of them, William perhaps, must have been the grandfather of the William and Ralph Shawe we meet in 1590.[4]

What the manorial records of 1590/91 tell us is that that William Shawe held a substantial tenancy. He paid an annual rental of 10s 9d, and at Pentecost, on 23 May 1591, he was due to pay a half year rental of 5s 4d. An immediate neighbour at Boarshurst, and probable near relative, was Gyles Shawe, whose family is described in chapter 10. Shortly after the arrival of the new Lord of the Manor, William and Gyles jointly held an additional, smaller tenancy for a time, constructing a building that was funded by a loan from the Lord of the Manor, and paying a rent for it of 2s. 8d.[5]

In addition to rental payments, a tenant was required to pay a 'garsome' – an entry fine payable upon taking up or renewing a lease. Garsomes reflected the extent and quality of the land and could be quite substantial: for this reason they were often paid in two or more instalments. William made garsome payments in 1594 and 1595 totalling £16.9s.7d. Tenants often had to turn to the Manor, or to others, for financial loans, as records show, in April 1601: 'lent to William Shawe wife vijs till June'; and in November 1611: 'Lent to William Shawe 4li till Easter'. Easter Sunday fell on 23 April 1612, and on 13 April 1612, William made a first garsome payment of £12 & 22d. Ten months later, he made a second payment, in kind, of two oxen, 'a branded and a fleckt', worth £4.[6]

William and his wife Katrine had five children, whom we describe more fully in the next chapter. These were an unmarried daughter named Agnes, a married daughter named Marie Whewall, and three sons named Edmund, Robert and George. In 1612, Edmund is named as an additional tenant at Boarshurst, apparently taking over some

acres from his father.[7] Five tenants are recorded at Boarshurst
in 1590/1: our ancestor William Shawe, his brother Ralph Shawe, his
relative Gyles Shawe, Thomas Platt and Arthur Scholefield.

Information from wills, rental records and a survey of the manorial
estate in 1770 shows that descendants of four of them were still farming
the same land almost two centuries years later. This enables an
approximate calculation of the size of their tenancies in 1590, when
William's payments were about two-thirds as much as Gyles's. The table
below lists their rental and garsome payments in the period 1590-1612.
The last two columns show the tenancies occupied by their descendants,
as recorded in the manorial survey of 1770 (in acres, roods and perches).
The exception is Gyles Shaw of Boarshurst, whose descendants were no
longer tenants by 1770; but at the time of his death in 1634, he is said to
have held two manorial tenancies totalling 30 acres.[8]

Tenants	1590/1: Rent pa	1594/5: Garsome	1612: Garsome	Tenancy	Acres
William Shaw	10s. 9d	£16.9s.7d	£16.1s.10d*	Lower Hse 136 & 5	22.2.13
Edmund Shaw	--	--	£11. 12s. 6d		
Ralph Shaw	2s. 10d	£10.0.0	£6.0s. .0d	Boarshurst 137	10.0.17
Gyles Shaw	17s.10d	£26.6s.3d	£40.2s. 2d*	Boarshurst	30.0.0†
Thomas Platt	5s. 6d	£8. 2s. 6d	£12. 7s. 6d	Boarshurst 4	7.0.32
Arthur Scholefield	2s.10d.	£10.0.0	£13. 6s. 8d	Arthurs 128	14.3.3
William & Gyles Shaw [9]	2s. 8d.	--	--	--	--

*Abated for Chief Rent;

† The figure of 30 acres relates to 1634, the year of Gyles Shaw's death.

William prepared his will on 23 October 1623, in the knowledge
that he was dying. He would have recognised the symptoms. His eldest

son Edmund had died just three weeks earlier, and his second son Robert apparently more recently still. William succumbed on 1 November: he was about 64 years old. 'Spotted fever', that had swept across the country following successive poor harvests, may have caused this cluster of deaths. His will was written 'in the one and twentieth yeare of the Raign of our Soverign Lord James by the grace of god of England, France and Ireland King defender of the faith And of Scotland the sisth'. It is a post-reformation, protestant document, and there are no references to saints or the Virgin Mary.[10] The will may have been signed by William himself - 'by mee Willm Shawe' - in a neat and accomplished hand that is nevertheless distinct from the rest of the clearly written document (although the signature may have been written for him). It is a comprehensive, well-structured will that, with the detailed inventory, gives rise to numerous points of interest.

Most wills of the time mention only around a dozen names. But William mentions as many as 33 different people in his will; his son Edmund mentions 50, and his daughter Marie Whewall 45. Their wills not only provide valuable information about their immediate family, but also illustrate the importance attached to extended kinship and to neighbours.

William's will shows that he was primarily an arable farmer, growing corn on his fields and grass for hay on his meadowland. It was autumn, and his inventory lists 'corn and haye' valued at £8.15s as well as ploughs and harrows. (His great grandson, another William, who farmed the same land and died in early July 1701, would list corn and grass in his inventory: the grass had not yet been harvested as hay.) However, it was a mixed farm, less risky than monoculture, and he also owned cattle and sheep valued at £11.6s.8d and £5.0.8d respectively. There is no mention of a horse for ploughing or transport, though he owned two saddles: perhaps he rented a horse when needed or harnessed an ox.

His estate was valued at £41. 08s 11d, with debts inwards of £10.4s.4d and debts outwards of £3. 15s. 11d, leaving a net total of

£47. 17s. 04d. This was quite a reasonable sum for a tenant farmer, estimated to be equivalent to nearly 1000 days' wages for a skilled tradesman.[11] This was despite him apparently giving away part of his tenancy land, in 1612, to his eldest son. Edmund, who had died three weeks earlier, left an estate worth over £59, rather more than his father's. William's life was simple, but by the standards of the day and relative to his neighbours, he was by no means poor.

In the absence of a formal banking system, borrowing and lending money was common, especially when a major outlay, such as a garsome payment, was required. We saw earlier that William had borrowed money from the Manor, first with his neighbour Gyles to enable the construction of a building, and then in 1611 to help assemble his garsome payment of over £16. But the fact that, in William's will, 'debts inwards' exceeded 'debts outwards' is a positive financial indicator, and his finances were sufficiently sound that he could lend money at interest. At his death, William was owed 24 shillings by John Broadbent of Pinfold and Edmund Platt of Thornes - but only 'if they payes it at Xsmas next; if not then it is 6 shillings more'. One of the functions of the executors of his will would be to ensure that his 'debts inwards' were collected.

The tradition of godparents was well established. William left a legacy of 2 shillings to his nephew and godson, Thomas Shawe, a son of his brother Ralph. He also made this Thomas one of the Executors of his will, alongside his daughter Agnes. William's son Edmund also left 'to everie one I am Godfather unto ffyve shillings', while his daughter Marie Whewall in 1658 left 12 pence 'to everie one I am Godmother unto'. Hard-line puritans rejected the concept of godparents, but the custom survived here: it helped strengthen extended family ties and was of practical value in an age of uncertain life expectancy.

The period remaining on the lease of William's land and tenement, the 'reversion of the lease', was valued at £6.13s.4d, or about 20% of his total estate. He had paid a garsome of £16. 1s. 10d in 1612 to renew the lease. The value calculated in his inventory is broadly consistent with a remaining period of nine years on a 21 year lease.[12] Over four years later, the will of his widow Katrine, who had inherited three-quarters of the tenancy, valued her reversion of the lease at 55 shillings – also consistent with this profile of a 21 year lease.

William's will is consistent with his occupation of the tenancy at Boarshurst that was later named Lower House. We have seen that he managed a mixed farm: Lower House included fields for corn, meadows for hay and less fertile land for grazing. In his will he left three quarters of his farm to his wife Katrine for the remainder of the term of the lease: 'the half of my ffarme … or three parts of that I now occupie during the tearme' The fourth quarter was given to his daughter Agnes and to his youngest granddaughter Marie: Agnes remained unmarried but appears to have assumed a maternal responsibility for little Marie, her niece.

However, his will is unusual in not conferring inheritance of the tenancy onto his eldest son. He made provision for his widow Katrine, as was customary, and for his unmarried daughter Agnes, who would inherit the whole tenancy after Katrine's death. We shall seek to explain this in chapter 9.

William's wife Katrine died in January 1627/8. Her will, dated 25 December 1627, was prized three weeks later by her brother-in-law Ralph Shawe, her son-in-law Francis Whewall (husband of her daughter Marie), John Shaw (the eldest son of Gyles Shawe at Boarshurst) and William Cartwright, who we shall meet again in chapter 11.[13] Most wills in this period were prepared by, or on behalf of, men. Yet Katrine, and later her daughter Marie Whewall, are notable exceptions. Both women display in their wills a thorough command of their affairs, competence in financial and land management and well-planned inheritance arrangements. In Katrine's case, she does not sign her name, but marks it with a confident and elaborate symbol.

Katrine's will tells us that she had sub-let her land to generate a cash income: her under-tenants were her brother-in-law Ralph Shawe and neighbour William Cartwright. These two under-tenants were to pay 5 shillings a year to her youngest son George, payable for the duration of the lease at 'Whitsonday cum twelmand' (ie every 12 months on Whitsunday). A further 15 shillings a year should be divided equally between all her grandchildren. For avoidance of doubt: 'the said Ralph Shaw and William Cartwright to paye the said muney forth of the ground that they have in occupation'.[14] The practice of sub-letting was not uncommon, and Katrine's great-grandson, another William Shaw (1653-1701) would also sub-let part of his Lower House tenancy. (see chapter 12)

Like her husband, Katrine left small legacies for her grandchildren, and a small annual income for her son George, but nothing for her son Robert, who we assume to have died in 1623. Like William, she made sure that her unmarried daughter Agnes was well provided for, bequeathing the tenement to her. Agnes was now in possession of her parents' entire tenancy (excluding the part given earlier to her brother Edmund). She was thus assured of a regular income from her under-tenants for the remainder of the term of the lease, which was probably about five years.

*****

William may have had a brother called George, who died in 1600/1. George's will was witnessed by Henry Cartwright of Boarshurst, and his inventory prized by William Shawe of Boarshurst, John Whewall of Tunstead and Thomas Platt, also of Boarshurst, while he owed 'iijs. ij2d' to Raph Shawe. Regretfully, he left to his widow Elizabeth Shawe 'all those my shepe which are in the handes of Alexander Shawe in recompence of that goodee of heres which was stoulne from me.' Sadly, we know nothing more of the unfortunate George.[15]

However, we do know for certain that William had a brother called Ralphe (c.1561-1637/8). Ralph adds colour to our understanding of the time and place, and in a remarkable record of his evidence to the Court Baron we can hear an authentic voice from the past.

The original 'Boarshurst' tenancy appears to have covered some 24 acres, a similar size to William's. However, by 1590 it had been divided into two, held by Ralph Shaw and Thomas Platt, a possible relative by marriage. Thomas Platt's tenancy later passed by marriage into the Bentley family, who in 1770 still occupied the 14½ acre farm 'Boarshurst No. 4'.[16]

Ralph's tenancy remained in his family for several more generations (Genealogical Table 4). Two decades after his death, the tenancy was held by his youngest son Richard, who is named in Marie Whewall's will of 1658 and who was also a witness to the will of Gyles Shawe's son, George of Boarshurst, in 1653. The manorial survey of 1770 shows descendants of Ralph and Richard still occupying the 10 acre farm, identified as 'Boarshurst No.137'. In 1791, when the manorial estate was broken up after the death of the Lord of the Manor, the tenant was James Shaw, who by now was also a shop-keeper. While the freehold of the Boarshurst tenancy was acquired by John Andrew, land tax records show James's son John Shaw continuing to occupy the tenancy until at least 1809.

Ralph paid an annual rent of 2s.6d. in 1590. To renew his lease in 1594/5, he made two garsome payments of £5 each, while in 1612/13 he renewed his lease with two garsome payments of £3 each.[17]

Ralph's own will has not survived, but he is mentioned in the wills of several members of William's family. In 1623 William's son Edmund named his uncle Ralph as Executor of his will, and Ralph was also one of the four men to prize it (that is, to assess the value of his estate). Edmund also left one Mark (13s.4d.) to Ralph, and named each of Ralph's children, to whom he left 3s.4d.: Henrie, Thomas, Edmund,

Richard, Elizabeth Rodes, Alice Heywarde, Margaret Shawe and Ellen Shawe – 'to everie of them 3s.4d.'[18]

William itemised a 'debt outwards' of 10s.7d. to Ralph Shawe in the inventory of his will in 1623, while his widow Katrine, as we have seen, made clear in her will of 1627 that Ralph Shawe and William Cartwright were managing her lands on her behalf. In 1634, Ralph witnessed the will of his Boarshurst neighbour Gyles Shawe, marking his name with a handsome letter 'S'. He also helped prize the estate and was no doubt grateful to receive the legacy from Gyles of his 'best paire of briches'.

In 1658, two decades after Ralph's death, his niece Marie Whewall bequeathed legacies in her will 'unto everie one of the children of my uncle Ralphe Shawe one shilling.[19] Clearly some of his children, the girls perhaps, were still living. Marie only names one of Ralphe's children, his youngest son Richard, who had by now inherited his father's old tenancy at Boarshurst. To him Marie left 10 shillings.

In 1636, Ralph of Boarshurst gave evidence to the manorial Court Baron. The court generally met two to four times a year to resolve disputes and enforce terms of tenancies, such as requirements to maintain houses and other farm structures. Jurors were drawn from the manorial tenants, as a condition of their lease. Fifteen jurors heard this case, one of whom was 'John Shawe de Boreshurst', eldest son of Gyles Shawe (see chapter 10.) The court case involved a dispute between two neighbours in Tunstead, whose fields bordered those of Boarshurst: Sara Wood, who had blocked a pathway across her field, and John Whewall. Ralph's evidence in support of John Whewall is paraphrased, but we hear his voice:

'Raph Shawe of Boarshurst sayeth that he is three score & fiveten years of age and he knowe every dweller in the Tunstead three score years ago and he never harde any controversie about this way. Furthermore he sayeth that fiftie yeares agoe he lead hay from the meadowe of John Whewall through the meadow of Sara Wood to Boarshurst which hay was bought of old John Whewall this old man's father and hath since then come and go on foote for all necessaries and never had any controversie about it.'[20]

The testimony was persuasive, and the court found against Sara Wood, ruling that John Whewall was entitled to use the path across the meadow: 'John Whewall and his successors may occupye the same with cartt and carriage and a footway'. Rights of way, then as now, were stoutly defended. Helpfully, the testimony makes clear Ralph's year of birth (1561) and that he was living in Boarshurst as a 15 year old in 1576. Ralph, his brother William and their parents were residents of Boarshurst long before the arrival of the Ramsdens as Lord of the Manor in 1590.

There were close relations between the Whewalls of Tunstead and the Shawes of Boarshurst. The two hamlets were less than a quarter mile apart, and old John Whewall's youngest son Francis had already married William Shawe's daughter, Ralph's niece, Marie. When old John Whewall drew up his will in December 1637, shortly after the death of his wife, he asked Ralph Shawe to be a witness. It transpired, however, that Ralph would die before him: the St Chad burial register for March 1637/8 records Radus Shawe (short for Radulphus or Ralph). He had lived to the grand age of 77.

9 : FIVE CHILDREN

William and Katrine Shawe had five children: Edmund, Agnes, Marie, Robert and George. The first three had no surviving children of their own, but the Shaw line was continued by Robert and George. Their lives shed light on the customs and relationships of the family at this time, the pestilence of the 1620s, and the complex inheritance of the Lower House tenancy.

Edmund (c.1578-1623) was the eldest son of William and Katharine, and his premature death in 1623 was the start of a catastrophic period for the family. His death had clearly not been anticipated: his will and inventory were completed on the same day, 3 October 1623, and his unsigned will describes him not only in the customary manner as 'fibble in bodie but perfect in memorie (praised bee god)', but also as 'late deceased'. The will names his wife Anne, but no children.[1] It also names his parents, William and Katherine, his sisters Agnes Shawe and Marie Whewall, his 'brethren' Robert and George and each of their children. His executors were his uncle Ralph Shawe and his brother-in-law Francis Whewall, husband of his sister Marie.

Edmund had held a manorial tenancy at Boarshurst since 1612. He appears to have acquired lands from his father William and uncle Ralph, both of whom paid reduced garsomes in 1612 compared to 1594, both in cash terms and as a proportion of Boarshurst garsomes.

We also learn from Edmund's will that he held two short-term leases of smaller fields at Hollingreave, where he was an under-tenant on the manorial estate: he rented the Little Bank (two acres) from

John Scholfield (123C in the 1770 survey) and the nearby Little Meadow (one acre) from Richard Scholefield of the Grange (122G). The practice of sub-letting parts of a manorial tenancy had evidently become commonplace, as demand for land increased from a growing population: manorial tenants were able to charge a market rent higher than the customary rent they themselves paid.

Edmund left half his tenement at Boarshurst and half of his short term leases at Hollingreave to his wife Anne, following the custom of the manor. He left the other half to his brothers Robert and George. In common with many wills of the time, Edmund placed conditions on his legacies to his wife Anne. If she were to 'either marrie, miscarrie or dye', (that is, re-marry, misbehave or die), then the lands bequeathed to her would pass to Edmund's brothers Robert and George. This gave Anne a secure living as a widow (at least for the remaining term of the lease) but ensured that the tenancy would remain within Edmund's blood family in the longer term. The fact that Edmund left his tenancy to be shared by his two brothers set a precedent for inheritance of land in the family in years to come.

There was a further condition. His brothers Robert and George were to occupy their half of the lands 'if they can agree with my said wife'. In the event of disagreement, his uncle Ralph Shawe and brother-in-law Francis Whewall were to occupy and manage the lands on behalf of Robert and George, 'to the onely behest and behoof of the said Robert Shawe and George Shawe'. Was this indicative of tensions in the family, or just a sensible precaution?

In his will, Edmund left his 'cloake' to his father. If the cause of Edmund's death was the dreaded 'spotted fever' that was raging through England at the time, bequeathing his cloak to his father may not have been a smart thing to do. Whatever the reason, three weeks later, William too was dead.

Edmund left numerous small legacies, naming the eight children of his brother Robert and the three children of his brother George, his two sisters-in-law Elizabeth and Marie, his sisters Agnes Shawe and Marie Whewall, and others besides. He also left legacies to neighbours at Boarshurst, including Thomas Platt and his children, who were possibly related through an earlier marriage. Edmund had no children of his own, but he was uncle and godfather to many.

The inventory of Edmund's will reflects his occupation as a husbandman, itemising corn, cattle and 'husbandrie geere' valued at £44, 'tackle of ground' and, in the house, stores of 'Beefe Bacon butters Cheese and meale'. He owed a debt to the Manor of 36 shillings for 'loosing three beasts': the manorial court was strict in imposing 'amercements' (penalties) for failures to maintain buildings and fences or to keep animals under control. Like his father, he had borrowed money but lent more: his estate was owed 3s.8d. by his Boarshurst neighbour Thomas Platt, for example, and £4.13s.4d. by John Scholfield of Hollingreave, from whom he was renting the field called 'the little Banke'. His goods were valued at £62.7s.6d. net of debts inward and outwards, rather more than that of his father William.

*****

Agnes (- 1633), also known as Annis, remained unmarried. Perhaps for this reason, she was well provided for by her parents. Her father left her a part of the tenancy and half of his goods, while four years later she inherited from her mother 'all the whole tenement and housing which I doe occupie under the right worshipfull Ser John Ramsden Knight during the tearm.' Acting as executor of a will was a responsibility generally given to men, but both William and Katrine made Agnes one of the two executors of their wills. This was recognition no doubt of her personal interest in ensuring their wishes were carried out, but also of her competence and reliability: she was being given the responsibility to manage a transition to the next generation.

Why then did Agnes inherit the Lower House tenancy, and not her brothers? There appear to be two reasons. First, she was unmarried and well past a marriageable age. In the absence of a husband, she therefore needed financial security: she was in a comparable position to a widow, who by custom would inherit a share of her husband's estate. So William provided for his widow Katrine to occupy three-quarters of the tenancy for the remaining years of her life, as was the custom; but she in turn, four years later, would bequeath the entire tenancy to their daughter Agnes. In doing so she ensured that reliable under-tenants, her brother-in-law Ralph Shaw and the neighbour William Cartwright, would manage the land for Agnes and pay her a rental income. Since Agnes would have no children of her own (apart from her niece Marie), the tenancy would pass, on her death, to her brothers or their heirs.

The second reason, which we shall explore below, is that her brother Robert also appears to have died, leaving children short of an age when they might take responsibility for a manorial tenancy. Agnes therefore was charged with managing an equitable continuity of the family at Lower House. How she achieved that will become clear later. She was buried at the chapel of St Chad on 3 November 1633. The lease for Lower House, both William and Edmund's parts, would probably have been due for renewal, in the spring of that year.

We might have anticipated that Agnes, like her mother before her and sister Marie after, would have prepared a detailed last will and testament. That would undoubtedly have clarified the Lower House inheritance for us. Unfortunately, no record has survived, so we have to rely on interpretation.

*****

Marie (- 1658), whose name was later spelt Mary, was already married at the time of her father's death. Her husband was Francis Whewall, youngest son of the family's neighbour, John Whewall of Tunstead – the same 'old man' referred to by the 75 year old Ralph Shaw in his evidence to the Manorial court in 1636. In his will of 1637, old John Whewall makes clear that he had three sons (George, John and Francis), three daughters (Joane, Agnes and one other) and a number of grandchildren. The unnamed daughter had died, leaving a child named Margaret.

This was not the only marriage between the Shaws and the Whewalls: there were marriages in the next generation too. In May 1638, John, grandson of William Shawe and son of Robert Shaw, married Agnes Whewall, who unfortunately died two years later. In May 1641, another John Whewall, grandson of Old John and nephew of Francis Whewall, married Sara Shaw, probably Robert's youngest daughter. So although Francis and Marie had no children of their own, they had plenty of nieces and nephews to take an interest in. Their wills provide a roll call of their extended families, and rich insights into their social life.

For several years before their death in 1658, Marie and Francis lived at Ballgreave, holding a tenancy on behalf of the three children of Edmund Radcliffe deceased, until they reached the age of 17. These were the grandchildren of 'widdowe Radcliffe at Shawhall' and descendants of the previous owners of the Schaghe estate. We shall find other examples of an inheritance being managed on behalf of children until they reached adulthood.

Marie and Francis died during Oliver Cromwell's Protectorate. Both left wills, but since bishops were not allowed to act as probate officials in the Commonwealth, their wills had to be proved at a civil registry in London. Only 13 Saddleworth wills are known to have been proved in the period 1649-1660, and fortunately those of Marie and

Francis are among them.[2] Earlier wills had begun by identifying the date and regnal year, the king being the Defender of the Faith: these two wills, in the changed times, did not.

Francis drew up his will in 1650, and signed it in his own stylish hand: it was proved after his burial on 19 May 1658. Two months later, on 8 July 1658, Marie drew up her own will, marking it with a sign: she had a short time to live and was buried at St Chad on 18 August. It was a pestilential year. After a long and intensely cold winter, an outbreak of catarrhal fever or influenza began in mid-April. This was followed in the summer and autumn by what the contemporary physician H.Whitmore described as 'a putrid, continued and malignant fever containing in it the seeds of contagion'.[3] Mortality rates were high, especially among older people: Francis and Marie died just three months apart.

The wills of Francis and Marie provide strong evidence of the support that an extended family network brought. Two of Francis's nieces should be mentioned. One was Margaret, whose mother (Francis's sister) had died when she was a child. It was a reflection of her vulnerability that Margaret was the only grandchild named by old John Whewall in his will, and that Marie became her god-mother. In his own will of 1650, Francis bequeathed the sum of £13. 6s. 8d. to his ailing brother John Whewall of Tunstead, but left this money 'in the handes and Custodie' of his niece Margaret for the 'maintenance' of his brother. After John's death, which took place in January 1655/6, whatever money was left over from this sum was to be kept by Margaret. Money and responsibility were held by women as well as men.

Another niece of Francis was Ann, wife of John Shaw of nearby Shawhouses (only distantly related now to the Boarshurst Shaws – see chapter 14, including note 1). John and Ann had two children named Mary and Ann (the latter baptised in 1649), and in his will, Francis bequeathed 'to Ann the wiffe of John Shaw and her children the somme of tenne poundes'. Francis had written his will in 1650, but by the time of his death in 1658, his niece Ann had also died, and John Shaw had remarried. Marie Whewall therefore bequeathed legacies in her own will to 'Mary and Ann Shaw, daughters of John Shaw of Shawhouses by his first wife, either of them …when they shall accomplish the age of one and twentie yeares.' Among her legacies to the two girls was 'a great Bible'. A century after Henry VIII had banned the reading of the bible by husbandmen, the bible had become a central feature of family life, and both male and female family members were seemingly literate enough to read it.

In her own will, Marie left ten shillings to a nephew of Francis, John Whewall of the Lane. He had married Sara, daughter of Marie's brother Robert Shaw, and Marie left a further ten shillings to John's 'familie'. She also named two nieces of her own, leaving legacies of 10 shillings each to Mary Bottomley of Longland in Slaithwaite and Sarah Pilling, seemingly daughters of her youngest brother George, who were now married with children of their own.

Marie also took care to acknowledge the children of her uncle Ralph, who had died in 1637, and in particular his son Richard Shaw. Francis had named George Shaw of Boarshurst as the Overseer of his will. George, one of the five sons of Gyles Shawe (see chapter 10), had remained at Boarshurst where, in his later years, he lived with his brother John. When George drew up his own will in 1653, a 'Richerd Shawe' was a witness. This Richard was the youngest of Ralph Shaw's four sons, who had inherited his father's manorial tenancy at Boarshurst. The sequencing of Marie's will makes this clear, as she leaves '…unto Richard Shawe of Boarshurst tenn shillings. Also I give unto everie one of the children of my uncle Ralph Shaw one shilling.' As we have seen, descendants of Ralph, through his son Richard, continued to farm their Boarshurst tenancy until as late as 1809.

Marie's will contains many other points of interest and leaves us with the impression of a wide and supportive extended family network, reaching not only across Lordsmere, Shawmere and Quickmere, but also eastwards across the moors to Marsden and Slaithwaite. She mentions several other Shaws, although the precise relationship is not known:

- Abraham and Elizabeth Shawe of Marsden;
- Anne the wife of Michael Shawe of Ryetop, in Lordsmere: 130 years later, our ancestor John Shaw would spend the first four years of his married life at Ryetop, where the manorial tenant was a descendant of this Michael Shaw;
- Henry Shaw of the Lane, a son of Gyles Shawe of Boarshurst, who had bought land in Quick Mere (see chapters 10 and 17), and who was named as an overseer of her will.

Marie owned linen, spun from flax or hemp, which was grown and woven in Saddleworth. She left her 'best Cambrick neckcloth' to Elizabeth, the wife of Abraham Shawe of Marsden, and 'one linen apron, the best I have' to the widow Mary Radcliffe.[4]

She employed two 'servant maids', Jane Cartwright and Mary Wild, and left them each ten shillings. The Cartwrights were close neighbours and well known to the Shaw family. When Jane Cartwright found herself orphaned and disinherited, in circumstances described in chapter 11, Marie employed her as a paid domestic worker, providing the girl with security, a roof over her head and some income.

From the perspective of this narrative, Marie's will is important for two further details. First, in appointing her nephew John Shaw as an executor of her will, she needed to distinguish him from John Shaw of Shawhouses. She did this by making clear first, that he was her kinsman, unlike the other John who was not a close relation; and second, by identifying his tenancy as Lower House, as distinct from Shawhouses. This is the first known record to name the farm occupied by our Shaw ancestors as 'Lower House', distinguishing it from the four other 'Boarshurst' tenancies held by the descendants of Ralph Shawe, Thomas Platt, Gyles Shawe and Arthur Scolefield. We shall read more about Lower House in later chapters.

Secondly, Marie's will identifies not only her nephew John Shaw, son of her brother Robert Shawe, who was now aged 44 and managing the Lower House farm; but also two young boys, William and John Shaw, aged about five and three respectively, who were sons of her recently deceased nephew Thomas Shaw. Marie provided generously in her will for the young fatherless boys and their recently widowed mother. William and John would live with their uncle at Lower House, and in due course William, our ancestor, would inherit the entire tenancy, as we shall see in chapter 11.

At the end of her will, Marie refers to 'my good friends and neighbours'. It is a warm and inclusive last will and testament of a woman who had no children of her own, but who was a matriarchal figure for a wide circle of others.

*****

Robert (c.1585-1623) was the second son of William and Katrine Shaw. His must have married his wife Elizabeth soon after 1605, producing some ten or more children over the next 15-18 years. Only three are recorded in the St Chad baptism register – Joane in April 1613, John in March 1614/5 and Edmund in February 1618/19, although we can deduce that two other boys, Robert and William, were born before Joane. The wills of his brother Edmund and his father William list the following eight as Robert's surviving children in autumn 1623: Robert, William, John, Henrie, Joane, Ellen, Susan and

Sara. Edmund also names a 'Marie Shawe alias Kaye' among Robert's children: an illegitimate child perhaps, or already married?

In 1623, William left small legacies to all of his grandchildren, though not to his eldest grandson Robert, who appears to have died in the three weeks since Edmund's death. He made additional provision for three: to Robert's now eldest son, William, he gave 'one of the meane lambs'; to Robert's eldest daughter, Joane, he left 12 pence; and to Robert's youngest child, Sara, he gave 'a lambe'. By December 1627, only five of Robert's children had survived to be mentioned in the will of his mother Katrine: William, John, Henery, Ellen and Sara.[5] William and Henrie are not mentioned in Marie Whewall's will of 1658, which is nothing if not thorough in naming her extended living family. It was therefore John who would become Robert's eldest surviving son and who would eventually inherit a part, at least, of the Lower House tenancy.

There is no evidence that Robert survived the pestilence of 1623. On the contrary, indications are that he, and his eldest son Robert, both died in the three weeks separating the death of his brother Edmund and the will of his father William. Robert was alive on 3 October 1623, when Edmund bequeathed to him part of his tenancy, but he received no direct mention or legacy in the will of his father William three weeks later, nor in that of his mother Katrine four years after that. Their wills treat him in exactly the same way as his recently deceased brother Edmund and their recently deceased grandchildren: none are directly mentioned. By contrast their wills are scrupulous in naming and granting legacies to all their living children, Agnes, Marie Whewall and George, and to all their living grandchildren. Robert himself receives no legacy whatsoever, which would be surely implausible had he still been alive. The last lines of his father's will seem clear in their implication. Having distributed numerous legacies, he concludes: 'And the rest I give to my sonne George Shawe, and the children of my sonne Robert Shawe, William John Henrie Ellen Susan Sara, children of Robert Shaw which I am grandfather to, to be divided equally amongst them.'

It is also noteworthy that by 1623 Robert had fathered at least ten children over 15 years or so, but between October 1623 and Katrine's will in December 1627 no more children were born to him. In or soon after 1628, a male child called Thomas (our ancestor) was born into the Shaw family. We have to conclude that Thomas was a son of Robert's younger brother, George, whose family was then small and still growing.[6]

*****

George (c.1695-1638/42) was William and Katrine's youngest son: Edmund's will refers consistently to his brothers Robert and George in that order. The same document also tells us that George's wife was named Marie, and that by 1623 they had three young children: William, Margaret and Marie. By 1627, they had added a fourth child, Sara, who received a small legacy in her grandmother Katrine's will of 1627. Their family was still growing, which suggests that when our ancestor Thomas was born soon afterwards, he was the fifth child of George and Marie. This Thomas, as we saw from Marie Whewall's will, went on to father two sons of his own before dying prematurely in 1657. We shall pick up this thread in chapter 11.

We have seen that in 1612 William Shawe divided his tenancy to make provision for his eldest son Edmund. The remaining part of his tenancy passed to his unmarried daughter Agnes in 1627/8. George, however, was also provided for, and retained a stake in the family farm. With his brother Robert, he inherited half of Edmund's tenancy in 1623. With his sister Agnes, he shared one third of his father's goods in 1623, about £5 each, while his father, at his death, owed 6 shillings 'to George Shawe my son'. George was also an overseer of his mother

Katrine's will, which bequeathed him an income of 5 shillings a year, payable by Agnes out of the profits of the tenancy.

We cannot be certain how long George lived, but he had clearly died well before Marie Whewall wrote her will in 1658. A George Shaw died in Saddleworth in 1638 and another in 1642: it is probable that one of these was George, the youngest son of William and Katrine, and our ancestor.[7]

*****

What, then, happened to the manorial tenancy at Lower House after the death of Agnes in 1633? We have seen that William seemingly divided the Lower House tenancy into two parts in 1612, one held by himself and the other by his eldest son Edmund. Edmund's tenancy passed to his brothers Robert and George in 1623. The remainder of William's tenancy passed through his widow Katrine to their daughter Agnes in 1627/8: after the death of Agnes in 1633, this tenancy also appears to have passed through Robert and George to their eldest surviving sons, who by then were John and Thomas respectively.

Thus, although Robert appears to have died in 1623, his eldest surviving son, on reaching maturity, was in line to inherit his father's share of Edmund's tenancy at Boarshurst. On the death of his aunt Agnes in 1633, he was also in line to inherit a further share of his grandfather's tenancy. This surviving son was John Shaw, born in 1614/15, whom Marie Whewall confirms, in 1658, was her 'kinsman John Shaw of Lower House'.

Like Robert, William's youngest son, George, had also inherited one half of Edmund's tenancy in 1623, and after the death of Agnes in 1633, he too was in line to inherit a further share of his father's tenancy at Lower House. Following his own death, George's inheritance passed to his eldest surviving son, who by then was Thomas, born in about 1628, and still a minor.

It was common for the rights of children to be protected during their minority, and for lands to be held in trust on their behalf until they reached maturity. Francis and Marie Whewall were occupying Ballgreave on behalf of the Radcliffe children, for example, and, later, the will of Thomas Hawkyard made a similar arrangement for his infant son in 1731. Agnes, an unmarried woman, was protected by her parents and received control of the larger part of the family tenancy. But her role was also to assure the rights of the next generation.

Thus the Lower House tenancy remained in the Shaw family via a slender thread. We can infer that, from William and Edmund onwards in 1612, it was shared between at least two family members. When Robert's son, John Shaw, died without issue in 1696/7, it was George's grandson, another William, who was in line to inherit the whole tenancy, as we shall see in chapter 11.

10 : THE GYLES SHAWE INHERITANCE

The largest tenant farmer at Boarshurst in the early 1600s was Gyles Shawe. (Genealogical Tables 5 & 6) He was probably a close relative of William Shawe, and a network of connections between the two families continued over many generations, but the fortunes of their descendants diverged. Gyles and William were both husbandmen. But while William's descendants remained tenants, without ever owning the land they farmed, Gyles's sons went on to become freeholders and yeomen of some standing in Saddleworth.

Gyles was the only son of Adam Shawe of Boarshurst, who had died in 1583. Was he perhaps descended from Adam de la Grene, who held lands in the area in 1322, or from Americ Shawe who in 1545 was the largest taxpayer in Boarshurst? Unfortunately, there is no firm evidence. At his death, Adam Shawe's goods and chattels were valued at £35.9s., and following the custom of the lordship he left half to his wife Alice and the other half to his son Gyles.[1] Alice died in 1609, when her goods were valued at over £22 by four prizers: Willim Shawe, Raphe Shawe and Arthur Scolfiele (all of Boarshurst), and Willim Knight (of Tunstead). Her estate, including her half of the manorial tenancy, would pass to her son Gyles.[2]

From 1590 onwards, manorial records show Gyles Shawe paying the highest rents and garsomes in Boarshurst, about one third more than William. It was later said that, at the time of his death in 1634, Gyles held two manorial tenancies, one of 20 acres and the other of 10 acres, yielding an estimated net annual profit of £10 and £5 respectively.[3] His estate was valued at £203.13s.8d – a very large sum for a husbandman. His 'farmed ground' was valued at £54 in his inventory, his animals (cattle, oxen, kine, a gelding and sheep) at £55 and his 'corne and grasse' at £8. He also had wool, yarn and cloth worth over £30.[4]

William and Gyles had borrowed money together from the Lord of the Manor in 1591 to build a house. This was perhaps the building identified as 'new house for a workhouse or shoppe' in Gyles's will of 1634, and again in a court dispute of 1666 described below. His will was witnessed with a mark, not a signature, by his son Henry and by William's brother Ralph Shawe. Ralph, now in his 70s, was also one of the prizers of the inventory, and Gyles bequeathed him his 'best paire of briches'.[5]

Gyles was survived by his wife Joane (who lived another ten years), a daughter Sarah (who had married Lawrence Kinder) and five sons: John, George, Thomas, Henry and Giles. The youngest son, Giles, mentioned in his father's will of 1634, died early. But the other four sons became yeomen, and two, Thomas and Henry, founded lines of Shaws for generations to come, in Lordsmere and Quick Mere respectively.

The sons inherited at an opportune time. Sir John Ramsden, who had succeeded his father as Lord of the Manor in 1625, was looking to sell land to raise cash, especially in the approach to the civil war. Both John and Thomas bought lands from him in Lordsmere in 1637, using the money they had just inherited. In Quick Mere also, the major absentee landowners Sir George Booth and Thomas Leigh were also keen to dispose of land in the 1630s, leading to an increase in freeholders in the district: one of these was Henry Shawe.

Land ownership, as distinct from tenant farming, made it easier to borrow funds for investment, as well as providing a greater incentive to invest. Wool weaving was a growing market, and bigger looms were more efficient. Gyles had already built a workshop on his manorial tenancy, and his sons had sufficient entrepreneurial spirit to invest in weaving.

*****

We will return to the 18th century descendants of Thomas and Henry Shaw in chapter 17. Meanwhile, it will be helpful here to have a brief account of the lives of these four sons.[6]

John (d. 1665), the eldest son, was one of the appraisers of Katrine Shawe's inventory in 1627 and also a juror at the manorial court that heard evidence from Ralph Shawe in 1636. After his father's death, he remained at Boarshurst where, with his mother, he inherited Gyles's tenancies. Three years later, in 1637, he was able to buy freehold land, together with his brother in law Lawrence Kinder, the husband of his sister Sarah, and at his death in 1665 he was identified as a yeoman. Among his possessions were a pair of woollen loombes as well as wool and yarn: he was supplementing his income from the land by weaving cloth. However, his finances were not entirely robust: his estate was valued at £108, but reduced by debts of £36, and his death triggered a legal dispute over money that we describe below.[7]

John had one surviving child, a daughter named Sarah, who, a year before her father's death, had married Raph Andrew, a husbandman.[8] Descendants of Sarah and Raph would remain at Boarshurst and adjacent Foulrakes for several generations, becoming yeoman farmers and later proprietors of 'Andrew Mill'. In 1791, when the estate of James Farrer was broken up and sold in separate lots, James Andrew would acquire the freehold to the Boarshurst tenancy that was still occupied by a descendant of Ralphe Shawe.

George (d. 1653) drew up his will in 1653, the year of his death, making no mention of a wife or children of his own. For several years before he died, he 'did live and table himselfe' with his brother John at Boarshurst. He was a yeoman, and his goods and chattels were valued at about £230. They included cows and sheep, but also 'woolle yearne oyle and dyeing stufe … Looumbes …and all furniture for Cloth making'. He too had a wool weaving business, and a thriving one too.[9]

Thomas (d. 1650), as a younger son, had to leave Boarshurst to make his own way in life. Initially he bought some land at Brownhills in Quick Mere before also acquiring the freehold of a manorial farm at Overmillne (Uppermill) in Lordsmere in 1637. He died young in 1650, but his two children, Giles and Sarah, lived into adulthood.[10] A long line of Shaws is descended from this Giles, through his own son Thomas of Uppermill (d.1727), grandson Giles of Fur Lane (d.1748) and great-grandson Giles of Fur Lane (1726-1800) (Genealogical Table 5). In 1776, this latter Giles commissioned a survey of his lands at Fur Lane, Uppermill and Carr Barn: by then they constituted a 50 acre estate.

View northwards, from the 'Upper Meadow' at Lower House, towards Fur Lane, re-built early/mid 18th century. To the left is Kinders, and beyond it the large, bald hillside of Wharmton, wooded until the early 20th century, and once called' la Shaghe'.[11]

Henry (d. 1689) also had to move away from Boarshurst, and he was able to buy land at Lane, in Quick Mere. He also bought the Brownhills farm in 1655 from his nephew Giles, as well as enclosed lands at Greengate Foot, later known as Hills. Here in Quick Mere he founded another line of Shaws. (Genealogical Table 6)

Henry was named as a witness to his brother Thomas's will in 1650, and appears to have taken a paternal interest in Thomas's children, Giles and Sarah. He was also named as executor of his brother George's will in 1653, an overseer of the will of William Shawe's sister Marie Whewall in 1658, and an appraiser of his brother John's will in 1665. When he died in 1689, his inventory listed livestock, farming equipment and also 'Instruments of clothmaking' and quantities of 'cloth, woll yarn and oyle'. His bequests included two loombes each to his sons John and James: he had diversified into wool weaving at scale. His also left 'Bookes' valued at £1.2s., suggesting that he could read, though there is no evidence that he could write.[12]

*****

William Shawe's family had been ravaged by pestilence in the 1620s, and the Lower House tenancy had passed for safe keeping to the unmarried daughter Agnes. The four sons of Gyles Shawe, on the other hand, prospered, becoming freeholders, investing in wool weaving, and increasing their wealth. But land ownership and money can be sources of conflict too. The Court of Chancery, restored and reformed after the Commonwealth, was kept busy with disputes over family inheritance, land and property. One such dispute involved the descendants of Gyles Shawe, and is recorded as the case of Shawe v Shawe.

With the death of John Shaw of Boarshurst in July 1665, Henry was the only surviving son of Gyles Shawe. John's only child Sarah had recently married Ralph Andrew, a husbandman, who now stood to take over John's estate through his wife. The prospect of his father's lands passing out of the family proved a tipping point for Henry, who felt he had a right to more of the family estate than he had already received. In 1666 he submitted a Bill of Complaint to the Court of Chancery demanding justice, equity and satisfaction to the tune of £400. He was joined in his complaint by Giles and Sarah from Uppermill, the children of his brother Thomas. The defence was mounted by John Shaw's widow Mary, their daughter Sarah and son-in-law Ralph Andrew: these three defendants were summoned later that year to answer the questions raised by Henry. Initially, most of their answers claimed ignorance, but by 1668 they were more organised and filed their own counter-complaint.[13]

To a modern and non-legal eye, the court documents are written in convoluted and repetitive language, liberally smattered with phrases such as: 'aforesaid', 'before mentioned', 'hereunto', 'heretofore', 'the said last named', and so on. A single word is rarely deemed sufficient if the author can add others of similar meaning, such as 'moneys due or appurteining to'. Gyles's estate is referred to repeatedly as: 'the aforesaid lands hereditaments tenements goods chatells personal estate and premisses'. The laborious style is not helped by the need to distinguish between Giles the father, Giles his son, and Giles his grandson (son of Thomas). There are also two Sarahs to contend with, one on each side of the argument, although they receive scant mention.

There is not much punctuation to help the modern reader, as in: '... the said John Shaw entred into & upon & possessed himselfe not onely of the said moyety of the said premises given to the said Joane after the death of her the said Joane but alsoe that part of the housing called the new house...' On the other hand, the language is often colourful and entertaining. Pairs of words provide numerous opportunities for alliteration, as in: 'Residue and Remainder', 'Combinacion and Confedracy', 'all and eny', 'all & everie', 'damage and detriment', 'Imbouldened & Incouraged', 'defraud & deprive', 'dealings and demeanours', 'practices and proceedings'.

Turning to the evidence, there was broad agreement between the two parties on the main provisions in Gyles's will of 1634, and although the actual document could not, allegedly, be traced at the time, the accounts of his will were accurate. Henry, after all, had been a witness to his father's will. Gyles's moveable goods and chattels were divided into three parts: the first for his wife Joane, the second to be divided between his five sons, and the third (after 'the deads part', which included funeral expenses, probation of the will etc) was to be divided between his four younger sons. As for his land and buildings, in accordance with the custom of the Lordship, half was for Joane 'during her widowhood and honest conversacion', and the other half for his eldest son John.

However, two other provisions proved more contentious. First, Henry argued, Gyles's will had bequeathed 'that part of houseinge … called ye Newhouse for a workehouse or Shopp & ye outhouseing belonging to the same unto and for the use of his said ffoure yonger sonnes' for the remainder of the term of the manorial Lease. On this point he was correct, and his wording mirrors that in his father's will almost verbatim.

His second argument was that, after Joane's death in 1646, her half share of the land and buildings and goods and chattells should have been shared between the four younger sons. This is more contentious. Gyles provided for his widow Joane according to the custom of the Lordship, and required John to pay the reversion of the leases. He did not explicitly state what should happen after Joane's death, but the implication is that her share should pass to the eldest son, John. There was, however, no dispute that after Joane's death, John had occupied both her half of the tenancy and the workshop and outbuildings called the New house, and that he also took Joane's share of the goods and chattels of Gyles.

Henry had not raised any objection at the time of his mother's death: he was after all building up his own land holdings in Quick

Mere and may have had little use for a workhouse in Boarshurst. However, 20 years later, after the death of his brother John, he could not accept that Raph Andrew, who had married John's daughter Sarah, should:

'possess themselves not onely of that parte of housing called the new house but alsoe of all and eny the aforesaid mesuage tenements lands goods chattells personall estate and premisses of the said Gyles Shawe the testator and belonginge to his said foure yonger sonnes and being of such value as aforesaid whoe have ever since by Combinacion & Confedracy betwixt themselves and of evill Intent towards your Orators held and Enjoyed the same without satisfieinge the moneys due or appurteigninge to the said foure yonger sonnes of the said Gyles the testator ... And alsoe Received & tooke the issues profitts & Revenues thereof and shared & divided the same amongst themselves and converted the same to their own uses.'

In response, John's widow Mary, his daughter Sarah and her husband Ralph Andrew did not directly answer Henry's challenge. They pointed out, reasonably enough perhaps, that Gyles the father had been dead for 32 years, and that 'in all that tyme noe Clayme or Demand whatsoever hath bin made'. They also argued, less convincingly, that John had gained nothing from the lands in question. What's more he owed nothing to Henry: 'ye said Henry Shawe Giles Shawe sonne of ye said Thomas Shawe and Sarah Shawe doe very well know that ye said John Shawe did not owe one peny to any of them at ye time of his death in any manner of wise'.

They also told how each of the complainants came to see John shortly before his death, not so much to pay their last respects, but rather to claim the money John owed them before he died. Giles and Sara (the children of Thomas) claimed 1s.8d. and 1s.6d. respectively. As for Henry:

'The said Henry Shawe did within ten houers before ye death of ye said John Come to an Accompt with the said John of all such sume & sumes of money Claymes & Demands as he could or might clayme from the same John Shawe ... and the said Henry did then onely Clayme eight shillings and eight pence from the said John Shawe and noe more which said sume the said John Shawe did appoint ye said Orator Mary Grotten wife to pay him which was Accordingly done. And ye said Henry did then receive the same and Acknowledged it in full satisfaccion of All Amounts Claimes & demands betwixt them'.

They also argued that, just after John's death, they had laid out various documents upon a table, when 'Henry violently snatched and tooke away severall of them and denyed to Returne them backe'. The implication was that these documents may have acquitted John of any debts or obligations in respect of Gyles's estate.

There now followed some proper mud-slinging, and neither party held back. Henry considered that Mary's party were acting 'by Combinaccion and Confedracy betwixt themselves and with evill Intent'; and that they were 'myndinge and Intendinge as it seems the damage and utter undoeing of your Orators'. For their part, Mary, Sarah and Ralph Andrew countered that Henry and his confederates were 'bearinge ill will' towards them and 'doe give out in speeches that they will molest and trouble' them.

Both sides claimed to know witnesses who would support their version of the facts. Unfortunately none of the witnesses could be found. They were 'either dead or gone into remote & obscure partes & places unknown to ye Orators to Inhabit & dwell so that ye Orators cannot procure them to be sent at a Tryall at a Common Law.' It was after all 'thirety twoe yeares at ye least since ye decease of ye said Giles Shawe first mencioned'

The Court of Chancery aimed to provide a fair and merciful justice, as distinct from one bound by the strict rules of the common law courts, but there were long backlogs and delays in reaching decisions. We do not know the outcome of the case. Henry was asking for £400 in compensation, but a compromise agreement may have been reached. Indeed, in a Quit Claim of 5 January 1666/7, Henry, Giles and Sarah renounced their claims 'ffully, cleerly and Absolutely'.[14] Despite that, the court case continued.

We might think that relations between Henry, Giles and Sarah on the one hand, and Mary, Sarah and Ralph Andrew on the other, had been permanently damaged by the ferocity of the claims and counter claims. But there appears to have been reconciliation. When Henry died in 1689, both his nephew Giles (the son of Thomas) and Ralph Andrew (the husband of his niece Sarah) were named among those prizing his Inventory.

11 : LOWER HOUSE

The year 1623 had decimated the Shaw family of Lower House Boarshurst. William, his two sons Edmund and Robert, and at least one grandchild, had all died within a month, as 'spotted fever' swept the land. But the family held on to its tenancy of around 22½ acres. William's sons, Robert and George, had at least one son each who survived into adulthood. William had already divided the tenancy in 1612, between himself and his eldest son Edmund. A division now continued – through Robert to his son John, and through George to his son Thomas and grandson William. Our ancestor is Thomas, but we will follow the fortunes of both cousins, who shared the Lower House tenancy at Boarshurst.

Thomas Shaw (c.1628 – 1657) was not yet alive in 1627/8, when his grandmother Katrine drew up her will. However, the youngest of his siblings, Sara, had been born between 1623 and 1627, and Thomas must have followed shortly afterwards. Seemingly the fifth child of George and Marie, he was named Thomas after a son of Ralph Shaw, to whom his grandfather William had been godfather. Perhaps this godson Thomas had recently died, for there is no further mention of him. However, the name Thomas recurs numerous times in the following generations.

There are no baptism or marriage records for Thomas because of gaps in the church register, but we know from the will of his aunt, Marie Whewall, that his wife was called Sarah. He married her in about 1651, and they had two children, with familiar names: William, born about 1653; and John, baptised on 18 July 1655. By 1657,

Thomas seemed well set in life: he was about 29 years of age, married, with two sons and a half share of a large tenancy on the manorial estate. But, once again, as in 1623, death 'crept from house to house'.

The summer of 1657 was intensely hot and dry, and by July an epidemic had broken out. This 'New Disease' was characterised by fevers, vomiting and diarrhoea. It was at first more common in the countryside than the towns and cities, but by August it was spreading 'far and near', and in the autumn it 'raged throughout all England'.[1] Thomas died in August of that pestilential year, leaving a widow with two young children.

Marie Whewall wrote her will in the summer of 1658, a year after the death of her nephew Thomas. To 'Sarah Shawe widdow' she bequeathed one pound, her best brown cloth hat, a brown waistcoat, a brown apron and 'a little Arke in the parlour'. To the five year old William and the three year old John, 'children of Thomas Shaw deceased', Marie left 'tenn shillings' and 'twentie shillings' respectively, as well as 'a great brass pot, and to the longer living of them to be left as an heirloom at that house.' William received less than John, but as the elder son he was first in line to inherit his father's share of the Lower House tenancy. The term 'that house' refers to Lower House, the house at Boarshurst where Marie had been brought up as a child, and where the two young boys lived with their uncle John.[2]

The phrase 'to the longer living of them' is an indication that Marie could not be confident that both of Thomas's sons would survive to adulthood, and who could blame her? But on this occasion, pessimism was misplaced. William survived to become our ancestor, while John became a trained weaver and the father of two children. What happened to the great brass pot is lost to the mists of time.

View southwards from Fur Lane to Boarshurst: the top floor of Lower House Farm is visible just to the left of the trees. Beyond, left to right: White Gate, Bucton Moor and Noonsun Hill, which overlook Mossley and Stalybridge.

John Shaw (1614/5 – 1696/7) was the eldest surviving son of Robert Shaw, and about 14 years older than his cousin Thomas. When Thomas died, at the age of 29, leaving two young sons fatherless, John effectively adopted the boys as his own. It was not unusual for a family member to take in the children of a deceased relative. John had no children of his own, and the elder boy, William, also had a right to a share of Lower House, when or if he reached his majority. As for the second son, John sponsored him through an apprenticeship with the master weaver Joseph Scholfield, of the neighbouring tenancy at Boarshurst called Arthurs. Over two centuries later, in 1872, Eli Shaw would similarly adopt his cousin's orphaned son and train him for a career in education (see chapter 20)

John Shaw of Lower House had been baptised at St Chad on 5 March 1614/5, the St Chad register identifying him as 'sonne of

Robert Shaw'. He appears to have married three times. His first wife was Agnes Whewall, a niece of Francis Whewall of Tunstead. They married in May 1638, and had a son baptised with the name William in June 1639. Agnes, however, died the next year, and there is no further mention of their young son. John's second wife, Ann, to whom Marie Whewall bequeathed her best hat, died in January 1676/7. A year later, on 4 December 1677, at the age of 63, John married for a third time: this marriage, with Margaret Kenworthy, would last for 19 years, until John's death.

We can trace John of Lower House through tax records in the mid-17th century. The Hearth Tax was introduced in 1662, in the early days of the reign of Charles II, and required every household to pay an annual tax of 2 shillings for each firehearth and stove. The tax was payable in two equal portions of one shilling, at Michaelmas (29 September) and Lady Day (25 March). No tax is popular, but this one caused particular resentment: because of its inequality, which 'pressed heavily on the poor and lightly on the rich'; because of the behaviour of the collectors, 'who were empowered to examine the interior of every house in the realm, to disturb families at meals, to force the doors of bedrooms...'; and because it exposed 'every man's house to be entered into, and searched at pleasure, by persons unknown to him'.[3]

The Hearth Tax was abolished in 1689, in the reign of William and Mary, and replaced by a tax on windows, which could be counted from the outside of a house without invasion of privacy. Unfortunately, this latter tax incentivised people to block their windows, which reduced not only the aesthetics of some buildings, but also their ventilation, thus aiding the spread of infection.

A very large majority of Hearth Tax returns for Saddleworth, in the period 1664-1674, are for a single hearth, although a few declared two and the Minister at St Chad paid tax for three. In Quick Mere, James Kenworthy Senior paid for five hearths in 1664, but this reduced to three in later years, when he had perhaps blocked up two hearths to reduce his tax liability. 'John Shaw de Lowerhouse' paid tax of 2 shillings for one hearth throughout the period.[4]

In 1669 the restored monarchy attempted to support the Church of England through the introduction of a further tax in the form of corn tithes. The tax was of course unwelcome, and the tax collectors appear to have met with some sullen resistance from the farmers of Saddleworth. Their report provides 'a particular of every man's Tythe Corn in Saddleworth for the yeare 1669 and the value thereof, being all Oats and no other Grayne as I am informed. But as to the Privy Tythes noe Account can be given for that yeare for they all refused to give any Account to the viewers'.[5] Oats may have been a staple cereal in Saddleworth, but they were not the only crop, contrary to what the tax collectors seem to have been told: place names such as Barley Butt and Ryetop suggest otherwise.

One of the larger tithe payers was 'John Shaw de Borehust', with 2 acres and 3 roods of oats, for which he paid 9s.2d. in tithe, at a rate of 3s.8d. per acre. The crop was probably grown on the Upper and Lower Fields (136 A & B: see table in chapter 12). These lay immediately to the west of the farmhouse, on the southern side of Boarshurst Lane, although today they contain housing. Higher, less productive land in the Diggle Valley paid a lower rate of 3s.4d per acre. Oats were grown on 102 farms in Lordsmere – a big increase in the number of farms compared to the early years of the Ramsden Manor.

We can identify Boarshurst residents from the Hearth Tax and Corn Tithe returns of 1662-1674, and these support the conclusion that John Shaw held the lease to the whole of the Lower House tenancy during that period. Soon after the last Hearth Tax record of 1674, however, he must have passed half of the tenancy to his nephew William, who attained his majority at that time and became entitled to a share of the farm. John's will, which he wrote in 1692, identified the fields he wished to bequeath to his wife as: 'the field at doors, the upper meadow and snipe rode', and to William 'the lower field, the lower meadow'. These field names confirm that by then he only occupied half of the Lower House tenancy (no. 136 in the later manorial survey of 1770), comprising housing and a little over eight acres. This part of the tenancy is referred to in 1719 rental records as 'half of Lower House': the other half (no. 5 in the 1770 survey) comprised some 14 acres of land, to the south west of Lower House, but no housing. We can deduce that in 1692 John occupied the former half of 8 acres, while his nephew William farmed the latter half of 14 acres closer to the Greenfield River.

John Shaw's will was written on 1 May 1692, 4½ years before his death on 7 January 1696/7, and he marked it with a symbol that resembled the letter 'J'. He lived to be 81 years old, two months short of his 82nd birthday, and was survived by his third wife Margaret, who lived on until 1703. He divided his portion of the farm into two parts: one for his eldest nephew and heir William; the other for his wife Margaret, 'for six years After Candlemas next Ensuing if she so long live'. He intended that, after Margaret's death, the whole farm would pass to William. However, yet again, premature death would intervene to thwart the plans.

The inventory of John's will valued his 'goods chattels and cattell' at a modest £28, including the reversion of the lease valued at £6. 6s. He had no inward debts, and only small outward debts of £1.4d., most which was owed to Mary, the wife of his nephew William. His inventory refers to 'Corne And hay And Cattel' valued at £12, to husbandry gear, and to butter and cheese, but gives no evidence of wool weaving. The will was witnessed by William's wife Mary, and by Robert and John Kenworthy, who may have been relatives of Mary and/or of his own wife Margaret.[6]

Our impression of John is a man who was unfortunate in marriage (thrice married, twice widowed and childless), but a survivor in a pestilent age, living to the age of 81. He appears not to have taken up weaving as an additional source of income, failing to move with the times. By the end, he had little extended family beyond his two nephews and their children. But in adopting the sons of his cousin Thomas, in paying for the younger son to serve an apprenticeship as a weaver, and in positioning the elder son to inherit the whole of the Lower House tenancy, he shows fairness and humanity.

*****

John's humanity was also evident in the long-running Chancery court case of Shawe v Broadbent. It was an inheritance dispute that juxtaposed a claim justified by legal documentation with an appeal based on traditions of custom and fairness. The case involved a number of people we have met before, notably the Cartwright family. It began in 1662, and the Complainants were John Shaw of Grotton, his recently married wife Margarett Cartwright and her younger unmarried sisters Jane and Elizabeth Cartwright. Among the many to give evidence was John Shaw of Lower House.

William Cartwright was well known to the Shaws of Boarshurst, as a neighbour and possibly a relative by marriage. He received a legacy of 12d from William Shawe in his will of 1623, to which he was also an overseer and a witness. He was also a witness of Katrine's will and a prizer of her inventory. After William's death, Katrine sub-let her tenancy to two neighbours: her brother-in-law Ralph Shawe of Boarshurst and William Cartwright. By then, or soon after, Cartwright had become a yeoman, purchasing a nearby farm at Greenfield Stye, also called Fur Lane, a five minute walk northwards from Katrine's house at Boarshurst. His farm was said to yield a net profit of eight to ten pounds a year.

William Cartwright died in March 1656/7, leaving a widow called Margarett but no children. His younger brother John, a mason, had died three years before him, leaving three young daughters: Margarett, Jane and Elizabeth. At his death, therefore, William Cartwright's estate should normally have passed to his widow, and through her to his three nieces. But it did not.

A William Broadbent had smartly occupied the housing and lands, claiming that William Cartwright had given them to him while he was still alive. On the face of it, William Cartwright's widow Margarett, and their three nieces, had been denied their inheritance. They must have fallen on hard times, and we saw that Marie Whewall (the aunt of John Shaw of Lower House) took the second daughter, Jane, into her house as a 'servant maid', and left her 10 shillings in her will of July 1658.

A few years later, the eldest of the three girls, Margarett Cartwright, married John Shawe of Grotton, a yeoman who was the eldest son of Henry Shaw of Lane, and a grandson of Gyles Shawe of Boarshurst (Genealogical Table 6). The newly married couple promptly lodged a Bill of Complaint. The case of John Shawe & Cartwright v Broadbent began in May 1662, continuing for years afterwards, with further hearings in 1666-1668, 1675 and 1679-1680.[7] By 1679, two of the three nieces, Jane and Elizabeth, had died, as had several witnesses, but still the case continued. Hearings took place in locations as varied as Huddersfield, Marsden, Manchester and Brook Bottom in Quick Mere. The Complaint alleged deceipt and trickery of an elderly and confused man, and, as ever, it was laced with venom:

'one William Broadbent, A meer stranger and of noo relation att all unto the said William Cartwright, having in the life tyme of the said William cunningly and surreptitiously obtained from him all such evidences and writeinges which did concern the estate of the said William – he then beinge of very weake and unsound memory – hath wrongfully entered into the messuages, tenements, lands and hereditaments of the said William, and receiveth the issue and profitts therof And hath also possessed himselfe of all the personall estate of the said William Amounting to the value and summe of tooe hundred poundes and onwards.'

The case for the defence presented matters rather differently. Broadbent was in fact William Cartwright's 'nephew by marriage': Broadbent's mother was the sister of William Cartwright's wife. What's more, the Cartwrights, having no children of their own, had raised the boy in their own house from the age of one. A deed of 1645 and an indenture dated 1653, witnessed by reputable Saddleworth residents, allegedly proved that William Cartwright had given away the land. Broadbent had even made payments from the profits of the land to Cartwright's nieces, as the indenture required. One of the witnesses to that indenture was Francis Whewall, husband of Marie Whewall: he had since died, but his signature was recognised as genuine.

An unflattering picture emerges of the Cartwright brothers. Despite owning land that yielded an annual profit of £8-£10, William Cartwright was constantly in debt. His younger brother John, a mason, drank too much and kept rough company: Almondbury Manor court records reveal that in 1627 he was beaten up by two other men, while in 1633 he was fined 10 shillings for another affray in which he 'drew blood'.

On the other hand, several witnesses vouched for Broadbent's character: he was 'reputed to be an honest man amongst his neighbours' and had paid off numerous debts for William Cartwright. A vicar of Birstall recalled William Cartwright saying that he had already provided quite generously enough for his nieces. John Whitehead of Pinfolde, a husbandman, used more blunt language, having 'oftentimes heard him saye that he would make the defendant his heire and give him his estate... whereupon he askt him why he would not give the estate to John Cartwright late father to the Complainants Margrett Jane and Elizabeth, wherefore he sayeth he would not give it to him for if he did he the said John would pisse it against the walls.'

In this small community, everyone knew each other, and many were related through marriage – not only William Cartwright and William Broadbent, but also several witnesses to the case. The court would have to decide whether this prejudiced the objectivity of their evidence. John Kaye the Younger of Marsden, for example, explained how the defendant William Broadbent, (who turns out to be his brother-in-law) had borrowed £12 from John Kaye's father in order to pay off one of William Cartwright's debts. The sum was an advance of the 'marriage portion' that William Broadbent was set to receive when he married John Kaye the Younger's sister. James Lees of Scout Heath, on the other hand, told how, when his sister Jane had married John Cartwright, their father had doubled the value of his daughter's marriage 'portion', from 20 Nobles to 20 Marks, against a promise that John Cartwright would inherit William Cartwright's property.

The evidence of John Shaw of Lower House Boarshurst, in 1666 and 1679, did not challenge the legality of the documents, but appealed to a sense of fairness and made clear where his sympathies lay. He knew very well all the parties to the dispute and the property that William Cartwright had owned. He added the detail that William and John Cartwright were in fact half-brothers, having 'had both one father but borne by severall women'. John Shaw had himself adopted the two sons of his cousin Thomas, and he confirmed that, similarly, 'William Cartwright tooke the Defendant when he was a child and kept him, and William Cartwright's wife was Ant unto him.'

In 1666 he gave evidence that Broadbent had used underhand tactics against the Complainant, causing him to be arrested on a trumped up charge of 'utlegary' (outlawry). He had then told him that if he and Margarett would just drop their complaint against him, 'he would freely discharge him from his said Imprisonne'.

Poignantly, and alone amongst the deponants, John focused on the plight of William Cartwright's widow. While many people claimed to have seen the deed in which William Cartwright gave away his wife's inheritance, it seems that she was not among them. She had been betrayed by a debt-ridden husband and by the nephew she had adopted and raised as her own child. She would not recover from these betrayals. John's evidence concluded:

'Margarett the wife of the aforesaid William Cartwright did in her life tyme tell this deponent that ye Defendant Broadbent had stolne away her husbands writinges and that hee had broken her heart. And verily at this same tyme the said Margarett, wife of the said William Cartwright, was very sickly and went and Laid her downe upon a bedd and that the said Margarett dyed about three monthes after or thereabouts.'[8]

12 : THE LAST HUSBANDMAN

When Thomas Shaw died in 1657, he left a young widow, Sarah, and two children aged about five and three years old. But families were used to sudden mortality: the children would be well looked after.

The eldest child, William, is our ancestor. He was born in about 1653, during a gap in the church registers, but there is a record of his marriage on 22 October 1678 to Mary Kenworthy. The marriage took place ten months after his uncle John's marriage to Margaret Kenworthy in December 1677. It is not clear if the two brides were related.

William's wife Mary may have come from Quick Mere, the daughter of William Kenworthy, whose baptism was recorded, in an occasional use of latinised names: 'Maria filia Gulielm Kenworthy, de Quicke 22 Feb 1662'. There were social links across the width of Saddleworth, strengthened by compulsory attendance at St Chad, the only Anglican church in the township. William also had relatives in Quick Mere: Henry Shaw, son of Gyles of Boarshurst, lived at Lane until his death in 1689, and William would have known his sons John (involved in the court case described in chapter 11) and James.

William lived with his uncle John at Lower House, and in 1674, on reaching the age of 21 he may have formally inherited his share of the family tenancy, occupying, it seems, the 14 acres that later formed tenancy number 5. With his wife Mary, he had five children. The first, named John after his uncle, and baptised in February 1679/80, died young. But four others survived: Thomas, named after William's father and baptised on 30 April 1682; William, born in about 1684; Martha, baptised on 13 November 1687; and Hugh, born in about 1690.

When his uncle John died in 1696/7, William occupied the entire Lower House tenancy of 22½ acres – but not for long. Death once again intervened. First to be struck down was his wife Mary, who is mentioned in uncle John's will of 1696/7, but not in William's of 1701. Then in the summer of 1701, William too died, aged just 48. He signed his own will clearly on 7 June 1701, but died on 30 June and was buried on 2 July.[1] He must have known he was dying, and he made sure to leave his affairs in good order, taking especial care to provide for his young children.

In contrast to wills written before the civil war, William's will makes no mention of the reigning monarch, nor of saints' days. It has the feel of a more modern piece of writing. He describes himself as a husbandman, the last in the family to do so. Like his forebears, he was primarily an arable farmer, cultivating 'Corne and Grasse growing upon y aforesaid tenement'. It was June, and the grass had not yet been harvested as hay. His inventory contains a detailed list of husbandry gear: 'plow, plowirons, harrow, carts, steads sadels, horse gayre, yoaks, swingeltree...' He had few animals, just 'one meere and three cowes, two yong lambes and one ould sheep'. There is also a long list of hand tools, including: 'Axes, nogers, chizels, sawes, spades, shovels, forkes, syth and sickels'.

However, unlike his uncle John's will, the inventory also mentions materials used for weaving: 'woll combes and combestock, weighbeames and scales'. The time was nigh when most husbandmen would call themselves clothiers, and their principal income would derive from weaving. His younger brother, John of Fur Lane, had already served an apprenticeship as a clothier (see below).

William's probate inventory mentions four rooms in his house: 'parlor, chamber, nearer parlor and further parlor', as well as another 'little house' containing chairs and tressels. We shall re-visit these houses in the next chapter. He had no debts, either inwards or outwards, and his goods were valued at £59 1s 8d.. A third of this amount (£22) was accounted for by 'the Remainder of the terme in Lease', three times more than the value of uncle John's lease.[2]

Yet although William's goods were valued at more than double those of his uncle John four years earlier, there is no indication of increased prosperity from the times of his great-grandfather William Shawe, who had died in 1623. On the contrary, the latter's valuation of 1623 equated to almost 1,000 days' wages for a skilled tradesman, while in 1701, his great-grandson's valuation in 1701 equated to about 650 days.[3] Upland agriculture was perhaps becoming less productive and profitable. There was a growing need to supplement farming with other forms of more profitable economic activity: Weaving would be the answer.

William bequeathed the Lower House tenancy to his eldest surviving son Thomas, then just 19 years old, 'to have hold and enjoy the messuage and tenement'. However, he also provided for his three younger children. Part of the land had been sub-let for a term of six years to John Whitehead of Kinders, providing a rental income of £6 per annum. This income was to be shared equally 'for the use and behoofe' of his younger children, William, Martha and Hugh. When the sub-lease to John Whitehead expired, the payments to his youngest three children would increase to £7.10s. per annum until the expiry of the manorial lease for the whole Lower House tenancy (in 1713/14).

The sub-letting of part of the tenancy indicates that William was the manorial tenant of the entire 22½ acre Lower House farm, and had seemingly agreed a contract to sub-let part of the tenancy after the death of his uncle John in 1696/7. The fields that he sub-let to John Whitehead of Kinders were almost certainly the 14 acre portion that William himself had farmed during his uncle's lifetime and that would later became Tenancy no. 5, after the formal division of Lower House into two separate tenancies in February 1713/4.

The Two Halves of the Lower House Tenancy, recorded in 1770

Lower House 136	Fields	A.R.P	Lower House 5	Fields	A.R.P
	House & Garden	0.0.12	5A 5B	Pingot Blackearth	1.0.7 1.1.13
136A	Upper Field	1.1.31	5C 5D	Bentend Frostylee	2.2.32 2.0.5
136B	Lower Field	2.0.1	5E	Frostylee Meadow	0.3.26
136C	Upper Meadow	1.0.20	5F 5G	Knowl Waste	0.2.14 0.3.21
136D	Lower Meadow	1.2.39	5H 5I	Barley Butt Holm	1.1.36 2.1.22
136E	Snipe Road	1.2.34	5K	Shrogg	1.0.20
TOTAL		8.0.17			14.1.36

The executors of William's will were named as his neighbour John Whitehead of Kinders and his second son, also called William. And just in case the money was not paid to the younger children as stipulated in the will, the executors had the authority to take over the whole messuage and tenement and distribute the 'rents, profits and revenues thereof' equally amongst all four children. His eldest son Thomas was still, after all, only 19 years old.

John Whitehead of Kinders was an immediate neighbour of William's and a yeoman, whose own land adjoined Lower House and Fur Lane to the north. At his death in 1708, his goods were valued at £246. These included quantities of cloth 'nine peeses of milld cloth, three peeses of unmilled cloth' (£28.10s), 'Bookes belonging to the deceased' (4s) and 'one Gunn' (14s). He was also owed £4 by Thomas Shaw and John Bentley 'upon bond'.[4]

Uncle John's widow, Margarett, lived on at Lower House for two more years. William's will provided for 'my Auntt Margarett Shaw' to receive 40 shillings a year, payable in six-monthly instalments, for two years after his own death, 'if she so long shall live': this was consistent with his uncle John's will that provided for Margarett to remain at Lower House for six years after his own death in 1696/7. In the event, 'Margaret Shaw widow' was buried on 1 July 1703.

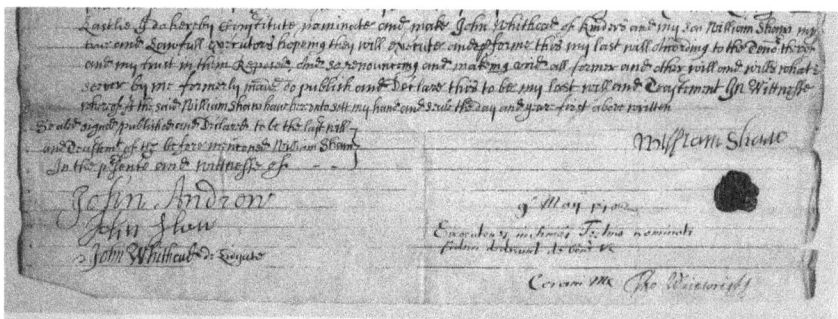

Will of William Shaw of Lower House, Boarshurst, signed by William and three witnesses in June 1701.

*****

There were three witnesses to William's will, each of whom signed their names confidently: John Andrew, John Whithead de Lidgate, and William's younger brother John Shaw. All three inform our understanding of William and his family.

John Andrew, who was also one of four to prize the inventory, was a near neighbour at Boarshurst. His father was Ralph Andrew, who had married Sarah the daughter of John Shaw of Boarshurst and granddaughter of Gyles. John Andrew's role in William's will is a further indication of the strength of ties across an extended family and between neighbours. The Andrew family would later acquire the freehold of Ralph Shaw's old tenancy (137) and build a water-powered mill, called Andrew Mill.

'John Whithead de Lidgate' in Quick Mere was a yeoman and a stapler (wool merchant or trader), a man of substance. On his death in December 1715, aged 78, a memorial tablet was placed over the vestry door in St Chad, recording that he was father to 14 children, grandfather to 51 and great-grandfather to 8, 'in all 73'.[5] Yet he was a witness to William's will. One reason is that he acted as an attorney in the township, and he appears as a witness to several wills at the time. He also gave evidence in the case of William Cartwright's inheritance, confirming that he recognised the handwriting of Francis Whewall. But there may also be another link. John Whithead's daughter Martha (born 1668) had married Edward Kenworthy of Quick Mere (born 1659/60). This Edward was just three years older than William's wife Mary Kenworthy and may have been her brother.

John Shaw (1655 -), William's's younger brother, was the third witness to his will. 'John sone of Thomas Shaw' had been born on 18 July 1655, and baptised on 28 July. We saw that his great-aunt Marie Whewall had left him 20 shillings in her will of 1658.

The will of his uncle John Shaw of Lower House tells us that, by 1692, young John was married with two children and living at neighbouring Fur Lane. Uncle John left small legacies of 2s. 6d. to each of these two children, Thomas and Mary. Fur Lane, previously known as Greenfield Stye, was part of a 54 acre estate that included land at Uppermill and Carr Barn. The estate was owned by Giles Shaw, a descendant of Gyles Shawe of Boarshurst (d.1634) through his son Thomas.[6] Continuing links across the extended family helped the fatherless young John to rent a cottage and workhouse in which to earn his livelihood as a weaver.

In about 1674, John's elder brother William would have come of age and inherited his share of the family tenancy. John therefore needed to find a different path in life. On 1 March 1674/5, at the age of 19, he was indentured as an apprentice clothier to Joseph Scholfield, 'Clothmaker of Boarshurst'. Joseph Scholfield lived at Arthurs, the tenancy that had been occupied by his grandfather Arthur Scholefield in 1590, and from whom the tenancy's name appears to derive. The record of indenture provides a fascinating account of the strict conditions that applied to apprenticeships: they were not a soft option. It records that young John undertook the apprenticeship 'of his own free voluntary will, as likewise by and with the consent of his uncle John Shaw of Lower House in Boarshurst'. He was required to complete a full seven year term as apprentice, and the document then set out strict conditions.[7]

The indenture was witnessed by John Whitehead (probably the yeoman farmer of neighbouring Kinders, rather than the attorney of Lydgate) and by uncle John Shaw of Lower House Boarshurst. Uncle John's agreement was necessary because he was required to stand as sponsor. The annual payment of fourpence, by Joseph Scholefield to his apprentice, was only a token contribution to his living costs, most of which, such as food, clothing and general upkeep fell to his sponsor, uncle John of Lower House.

'The said John Shaw apprentice to the said Joseph Scolefield his said Master well and faithfully shall serve. His secrets he shall keep and counsel, his commands lawful and honest everywhere he shall obey. Hurt unto his said Master he shall not do, nor consent to be done to the value of 12 pence by the year or above, but the same to his person shall hinder or immediately admonish his Master thereof. Taverns nor alehouses of infamy he shall not frequent, except it be about his Master's business there to be done. At the cards or dice or any other unlawful games he shall not play whereby his Master may incur any hurt. The goods of his said Master inordinately he shall not waste nor them to anyone lend without his Master's consent. Fornication he shall not commit. Matrimony within the said term he shall not contract, nor from his said Master's service by day or by night he shall not absent or prolong himself, but as a true and faithful servant ought he shall behave himself as well in words as in deeds during the said term.

'The said Joseph Scolefield, for and in consideration of the before mentioned service, doth hereby convenant in the craft, trade, science or occupation of a cloth maker, after the best manner he can, to teach, instruct and inform, or cause to be informed, instructed and taught, the said John Shaw his apprentice as much to the said craft belongeth, or in any wise appurtayneth, as dyeing of wool, mixing of colours, warping, weaving and looming of cloth, and in due measure to chastise him, and to pay unto his said servant or apprentice the sum of four pence upon every first day of the nativity of our Blessed Lord and Saviour yearly during the before mentioned term of seven years, being his wages.'

The conditions of the indenture were standard, as we can see from an 1842 indenture of apprenticeship for Thomas Hayes, who went on to marry Sarah Jane Shaw in 1859 (see chapters 18 and 20). This Thomas served a seven year apprenticeship to an engraver in Staffordshire. Yet despite the distance in time and geography, the wording of the principal conditions in the indenture is almost identical to that of John Shaw in the Saddleworth of 1674/5. Indeed these conditions are printed in Thomas Hayes' indenture, with space allowed for manuscript insertions regarding pay.

The main difference between the two indentures is that the wages paid to Thomas Hayes increased with each passing year, as he became more skilled and of greater usefulness to his master, rising from nothing in the first two years, to 2s per week in the third year and 7s per week in the 7th and final year. There were payments for overtime too, rising from 1d per hour to 4d per hour in the final three years. The indenture is also explicit that Thomas Hayes' father was responsible for the costs of his upkeep, being required to 'bind himself and his heirs Executors and Administrators to Provide his said son with sufficient meat, drink, washing and Lodging and all other necesaries during the said term and to Pay ... the sum of Five Pounds (Premium) with his said son.'[8]

13 : THE LAST SHAW OF LOWER HOUSE

The 18th century brought radical change. Saddleworth witnessed a rapid growth in domestic woollen manufacture as a commercial activity, and the stone clad houses built in this century typically provided generous workspace for looms. Lower House too would be redeveloped. The large majority of church records refer to 'clothiers', while 'husbandmen' are now rare. Population growth was placing unprecedented pressure on land, and younger sons moved further afield to find land to rent or, later in the century, into the growing towns for employment. There had been earlier examples of people moving across the four Meres of Saddleworth to live: Gyles Shawe's son Henry bought land in Quick Mere, for example. Now such movement became more commonplace. Church registers contain frequent references to 'sojourners in Saddleworth', to Irishmen and soldiers, to people from Oldham, Mossley, Ashton and Glossop.[1] Horizons were widening.

There had always been a number of yeomen in Saddleworth, who owned the freehold to their land, and their numbers now increased. Our own Shaw ancestors, however, had remained tenants of the Lord of the Manor, and to follow the fortunes of the next generation we need to understand the different kinds of leases on the manorial estate in the early 18th century. Manorial rental records for 1719 identify four types of lease, as below, with the number of leases in each category shown in brackets.[2] The first two types of lease were traditional or 'archaic', and they progressively gave way to rack rents.

Leases upon fine and Years (26): Most husbandmen on the manorial estate held this type of lease in the 17th and early 18th centuries. It covered a fixed term of years, but could be renewed at the end of the term, subject to payment of an entry fine or garsome, and could also be passed on to the leaseholders's heirs at his death. The rent was by custom held at a low level, but the entry fine evolved to become the principal element of the payment to the landowner. In 1731, for example, Thomas Hawkyard renewed the lease to his tenancy at Thamewater shortly before he died: his inventory records a 'fifty five pounds ffine paid for a Lease for 21 yrs.'

Leases for Lives (37): This type of lease became increasingly popular in the 18th century. With good judgement, and good fortune, the leaseholder could retain the property in the family for a longer time than a standard 21 year lease. Instead of a term of years, the lease endured for the term of three specified lives: the leaseholder and, typically, his wife and eldest son. A low annual rent was fixed for the entire duration of the lease, a significant benefit in times of inflation. The lease could also be renewed by replacing the names of those who had died with new names, subject of course to the payment of a new fine.

Leases upon fine for 999 Years (12): These were rare on the manorial estate, a recent initiative in 1719, and were to all intents and purposes a sale of the property while retaining rental income for the manorial estate.

Racke Rents (54): The manorial estate was keen to introduce rack rents where hereditary entitlement had lapsed, offering farms to new tenants on a more flexible basis. Rack rents strongly favoured the manor. Annual rents were high, reflecting the full market value of the property, land and buildings. There were no hereditary rights for the tenant, and no security of tenure. When the lease came to be renewed, the landowner could increase the rents or seek the highest market bid; and with a growing demand for land, he held the whip hand. There were nevertheless some benefits for the tenant, who could access housing and land without the large up-front payment of an entry fine, and who could then sub-let some or all of the land at a higher rent.

Unlike tenants with a lease for lives or years, they were not liable for payment of the land tax, introduced in 1692.

*****

Our ancestor William Shaw (1653-1701) and his wife Mary had five children, born at Lower House: John (1680), Thomas (1682), our ancestor William (c.1684), Martha (1687) and Hugh (c.1690). John appears to have died in childhood, and we know nothing of Martha beyond her being mentioned in her father's will; but we do know about the three surviving sons. They were all young when their father died in 1701 (between 11 and 19 years old) and needed to remain at Lower House for some more years; but since the eldest son inherited the tenancy, the others would have to leave in due course. This chapter will focus on the eldest son Thomas and his descendants, who were the last Shaws to live at Lower House. The following chapter will focus on the second surviving son, our ancestor William. First, a few words about the youngest son, Hugh.

Hugh (c.1690 – 1777), the youngest son of William Shaw, was perhaps as young as 11 years old when his father died. Initially, he would have remained at Lower House, supported by the annual payments of £2 rising to £2.10s., provided for him by his father's will. However, the lease on Lower House was due for renewal at Candlemas 1713/14, and at that point the payments to him would cease, and he would need to move on and find a living elsewhere. He had a plan.

On 7 May 1713, just a few months before the expiry of the lease, Hugh married Ann Buckley and moved to Halls in Shaw Mere. Here his descendants remained for several generations. Hugh had not moved far. Halls may have been in Shaw Mere but it was just half a mile or so from Boarshurst, touching the western fields of Arthurs. It was a large manorial tenancy of some 44 acres, with three 'dwelling houses'. Hugh was a sub-tenant, but acquired customary rights to retain occupation. Rental records for 1743 show that Joseph Lawton was the tenant of Halls, but that the farm was 'now lettt to Hugh Shaw and William Buckley'.[3] In 1740 Hugh was the Churchwarden for Halls,[4] and in 1745 he was elected as a Bylawman in support of the constable for the township of Quick.[5]

By the time he died, well into his 80s, Hugh had founded a numerous and often long-lived line of Shaws at Halls and neighbouring Arthurs. The gravestone at St Chad's of his eldest son, John of Halls, who had married a Mary Shaw of Tunstead in 1740, records that he died 'in his 80th year'.[6] Hugh's grandson James, who acquired the freehold of a farm at Arthurs, lived to over 86 years old. And one of James's sons, another James, who occupied a second farm at Arthurs, lived to 83 years of age. (See Table 8)

Thomas (1682-1747/8), and his descendants, are particularly relevant to our story. Whereas William and Hugh, as younger sons, were expected to leave the ancestral home at Lower House, Thomas, being the eldest, stood to inherit. He was just 19 when he inherited most of the 22½ acre Lower House tenancy. (He had to wait two more years to inherit four acres from his great aunt Margaret, John Shaw's widow, who died in 1703. His father's will was proved in May 1702, and Thomas lost no time in finding a wife, marrying Mary Broadbent in September. A child, another William, was born in 1703, but Mary died the following year. Thomas remarried, and his second wife, Ann, delivered him another son, to whom he gave his own name of Thomas. Ann died in 1736, leaving Thomas a widower for the last decade of his life.

Thomas's father, William Shaw, had held a 'lease upon fine and years' at Lower House, and at the time of his death in 1701 there were still 12 years remaining on the term. Part of the farm had been been sub-let, most recently to John Whitehead of Kinders, for an annual income of £6, and it was expected to yield £7.50 p.a. thereafter. When the term of the Lower House lease expired in 1713/14, Thomas made two important changes. First, he agreed to a 'lease for lives', which, as luck would have it, lasted until 1772. Secondly, he renewed the lease for only half of the tenancy, relinquishing the other half.

As we have seen, the tenancy had been divided for much of the preceding century. Sometimes the land was divided between family members, such as William and his son Edmund in 1612, while at other times part of the tenancy was sub-let, for example by Katrine in 1623 to William Cartwright and Ralph Shawe, or by William Shaw after 1696/7 to John Whitehead of Kinders. However, the family had always maintained the right to the entire tenancy of 22½ acres.

Why then, in 1713/14, did Thomas relinquish half of the lands that his ancestors had held for generations? The cost of renewing the lease upon its expiry was doubtless one consideration. While the annual rental for the whole of Lower House was held at the customarily low level of 10 shillings, the garsome to secure renewal of the lease was around £50. This was a sizeable sum, especially after Thomas had distributed to his younger siblings the income from sub-letting part of the farm, in accordance with his father's will. However, a part of Thomas's motivation was surely that he saw his future in weaving more than agriculture, and that is where he wanted to focus his attention and investment. Weaving was the future and offered greater profits. Twelve years after the death of his father, a 'husbandman', the new indenture of lease identifies Thomas as a 'Clothmaker'.

There was also a willing buyer. In 1701, the under-tenant for half of the tenancy was John Whitehead of Kinders, but he was later succeeded by John Bentley. John Whitehead's will of 1708 records that he was owed £4 upon bond jointly by Thomas Shaw and John Bentley, suggesting that Bentley was now sub-tenant for part of the Lower House tenancy. Bentley was keen to acquire lands. His father had married Ellen Platt, descended from the Platts of Boarshurst who were named in Edmund Shawe's will.

Through this connection, he had come into the 7 acre tenancy at Boarshurst (later numbered 4 in the estate survey).[7] He also held the lease to a 15 acre manorial tenancy at Saddleworth Fold. By the time of his death in 1749 he was a yeoman owning his own freehold land.

When Thomas Shaw's lease on Lower House came up for renewal in 1713/14, John Bentley acquired half of it in his own name. Hereditary leases rarely came on the market, but a leaseholder could, with the consent of the Lord of the Manor, sell all or part of a lease to a third party. John Bentley may have made a persuasive offer.

Lower House was now formally divided into two tenancies, although both parts retained the name 'Lower House'. At Candlemas, on 2 February 1713/4, they each paid a 'consideration' (or garsome) of £25, to be followed by an annual rent of 5 shillings payable in two equal instalments at Pentecost and St Martin the Bishop. Rental records from 1719-1743 show each of them paying 5 shillings per annum (2s.6d. at half yearly intervals) for their respective halves of the Lower House farm.[8]

The lease was for 'all that messuage or dwellinghouse and buildings in Saddleworth commonly called Lower House, all such closes, meadows and pastures as the same is now divided by the said Thos Shaw & Jnᵒ Bentley being the moiety or one half of the closes &c belonging to the aforesaid messuage'. Thomas Shaw and John Bentley each held a lease for lives for their respective parts of Lower House. Thomas's lease was held against the three lives of himself, Thomas Shaw 'Clothmaker', his wife Ann and his son William, 'or the longest survivor of them.'[9] By 1743 Thomas and his son William had again sub-let part of their diminished Lower House tenancy: 'Thomas and Wm Shaw for half of Lower house part lett to Henry Brearly.'[10]

Importantly, in dividing the Lower House lease between himself and John Bentley, Thomas retained the housing at Lower House Boarshurst. His 'moiety', later numbered 136 in the manorial survey of 1770, comprised 8 acres of arable fields and meadow land, including housing and two outbuildings. John Bentley's part, later numbered 5, comprised just over 14 acres, but with no housing or outbuildings attached; the fields were also a little further distant from Boarshurst, on either bank of the Greenfield River.

Thomas now set about improving the housing and providing better space for weaving looms. By 1770, when his son William still held the lease for lives, the manorial survey records a newly built house of two bays, an old one of two bays and recently repaired outhousing of two bays. The current buildings as we see them today reflect these changes, as well as later extensions up to the early 19th century which added a third bay and third storey to the main farmhouse, connecting it at right angles to the two storey cottage. The sturdy, stone-built houses, with their slate roofs and light windows, are strongly characteristic of this part of Saddleworth and are now Grade II listed. [11]

Lower House on Boarshurst Lane: the Grade II listed farmhouse and cottage as they appear today, constructed at various periods between the early 18th and early 19th centuries. A workshop for weaving looms once ran the full length of the main house on the third floor.

Thomas died in January 1747/8, aged about 65: the burial register records 'Thomas Shaw senior of Boarshurst', to distinguish him from his second son of the same name. But it is the fortunes of his first son, William (1703-1772), that are of most relevance to our story. This William moved around in his youth, as was now common, before settling at the family tenancy of Lower House. He was living at Wharmton Brow in 1724 when he married Esther Bottomley. His first two children were born at Boarshurst and his last two at Wellihole in Shaw Mere, where rental records for 1743 show him occupying the tenancy held by a Samuel Shaw, in yet another example of a supportive relationship between Saddleworth Shaws.[12] Several Shaw families now lived in close proximity in this part of Shaw Mere – at Wellihole, Gibbs, Barn and Lanehead.

This William was the third name on the Lower House lease for lives. His step-mother, Ann, had died in 1736, and on the death of his father in 1747/8 he inherited the tenancy. A Manorial Court Roll of 1750 notes that he was now the sole remaining name on the lease: 'William Shaw Tenant at boreshurst called Lower house leased for three lives, the said Willm Shaw ye only surviving life'.[13]

William was still listed as the tenant of Lower House in the Manorial Survey of 1770. However, although the lease was still in his name, William had moved to Grottonhead in Quickmere soon after his father's death, sub-letting the Lower House tenancy. Three Manorial Court Rolls make this clear. In 1762, the Court resolved to 'Lay a pain that William Shaw or the occupyers of Lower house in boreshurst Do put their barn in good Repair before the Eleventh day of November Next or forfiet to the Lord of the Manner ye sum of five shillings'. The next year came the threat of an increased penalty: 'We Lay in paine that William Shaw Seanier of grottenhead Repare his Barn at Borsherst before the first day of June next or forfet to the Lord of this Manner the

130

Sum of one pound.' In 1764, having still not repaired the barn at Boarshurst, he was amerced the sum of twenty shillings (£1) 'for non performance of the pain'.[14]

Grottonhead is where this William later died, of consumption, in January 1772. He was buried at St Chad, where a headstone marks his grave and records that he died 'in the 70th Year of his Age', and that his wife Esther died seven years later in her 77th year.[15] He was the last Shaw of Lower House, Boarshurst, and his move to Quickmere signalled an important change in our family history, as we shall find out in chapter 17.

IV SHAWHOUSES (1719-1798)

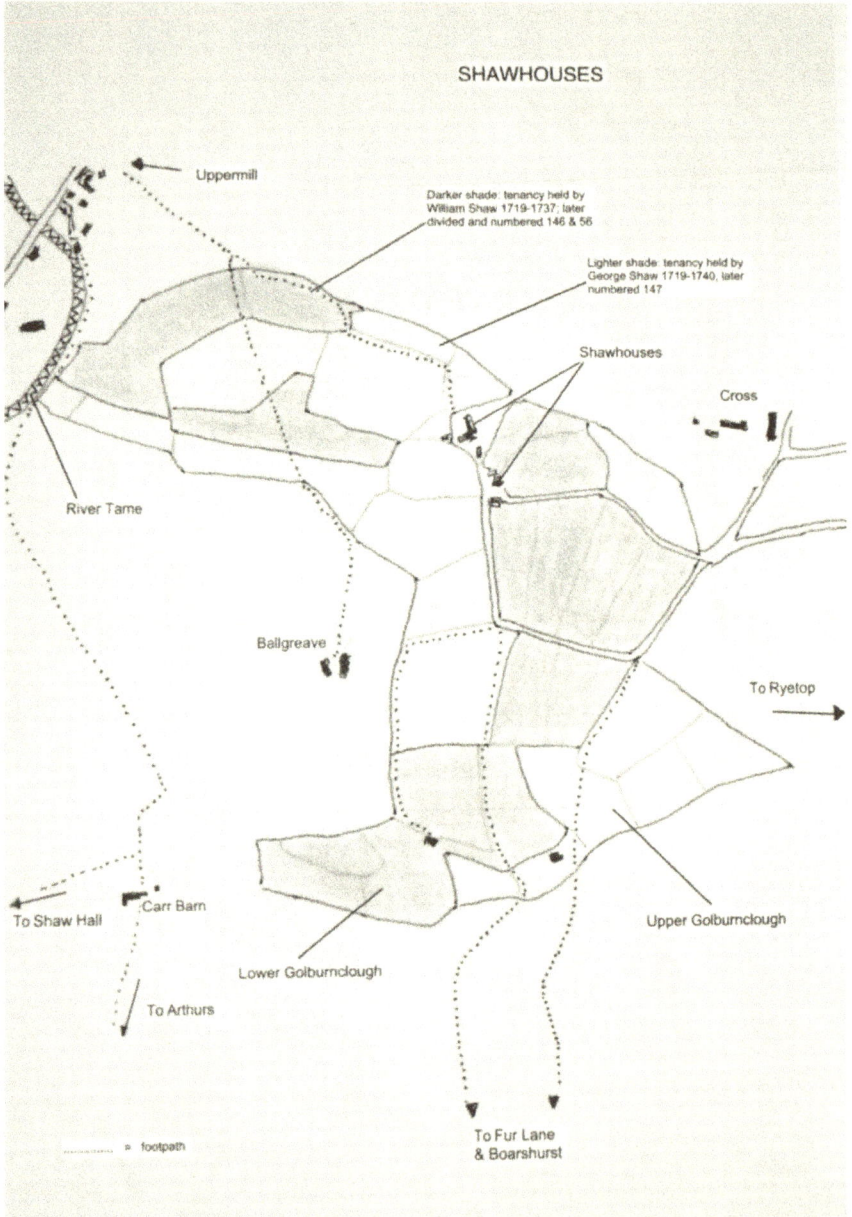

SHAWHOUSES

Uppermill

Darker shade: tenancy held by
William Shaw 1719-1737; later
divided and numbered 146 & 56

Lighter shade: tenancy held by
George Shaw 1719-1740, later
numbered 147

Shawhouses

Cross

River Tame

Ballgreave

To Ryetop

Carr Barn

To Shaw Hall

Upper Golburnclough

Lower Golburnclough

To Arthurs

footpath

To Fur Lane
& Boarshurst

133

14 : WILLIAM AND THE HAWKYARDS

We must now return to Lower House, Boarshurst, where William Shaw had died in 1701. His eldest son, Thomas, inherited the tenancy, as we have seen, while his youngest son, Hugh, moved away to live at Halls. What happened to his second surviving son, our ancestor William Shaw (c.1684-1737)? (Genealogical Table 1B)

There is no baptism record for William, because of gaps in the register, but he must have been born in about 1684, between his elder brother Thomas (1682) and his sister Martha (1687). According to his father's will, in which the 17 year old William was named as an executor, he would have benefited from £2 p.a. income from Lower House until 1707, followed by £2.10s, until the term of the manorial lease expired in 1713/14. By then, William, like his younger brother Hugh, needed to leave Lower House. He had probably done so by the time he married Sarah, in about 1706, and by 1719 he held his own manorial tenancy of some 27 acres at Shawhouses, ¾ mile north of Boarshurst, along the paths and cart tracks that led towards Uppermill. How did he come by such a large tenancy?

At the start of the 1590s, the earliest tenancy records of the Ramsden Lordship of Saddleworth Manor show two manorial tenants farming at Shawhouses: Ralphe Shawe and Barnarde Shawe, from which families the settlement's name seemingly derives. There is no evidence that these were particularly close relations of our line of Shaws, though they too must have been descended from the del Schaghes. The two tenancies were of a similar size: in 1770, Ralphe's old tenancy, now numbered 147 on the manorial estate, comprised 25 acres, while Barnard's old tenancy, now split in two and numbered

146 and 56, jointly comprised 27 acres. For ease of reference, we shall call these Shawhouses (147) and Shawhouses (146/56). Three wills from the period 1626/7- 1633/4 help us to piece together what happened to these tenancies.[1]

Ralphe's descendants managed to hold on to the lease of the 25 acre tenancy at Shawhouses (147) despite the recurrent pestilence of the times. Ralphe's son George paid the garsome in two instalments in 1612 and 1612/3.[2] When George died in 1632/3 (leaving £2 to his elderly father Ralphe, who outlived him by a couple of years), his eldest son, George Shaw junior, stood to inherit the lease, but died almost immediately in 1633/4. Fortunately, there was a second son called John who took over the tenancy. This is the same John Shaw of Shawhouses referred to in the will of Marie Whewall in 1658, and also listed in Hearth Tax returns of 1664. By 1719, the lease was held by another George Shaw, apparently descended from Ralphe through George and John, who paid an annual rent of 20 shillings. This tenancy was therefore still held on an hereditary basis in 1719.

The second Shawhouses tenancy (146/56) was occupied by Barnarde Shawe in 1590 -1595, but his family could not hold onto the lease for very long. Barnarde evidently died in about 1595, as he paid half his garsome in that year, but in 1596 the other half was paid on behalf of Barnarde's wife by a neighbour called Peter Greave. By 1612, Barnarde's son John was named as the tenant, paying a similar garsome to that of his Shawhouses neighbour, George Shaw. When John died in 1627 without issue, he left the tenancy to be shared equally between his wife Ellen and his brother Bernard. However, Ellen died in 1636/7, and brother Bernard seemingly had no male children (none were mentioned in John's will of 1627). So when this younger Bernard died in 1638, the lease passed out of the family.

Certainly, by the time of the Hearth Tax records of 1664, the line of descendants from Barnarde Shawe had ended, and thereafter the land was occupied by a series of tenants who had no previous family connection to Shawhouses, and no hereditary right to the land. By 1719, our ancestor William Shaw had become the latest to occupy Barnarde Shawe's old Shawhouses tenancy, on a non-hereditary basis.

We have seen that by 1719, the lease of Lower House, Boarshurst was now a 'lease of lives', in the names of Thomas Shaw, his wife and eldest son: it had a low, fixed annual rent and enabled Thomas's son to inherit. However, Thomas's younger brother, our ancestor William Shaw, was paying a Rack Rent for Shawhouses (146/56). We do not know all the conditions of the lease, but critically, unlike the lease for lives on Lower House, there were no hereditary rights, and therefore no guarantee that William could pass the lease on to his own son and heir.

Unusually for a rack rent, rental payments did not increase during the term of the lease. However, they started high. While Thomas at Lower House paid a low annual rent of 5 shillings for an 8 acre tenancy (around 7½ pence per acre), William paid an annual rent of £7 for his 27 acre tenancy (over 5 shillings per acre). William was thus paying 8 times more per acre in rent than his brother. George Shaw, who held the tenancy at Shawhouses (147) by hereditary right, was paying just £1 throughout this period for a similar acreage to that farmed by William (under 10 pence per acre). After William's death, the rent was reviewed, and the increasing demand for land from a growing population meant that this could only lead to steep increases.

Writing in 1691, the Reverend Richard Baxter was scathing of landlords who were exploiting demand for land by imposing rack rents, breaking up larger tenancies into smaller ones and letting them to the highest bidder. He described a national trend, but his words might have applied to the Saddleworth manorial estate a couple of decades later.

'The husbandmen are the stamen of the Commonwealth... Gentlemen say, oure Land is our owne and therefore we may make the best of it for our owne commodity, and he that will give most for it shall be our tenant. The old custome was to let Lands for Lives or for long terms of years, and to take a fine at first and a small yearly rent afterwards, and so, when a man, with his marriage portion, had taken a lease he lived comfortably afterward and got somewhat for his children. But now in most countrys (areas) the custom is changed into yearly rack-rents: or, if a man take a Lease for many years it is yearly to pay as much as the tenement is worth, and that is as much as any man will give for it.'[3]

For all that, William did not, so far as we know, have to pay a garsome, and we know that he was able to sub-let parts of the tenancy, potentially for even higher rents, so he should have been able to make a reasonable living. In 1729, a William Shaw was elected a Bylawman. The name was not common in Saddleworth at the time, and was quite probably William of Shawhouses. He was re-elected in 1733 and the next year became Constable for Quick, an important, if burdensome, role.[4]

All changed in 1735, when William's wife Sara died and was buried at St Chad on 9 November. Seven months later, on 17 June 1736, William re-married. His second wife was Martha Hawkyard, the widow of 'old Thomas Hawkyard de Tamewater', who we mentioned in chapter 7. She had married Thomas Hawkyard in 1725, after the death of his first wife Esther, when he was 62 years old. The marriage register records Martha as a spinster, but she already had two children, James and Martha Buckley, adopted nephew and niece perhaps, or the product of an earlier marriage. So many marriages at this time ended with the premature death of one spouse, and so many children were raised by step-parents.

The marriage of Thomas and Martha Hawkyard, despite Thomas's advanced years, was not an entirely platonic arrangement, for in 1726 Martha gave birth to a son, also named Thomas. This son would ensure her financial security. Five years later, in 1731, old Thomas, 'aged and decayed in body', died, leaving Martha with three children – two Buckley children and young Thomas Hawkyard.

On her husband's death, Martha inherited half of his goods (valued at £94), the other half being held in trust for the 'maintenance, education and preferment' of their infant son during his minority. She also occupied her late husband's 33 acre manorial tenancy at Tamewater, and held a third part of enclosed land at Wadehill.[5] Just before his death, Thomas had paid a fine (garsome) of £55 to extend the Tamewater lease for a further 21 years, so Martha's future was secure. Technically, she stood to forfeit most of her share of old Thomas Hawkyard's estate if she re-married, owing to the standard condition in his will: '… for so long as she continues my widow and keeps herself sole and unmarried.' However, since this share would then pass to her young child Thomas, the condition in the will made little practical difference.

William Shaw was in his early 50s when his wife Sara died, and marrying Martha Hawkyard must have seemed a sensible arrangement. After the wedding he moved to Tamewater to live with Martha and her then 10 year old son, leaving his own son John, our ancestor, to continue at Shawhouses.

However, as so often, the best laid plans foundered. Just 18 months after their marriage, 'William Shaw, of Taume-water, Clothier' was buried at St Chad on 8 December 1737. Whether the lease of Shawhouses was for a term of 21 years and therefore about to expire, or whether it was linked to the life of William and therefore would expire with his death, we cannot be sure. Either way, the lease would come up for review, and this was a problem for William's son John Shaw. We shall follow John's fortunes in the next two chapters.

Meanwhile, Martha's son, young Thomas Hawkyard, did not live long either. In 1743, at the age of seventeen, he signed his own will, dying some ten weeks later from a wasting illness. His will reflects the pitiful complexity that death had brought to his family ties, yet also the value of extended family relations. The first legacy in his will bequeathed three shillings 'to my cousin William Shaw', the five-year old grandson of his stepfather William Shaw. He also bequeathed legacies to his 'brother and sister', James and Martha Buckley, (including a gun for James) as well as funds to ensure his step-mother's livelihood.[6]

Martha lived on at Tamewater, though she sold her one-third share of land at Wadehill in 1748. In her lifetime she had lost a teenage son and probably three husbands. She did not marry again after William's death, and she herself died in 1752, the burial register recording: 'Martha Shaw, Thame-water, widow'.

*****

Before we leave the Hawkyards, we should note the extraordinary will of Ralph Hawkyard, son of old Thomas Hawkyard by his first wife, Esther Shaw.[7] Ralph made his way in life as a 'chapman' or pedlar, and was evidently good at it, for by the time of his early death in 1729, at the age of 39, he had amassed some wealth. Lacking children of his own to leave his money to, he bequeathed £50 for the renewal of the lease on his father's manorial tenancy at Tamewater. As we have seen, his father used the sum for that very purpose shortly before his own death two years later, thus enabling the tenancy to be passed to his widow, and through her to their three year old son Thomas (Ralph's half-brother).

Ralph bequeathed a further fifty pounds to be held in trust for his three year old half-brother Thomas, to be given to him when he reached the age of 21, which, sadly, as we have seen, young Thomas failed to do. And he bequeathed smaller sums of £10 each to his father and to a maternal cousin called James Shaw, as well as an annuity of 40 shillings per annum to his unmarried sister Esther.

Most remarkably, however, he left 'the full sume of Two Hundred pounds of lawfull British Money' to pay for the endowment of a free school (plus an extra £50 if his half-brother Thomas died before the age of 21, which indeed transpired.) He noted that there had been 'discourse' in the parish about a proposal to create a free school, but no contributions had been forthcoming. Yet there was a 'great want of learning' among children in the parish, 'especially among the poorer sort of people, who, not being of ability to send their children to remote schools, were in a great degree void of learning and not capable of reading the Divine Scriptures'.

He therefore instructed his executor to use the funds to build a new schoolhouse within half a mile of Tamewater, and to pay the wages of a schoolteacher 'able to teach the three tongues vizt English, Latin and Greek'. Wharmton Grammar School was subsequently founded, the first endowed school in Saddleworth, and a tribute to a young chapman, whose community spirit is celebrated in a tablet in Saddleworth Church. While the school closed in 1883, The Hawkyard charity continues to this day to provide educational grants to Saddleworth children. [8]

15 : SHAWHOUSES DIVIDED

William Shaw of Shawhouses (c.1684-1737) held his manorial tenancy on a rack rent, which provided no security of tenure for his children after his death. What would their future be?

William had five children by his first wife Sara. Most were born during a gap in the baptismal registers (1704-1715), but their marriage records show them each living at Shawhouses: John, our ancestor, born about 1709, Martha (c.1711), Thomas (c.1713), Ann (c.1715) and William baptised in 1717/18. In keeping with the usual pattern, the younger siblings would move away from the family home at Shawhouses, while the eldest son, John, would remain. We shall come to John below, but first, what do we know of his siblings?

Martha, born about 1711, married a James Shaw of Barn, near Saddleworth Fold, just north of Shawhouses, in 1731. This was probably the same James Shaw, a maternal cousin of Ralph Hawkyard, who received £10 in Ralph's will of November 1729. James's father Jonathan died just two days after Ralph Hawkyard, naming William Shaw, amongst others in his will.[1] Jonathan had acquired the freehold of his land at Barn, and although he left this to his wife Deborah, it would in due course pass to his only son James. As it was, James, just 19 years old in 1729, immediately inherited £20 and all his father's 'utensils, work loombes whatsoever belonging to the Clothmaking Trade', valued at £26. He also inherited his father's seat in the gallery of the nearby church of St Chad.

On 19 September 1731, the St Chad's register drily recorded the baptism of 'George, son of James Shaw, de Barn, Clothier, by Martha Shaw, Spinster, de Shawhouses'. No doubt the curate had a word with

James and Martha, for five weeks later, on 26 October, the pair were married. Later children included, inevitably, a William.

Thomas, the second son, was born about 1713 and married in 1736/7. His wife was Mary Bradbury and he married her seven months after his father William's second marriage to Martha Hawkyard. Thomas and Mary are both recorded as living at Boarshurst at the time of their marriage, and their first three children were born there. They lived at Lower House, where, as we saw in chapter 13, Thomas's uncle (Thomas Shaw Senior) held the manorial tenancy. Uncle Thomas had been widowed in 1736 and may have welcomed a nephew and his wife coming to live in the house.[2] Once again, the extended family helped out a young couple embarking on married life.

Ann married in 1737/8, two months after the death of her father had left her in need of security. The marriage register for 14 February 1737/8 records: 'James Mellor, Sojourner in Saddleworth, and Ann Shaw, Spinster, de Shaw-houses'. Their first child, James, was born in 1741, in Knott Lanes, just across the parish boundary in Ashton.

The youngest son, William, in another example of the value of an extended family, seemingly took the opportunity to farm alongside his uncle Hugh at Halls. He was living there when he married in 1743, and his children, who included a Hugh, John and William, were all born at Halls. (See Table 8)

We now come to John Shaw (c.1709-1789), our ancestor and the eldest son of William and Sara Shaw of Shawhouses. John married on 19 August 1731 at St Chad's. The register confirms him as a clothier from Shawhouses, and his wife as Mary Buckley from 'Saddleworth', probably Saddleworth Fold, a hamlet just east of Uppermill.

As we have seen, John's father, William Shaw, held the tenancy of Shawhouses on a rack rent from 1719 to 1736. After his first wife's death, he re-married and moved to Tamewater, but died unexpectedly in 1737. John, now in his mid-20s, succeeded his father as the tenant of

Shawhouses - but not for long. As he had no right to inherit the tenancy from his father, the lease would be reviewed.

Was there a garsome to be paid up front, that John could not afford? Or perhaps a bidding process, as described by the Reverend Richard Baxter? John's neighbours and sub-tenants, the Whiteheads, were certainly growing in numbers and keen to acquire more land: John Whitehead had two adult sons, John and Timothy, while his daughter also lived in Shawhouses with her husband David Harrop and their growing family. John Shaw, by contrast, was a young man, recently married, who had just lost both parents in the space of two years, and who may have struggled to make a case for managing a 27 acre estate, with sub-tenants and multiple buildings, boundary walls and ditches.

Perhaps also, just as his uncle Thomas Shaw had relinquished part of his agricultural tenancy in order to develop his weaving activity at Lower House, so John Shaw may have been content to farm a smaller and more manageable tenancy, while giving more of his time to weaving.

For two years, John Shaw continued to pay the same £7 annual rental as his father had done.[3] But in 1739, the tenancy was split in two: John retained half of it for one more year, while David Harrop became the tenant of the other half (tenancy 56 in the 1770 survey). In 1740, John Shaw relinquished his remaining half, which passed to John Whitehead the elder (tenancy 146 in the 1770 survey). In 1741, John Whitehead's second son Timothy replaced George Shaw on the 25 acres Shawhouses tenancy (147). The extended Whitehead family now shared 52 acres of land across the two old Shawhouses tenancies, and when John Whitehead the elder died in October 1743, his first son John replaced him as tenant of Shawhouses (146).

But neither of the Whitehead sons lived long. Young John Whitehead died just three months after his father, in January 1753/4, and his tenancy passed out of the Whitehead family. His will had not yet been executed by the time his brother Timothy also died in 1755. Timothy's will, however, tasked three executors with holding his tenancy and belongings in trust for his six year old son James, who eventually inherited on reaching maturity in October 1770. A good choice of executors could lead to the desired implementation of a will, even fifteen years after the testator's death.

Throughout the period 1740-1770, rents, which had been static since 1719, now rose steeply. The combined annual rental, for William and John Shaw's successors as manorial tenants, increased from £7 to £8 in 1740, to £11 in 1744, and to £35.3s. by 1777. In Shawhouses (147), the rent jumped from £1 to 10 guineas on the death of the hereditary tenant George Shaw.

Shawhouses 147: 25 Acres			Shawhouses. 146/56: 27 acres	
Year	Tenant	Rent - £sd	Tenant	Rent - £sd
1719	George Shaw	£1.0.0	William Shaw	£7.0.0
1736	George Shaw	£1.0.0	William Shaw	£7.0.0
1737	George Shaw	£1.0.0	John Shaw	£7.0.0
1741	Timothy Whitehead	£10.10.0	John Whitehead	£4.0.0
			David Harrop	£4.0.0
1744	Timothy Whitehead	£11.10.0	John Whitehead	£5.05.0
			David Harrop	£5.05.0
1777	James Whitehead	£12.01.0	John Winterbottom	£ 7.0.06
			James Harrop	£10.11.0

John Shaw, meanwhile, appeared to have lost his father's manorial tenancy. But all was not as it seemed, nor was he left landless.

John Whitehead the elder, and his son-in-law David Harrop, were both living in Shawhouses in the 1720s and 1730s respectively, when their children were listed in baptism and burial registers. They were immediate neighbours of William Shaw's family, and would have known John Shaw most of his life. They were also sub-tenants of William Shaw. Now, in 1739-1741, roles were reversed: John Whitehead and David Harrop became the principal manorial tenants of a divided Shawhouses tenancy, while William's son John Shaw became a sub-tenant of John Whitehead, occupying some 6½ acres in

Lower Golburnclough. There was, however, another important change: the tenants and their sub-tenant now appeared to hold lifelong and hereditary rights. It was an outcome that perhaps suited everyone.

The main housing for the two large Shawhouses tenancies, was at the northern end, close to Uppermill. The valley of Golburnclough ran from east to west at the southern end of Shawhouses. It held attractions for John Shaw. It was close to Boarshurst, a gentle ten minute walk away, where John had many connections. His uncle Thomas Shaw, held the Lower House tenancy at Boarshurst; and after Thomas was widowed in 1736, John's younger brother, also called Thomas, stayed at Lower House for some years, having married in 1736/7.

For several years after 1740, John and Mary may have continued to live at Shawhouses, until accommodation was built at Golburnclough. Their first two children died young: Alice (1733–1743) was buried on 29 June 1743, and William (1735–1737) on 22 January 1737/8, the second anniversary of his baptism. Others, however, arrived: a second William (1738–1798), our ancestor, was given the name of his dead brother, while Mary (1742–) was given her mother's name. For the baptisms of their last three children, John is identified as being 'of Golburnclough': John in 1749, Jonathan in 1751 and Thomas in 1754.[4]

In 1770, John Shaw of 'Gouburn Clough'served as one of the two church wardens at St Chad's. He was buried there in April 1789, and his wife Mary followed in February 1793, both approaching 80 years old. John did not leave a will, but his estate was valued at £339, equivalent to over 2,000 days' wages for a skilled tradesman, and appreciably more than his grandfather William, the last husbandman of Lower House, in 1701. The supplementary income derived from weaving, on top of small-scale farming, had led to a notable increase in affluence.[5]

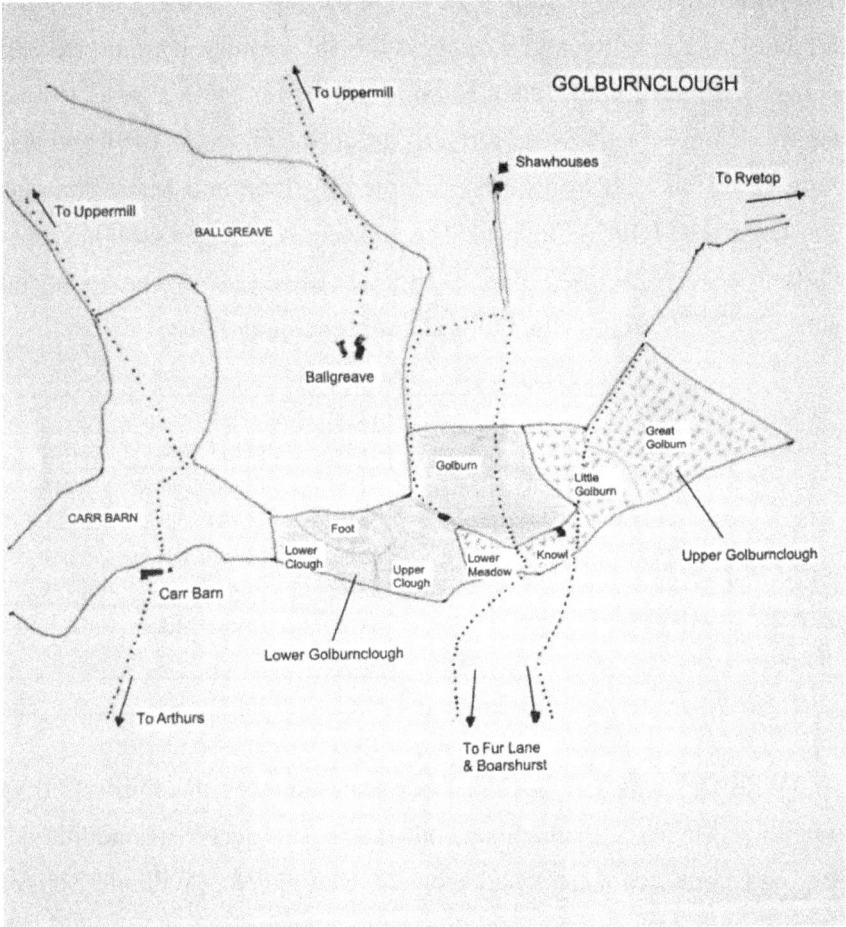

GOLBURNCLOUGH

To Uppermill

To Uppermill

BALLGREAVE

Shawhouses

To Ryetop

Ballgreave

Great Golburn

Golburn

Little Golburn

Foot

CARR BARN

Lower Clough

Upper Clough

Lower Meadow

Knowl

Upper Golburnclough

Carr Barn

Lower Golburnclough

To Arthurs

To Fur Lane & Boarshurst

16 : GOLBURNCLOUGH

The Golburnclough valley rises from the west to the east, in the direction of Knowltop and Ryetop. In the 18th century, it contained two parcels of farmland, each comprising over 6½ acres. Lower Golburnclough, to the west, formed part of Shawhouses (146), and was now, from the 1740s onwards, occupied by John and Mary Shaw as sub-tenants of John Whitehead. The adjacent land to the east, at Upper Golburnclough, formed part of Shawhouses (147). The manorial survey of 1770 records the fields at Golburnclough thus:

Lower Golburnclough			Upper Golburncough		
Field No.	Field Name	Acres *	Field No.	Field Name	Acres *
146C	Golbron	3.1.11	147M	Great Golbron	2.0.18
146D	Upper Clough (Meadow)	1.0.13	147N	Great Golbron	2.2.08
146E	Lower Clough (Meadow)	1.0.0	147O	Little Golbron	0.3.37
146F	Foot	1.0.30	147P	Knowl	0.2.25
			147Q	Lower Meadow	0.2.25
Total		**6.2.14**	**Total**		**6.3.33**
*1 Acre = 4 Roods; 1 Rood = 40 Perches					

William Shaw (1738-1798), our ancestor, was the third child of John and Mary of Shawhouses, but the first to survive to adulthood. He was baptised at St Chad's on 28 May 1738: 'William, son of John Shaw, Clothier, and Mary, his wife, de Shaw-houses'. In line with custom, he was given the name of his older brother, who had died fourteen months' earlier. His grandfather William had died just six months earlier too, so the choice of name was really a foregone conclusion.

In 1743, the year in which his sister Alice died aged ten, the five year old William had been left three shillings in the will of the seventeen year old Thomas Hawkyard, his grandfather's step-son.[1] Life was uncertain for the young.

On 6 January 1763, at the age of 24, he was married in St Chad's church. Banns of marriage tell us that his wife, Betty Stansfield, now 'of this parish', had come originally from Glossop, where she had been baptised in the parish church in December 1739. William signed the marriage certificate in a fluent hand, while Betty marked her name with a cross. Out of eight marriage records on the register page, seven grooms signed their names, but only one bride. William, like his father and grandfather, described himself as a clothier.

After marrying Betty, William initially moved away from his parents' house to live independently, as had become common practice. Their first child, our ancestor John Shaw (1764-1821), was born at Fur Lane, and their second, Thomas, at Carr Barn. They had not moved far: both farms were less than a quarter mile from Golburnclough, and, significantly, both were on the 54 acre estate owned by Giles Shaw, yeoman, of Uppermill.[2] Giles was descended from Gyles Shawe of Boarshurst (d.1634), the neighbour and relative of William Shawe of Boarshurst. The fact that William and Betty stayed on Giles Shaw's land after their marriage is further evidence that extended family ties, however distant by now, remained important, and could be relied on to support a young couple embarking on their married life.

By 1768, when their third child was born, William and Betty had moved again, this time back to Shawhouses, to occupy a farm at Upper Golburnclough, part of Shawhouses 147, where they would live for the rest of their lives. As we saw, the principal manorial tenant of Shawhouses 147, Timothy Whitehead, had died young in 1755 when his son James was still a child; so the tenancy was being managed on James's behalf by his father's executors. William and his father John knew the Whiteheads very well and would have been the first to learn of an opportunity at Upper Golburnclough. So by the age of 30 in 1768, William had acquired his own sub-tenancy.

While John and Mary Shaw farmed at Lower Golburnclough, (part of Shawhouses 146), their son William now farmed adjacent land to the east, at Upper Golburnclough (part of Shawhouses 147). From 1782 onwards, land tax records list John Shaw and William Shaw occupying lands next to each other in the 'Shaws' area of Lordsmere, and paying tax of 1s.10d and 2s.0d respectively.[3]

The 1770 manorial survey records five houses with outbuildings at Shawhouses, before noting: 'Also a new House (but a very indifferent one) built in Golbron Clough in which two families dwell'.[4] Had William and Betty perhaps moved in with his parents? It must have been a crowded household, at least until new housing was built at Lower Golburnclough a few years later.

In the 18th century, the Manorial Court met two to four times a year, usually at a Saddleworth inn, to resolve disputes that typically related to land and buildings. Cases often resulted in fines or 'amercements' being issued, although tenants could generally avoid this by carrying out repairs by a set date. In 1774, a case arose involving land at Golburnclough.

We saw that the 27 acre Shawhouses tenancy previously held by William's grandfather was divided into two parts. David Harrop and his descendants occupied 12 acres (at 'Shaws', no. 56), while tenure of the remaining 15 acres ('Shawhouses & Deanshaw Bankes', no. 146) changed hands regularly: in 1740 it was held by John Whitehead, in 1770 by John Winterbottom, and in 1774 by Philip Buckley.

A land tax record shortly afterwards shows: James Harrop, son of David Harrop, paying 4s.7d. in tax (for his land at Shaws); Philip Buckley paying 3s.4d. (for part of Shawhouses & Deanshaw Bankes) and Buckley's sub-tenant John Shaw paying 1s.10d (for 6.2.14 acres at Lower Golburnclough). At Shawhouses (147), James Whitehead, son of Timothy, was paying 9s. 0d. (for about 18 acres), while his sub-tenant William Shaw was paying 2s.0d. (for almost 7 acres at Upper Golburnclough).[5]

The lands occupied by Philip Buckley abutted both Upper and Lower Golburnclough. The fields were separated by boundary ditches, but these had fallen into disrepair. On 2 June 1774, the Manorial Court ordered Buckley to repair the ditches separating his 3-acre field Golbron from Lower Meadow (147Q) on William Shaw's land and Upper Clough (146F) on John Shaw's land:

'We lay in pain that Phillip Buckley of Shaw's do Remove the Ditch and set the same in the usual place, and sufficiently repair the same betwixt a certain close called Gowburn now in his occupation and a meadow called Gowburn Clough Meadow in the Occupation of William Shaw and likewise betwixt the said field and the next above in the occupation of John Shaw in the Manor aforesaid on or before the twentieth Day of August next or on failure thereof Do pay to the Lord of the Manor £1.19.6.'[6]

When John Shaw relinquished the Shawhouses tenancy in 1740 to become sub-tenant of 6½ acres of land at Lower Golburnclough, he may not have foreseen that this would deny his sons the opportunity of obtaining freehold rights. One year after John's death, the Lord of the Manor of Saddleworth, James Farrer Esq., also died, and in 1791 the estate farms were put up for sale. Most were acquired by the sitting manorial tenants. Thus, at Lower House, for example, the sitting tenant in 1791 was a Robert Buckley, and he was able to acquire the freehold. Similarly at Shawhouses, the freehold of Shawhouses (147) was acquired by the sitting tenant James Whitehead; that of 'Shawhouses

& Deanshaw Bankes (146) by Philip Buckley; and that of 'Shaws' (56) by James Harrop.

Land Tax records for 1794, shortly after John Shaw's death, show the new pattern of land ownership. The 'executors of John Shaw deceased' were now tenants of the new landowner Philip Buckley, paying land tax of 1s.6d., while William Shaw was tenant of the new landowner James Whitehead, paying land tax of 1s.8d. Subsequent records show the name of John Shaw's second son, another John, paying land tax, after inheriting the Lower Golburnclough sub-tenancy. The brothers William and John were now farming the adjacent lands.

In 1770, the housing at Upper Golburnclough had been described as new but 'very indifferent'. Now, with the change in ownership in 1791, a new three-storey stone house with slate roof would be built. Land Tax records from 1798 onwards record William Shaw paying an additional 6d for the 'Improvements'. Today the house has a large converted barn attached and is Grade II listed.[7]

William's wife Betty died in 1795 and was buried at St Chad's on 21 December 1795 aged 55. William died two years later and was buried on 16 April 1798 aged 59, one month short of his 60th birthday. The burial register is succinct: 'William Shaw – Goburn Clough'. He could not enjoy his new house for long, but his younger son of the same name would do so for some more years.

Church registers tell us that William and Betty had nine children, born over two decades. At least two died in infancy, and two others scarcely reached adulthood. Their names largely followed tradition: John, William, Betty, two Thomases (the first died aged 19, and the second was given the same name six months later). Mally and Sally were new names to the Shaw family. We should mention three of their children in particular.

William (1770-) was born in Golburnclough, baptised on 21 October 1770, and named after his own father, great-grandfather and other Williams before them. On 3 March 1794 he married Mary Lees in St Chad's, signing his own name. They initially moved away from the parental home, as was customary, but returned to Golburnclough after his mother Betty died in 1795. Of their five children, the first, Betty (1795), was born at nearby Kinders, and the next four at Golburnclough: Ann (1798), Hugh (1799), Hannah (1802-1807) and Robert (1804). Land tax records show that, after his father's death in 1798, William continued to live in the new house at Upper Golburncough until 1805.

Mally (1773 – 1801), whose name is a derivative of Mary, was born in Golburnclough and baptised in St Chad's in March 1773. By 1794 her older siblings had all married, in 1795 her mother died, and by 1798 her father was ailing. She was nearly 25 years old, and it was high time for her to marry, which she did on 5 February 1798. Neither she nor her husband, Jonathan Hurst, could sign their own names; but her brother William signed the marriage register as a witness, his signature matching that on his own marriage certificate five years earlier. Their father William was perhaps too ill to sign, and he died two months later. Mally's marriage was brutally short. In 1799, she gave birth to a son named Ralph: but Ralph died in August 1801, and Mally herself followed in September.

John (1764–1821) was the eldest child, and our ancestor. He was born at Fur Lane and named after William's father. As the 18th century drew to a close, John was starting his own family and would make a decisive move away from Lordsmere, where his ancestors had lived since medieval times.

V QUICK MERE (1764-1881)

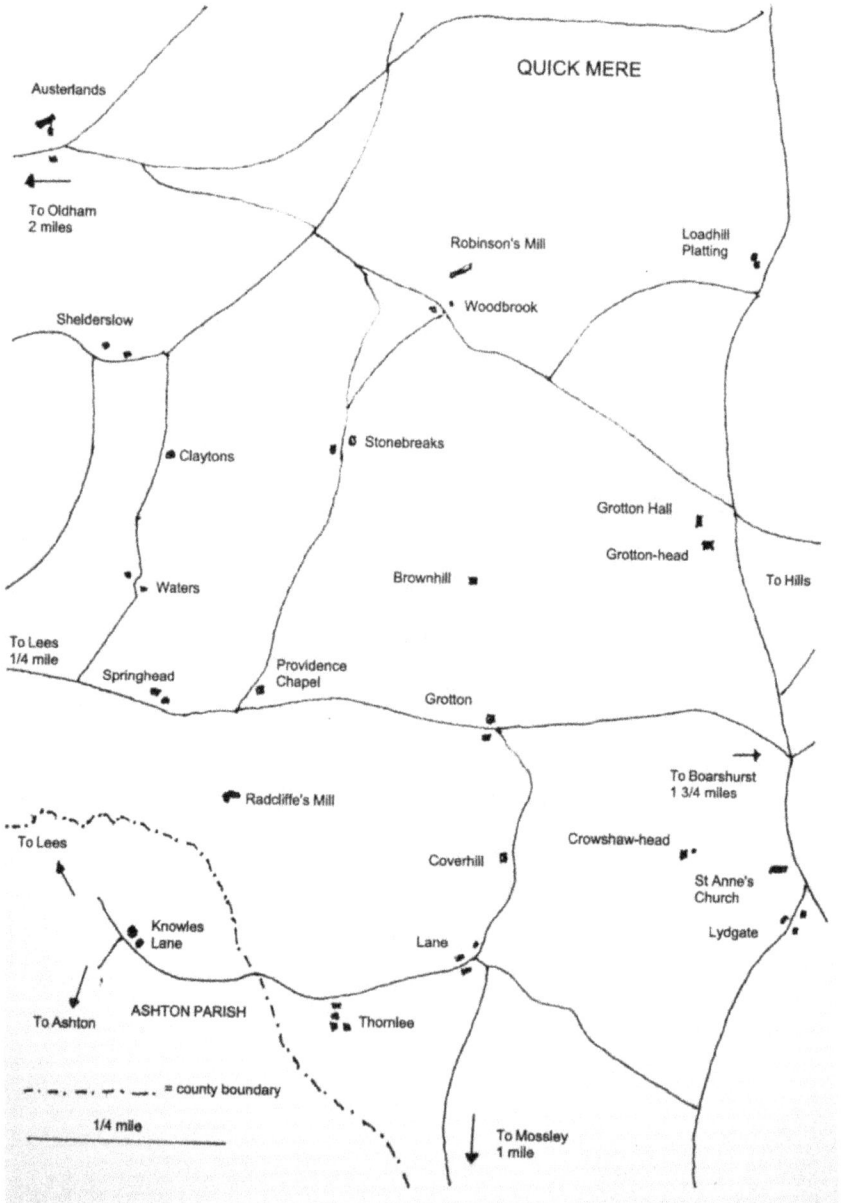

QUICK MERE

Austerlands

To Oldham
2 miles

Robinson's Mill

Loadhill
Platting

Shelderslow

Woodbrook

Claytons

Stonebreaks

Grotton Hall

Grotton-head

To Hills

Waters

Brownhill

To Lees
1/4 mile

Springhead

Providence
Chapel

Grotton

To Boarshurst
1 3/4 miles

Radcliffe's Mill

Crowshaw-head

To Lees

Coverhill

St Anne's
Church

Knowles
Lane

Lane

Lydgate

To Ashton

ASHTON PARISH

Thornlee

= county boundary

1/4 mile

To Mossley
1 mile

153

17 : THORNLEE

When our ancestor John Shaw (1764-1821) left Lordsmere to live in Quick Mere, he may only have moved a couple of miles away. But in the context of the times it was a move of some significance.

The eldest son of William and Betty, John was born at Fur Lane, on Giles Shaw's estate, and baptised on 12 February 1764: 'John, son of William Shaw, Clothier, and Betty, his wife, of Fur Lane'. He spent his childhood in Golburnclough, before marrying Mary Kenworthy on 30 March 1789 at St Chad's. He was 26 years old, and she 18. They both signed the marriage certificate with some confidence. Mary's signature does slope upwards a bit, but she is one of only two women, out of eight on the register page, to sign her own name. John's 50 year old father William witnessed the ceremony, signing his own name with a stylish flourish.

Mary had been baptised in the Heights Chapel, Friarmere, a new chapel built to meet the needs of a growing population. It stood on a bracing site, on the top of a hill, and had just been consecrated in 1768. The construction had been paid for by public subscription, suggesting a degree of wealth and community spirit.

Mary was the daughter of Thomas and Betty Kenworthy, who then lived in Waters, between Delph and Bleak Hey Nook, close to the site of the modern Castleshaw Reservoir. She was the eldest of six children born between 1770 and 1780. Initially her father was a clothier, but later a Cropper, then Ragman, moving regularly in the Delph and Diggle area.

Mary Kenworthy was baptised and married with the name 'Mary', but was referred to as 'Mally' throughout her married life, and this was the name on baptism records of her children. It was also the name of John's sister, who was just two years younger than Mary Kenworthy: John called them both Mally.

John and Mally began their married life in Ryetop, about 600 yards from the crowded paternal home in Golburnclough, distant enough for privacy, but near enough for support when needed. Even by Saddleworth standards, it was a bracing spot, at 300 metres altitude on the slopes of the moors. The manorial tenant at Ryetop was Michael Shaw, the latest in a long line of Michael Shaws, one of whom was mentioned in Marie Whewall's will of 1658. John and Mally's first two children were born here. In autumn 1792, one year after the break-up of the manorial estate, they moved to Thornlee, in Quick Mere, where they lived for the rest of their lives, and where Mally gave birth to a further five children.[1]

Why, then, did John move from Lordsmere, where his ancestors had lived for centuries, to Thornlee, in Quick Mere? It was only a distance of two or three miles, but it was quite a different part of Saddleworth, bordering Ashton parish.

As a 29 year-old father of two, he needed to find a tenancy where he could settle. He had established his independence as a married man on Michael Shaw's farm at Ryetop, but he could not wait to inherit the land at Upper Golburnclough, where his father was still relatively young. The location was in any case bleak and the land surely not very productive. The housing was also inadequate (though it would be replaced shortly), and more spacious buildings may have been needed to accommodate the larger, modern weaving looms. Change was in the air, and perhaps the break-up of the manorial estate, when the family failed to acquire the freehold of its farm, was also influential.

Quick Mere now seemingly offered better opportunities for housing and land, for access to the growing markets of Ashton, Oldham and Manchester, and for the supplement of paid employment in the burgeoning mills of the area. This was the cusp of the 19th century: horizons were widening and opportunities diversifying.

Importantly, there were now also multiple family connections in Quick Mere, which themselves offered opportunities. The Hearth Tax records, 130 years earlier, showed a concentration of 15 Shaw families in Lordsmere, but only four in Quick Mere. By the mid-18th century, Shaws had ramified exponentially in Quick Mere, and almost all could trace their heritage back to Boarshurst, to Gyles Shawe (d.1634) or to William Shawe (d.1623).

*****

Henry Shaw of Boarshurst and Lane (d.1689) was the first to move to Quick Mere. (Genealogical Table 6) We saw in chapter 11 that Henry, a younger son of Gyles Shawe of Boarshurst, had moved to Quick Mere, where in the mid-17th century he bought three farms: at Lane, where he lived, at Brownhill and at Hills. In his will of 1689 he left the first two farms to his eldest son John (who had married Margaret Cartwright and brought a complaint to the Court of Chancery in 1662). Henry left the third farm, at Hills, to his second son James. John was alive in 1689, but his wife Margaret had died six years earlier and they evidently had no children. So when John died, his younger brother James inherited all three farms, and, in his own will of 1733, James left them all to his son, Thomas of Lane (1696-1776).[2]

Until his death in 1776, aged 80, this Thomas was living at Lane, while his own son James was at Hills, and his grandson Thomas (son of James) was at Brownhill.[3] Old Thomas had already buried three of his four children in the same grave at St Chad's, leaving James as his sole surviving son.[4] But a serious rift opened up between them. Old Thomas's will contained the extraordinary stipulation that his son James, now aged 53, should come to Lane in person to collect a weekly stipend of 1s 6d from the hands of his own son Thomas. If he did not come in person he would not receive the money. The rift may have begun some years earlier, in 1750/1, when James fathered an illegitimate child, called Nelly. The child was born just one year after the early death of James's wife Esther, young Thomas's mother.

Whatever the reason, it was the grandson, young Thomas of Brownhill, who inherited all three farms, comprising some 35 acres. He continued to live at Brownhill, marrying the year after his grandfather's death. However, he died in 1785, aged just 38, leaving a widow, Sarah, two young daughters and a two year old son. He needed to provide carefully for his wife and children, and he turned to his extended family ties to establish a trust.

In his will, Thomas named as his executors the two eldest sons of Giles and Hannah Shaw of Fur Lane (called Thomas and Giles), who were of a similar age to himself, and who he made responsible for supporting the maintenance and education of his young children.[5] On reaching maturity, his surviving daughters were to share an inheritance of £1,000, raised from the income of his farms and held in trust for them, while his son (another Thomas) would inherit the three farms at Brownhill, Lane and Hills.

In the meantime, the executors would let the three farms to tenants. Land tax records up to 1832 show the farms still owned by Thomas Shaw's executors. Thomas's son and his widow Sarah both moved away from Saddleworth, returning only to be buried in Thomas's grave at St Chad, in 1828 and 1842 respectively.[6] Their farmland at Lane abutted John Shaw's tenancy at Thornlee, while the two houses owned by Thomas Shaw at Lane were less than 300 yards distant from John's.

*****

A second, much larger, concentration of Shaws was descended from the Shaws of Lower House. (Genealogical Table 7) In chapter 13 we saw that, after the death of William Shaw of Lower House in 1701, his eldest son Thomas inherited the family tenancy, while his second son, our ancestor William, moved to Shawhouses. After Thomas Shaw's death in 1747/8, the lease passed to his eldest son, another William (1703-1772). This William, the last Shaw of Lower House, moved with his wife Esther to live at Grottonhead in Quick Mere, and this is where they died, two decades later, William of consumption in 1772, 'in his 70th year', and Esther in 1779, aged 77.

It was not only William and Esther who moved from Boarshurst to Grottonhead: so too did their sons, William (1729-1782) and Hugh (1737/8-1814). The marriage certificates of these two brothers confirm that the elder son, William, was already living in Grottonhead in 1750, when he married Alice Scholefield. The second son, Hugh, was also living in Grottonhead in 1759, when he married his neighbour Mary Dronsfield, daughter of another Grottonhead tenant. Neither of these brothers showed any intention of returning to Lower House, or of paying a large garsome to renew the lease when their father, the last name on the lease for lives, died in 1772. In Quick Mere, they were tenants of John Buckley Esq., holding larger tenancies, with apparently better workshop facilities and closer proximity to urban markets in south east Lancashire.

In the 17th and 18th centuries, the Buckley family had compiled substantial landholdings of over 400 acres, in some 13 locations, centred on their ancestral home at Grottonhead. By the mid-18th century, they no longer lived at Grottonhead and, as absentee landlords, they needed responsible tenants to manage the lands on their behalf. John Buckley Esq.'s survey of his estate, in 1779, contains individual maps of his landholdings.[7] The estate included farms at

Hollingreave (in Lordsmere), Ashton, Oldham and Mottram; but the heart of the estate was in Quickmere, to the north and south of Grottonhead. A largely unbroken swathe of lands dominated the area, stretching from Loadhill Platting in the north-east to the fringes of Lane and Lydgate in the south. Two further farms completed this Quickmere estate: to the west, Claytons (30 acres), and to the south, Thornlee (11½ acres), the latter being separated from the rest of the Grottonhead estate only by Henry Shawe's farm at Lane.

The 150 acre central part of this Quickmere estate was split into five areas: Grottonhead (74 acres), Grotton (24 acres), Loadhill Platting (15 acres), Coverhill (7 acres) and Crowshawbent (29 acres). Each of these was let to a single tenant, except for Grottonhead, which had three tenancies. At the start of the 1780s, the largest of the three tenancies at Grottonhead (around 34 acres) was held by William and Esther's eldest son, William Shaw (1729-1782), with his younger brother Hugh also occupying a share of it. The second largest tenancy (around 28 acres) was occupied by Richard Dronsfield (whose sister Mary had married Hugh Shaw); and the third (around 12 acres) by John Bradbury. After John Bradbury's death in 1791, Hugh Shaw took over this smaller tenancy, holding it until his own death in 1814.[8]

William Shaw (1729-1782), the elder brother, died at the age of 52, having fathered seven children over a 15 year span. He was buried at St Chad's in the same grave as his wife Alice, who had died in 1767, and beside the grave of his own parents, William and Esther.[9] After his death, he was succeeded in the largest tenancy at Grottonhead by his son Hugh (1754-1831). This Hugh fathered nine children over a span of 26 years, and inherited or developed a successful textile business, referenced in Bailey's Directory of 1784: 'Hugh Shaw manufacturers of broad and narrow plain cloths textiles, Grottonhead, Saddleworth, Yorkshire'.[10]

Hugh Shaw (1737/8-1814), the second son of William and
Esther, remained at Grottonhead for 32 years after his brother's
death, until he was buried at the chapel of St Anne's Lydgate in 1814,
aged 76. During this period, he and his nephew of the same name
both occupied tenancies at Grottonhead. Land tax records show
'Hugh & Hugh Shaw' as joint tenants of the largest farm, while the
uncle Hugh also held the smallest farm. Hugh the Elder, as he was
now often called, and his wife Mary (nee Dronsfield), had no fewer
than eleven children over a 27 year period. Of these, three sons
survived to adulthood: they were living in the area when our ancestor
John Shaw moved to the neighbouring tenancy of Thornlee, and they
were close to him in age.

Hugh the Elder's first son was named William Shaw (1761-1797).
In 1780, this William married Ann Robinson of Ashton and was on the
look out for a tenancy of his own. When John Buckley Esq.'s tenant at
Thornlee died, in 1782, William was handily placed to step into the
11½ acre farm. Not long afterwards, however, another death gave rise
to an even better opportunity. John Radcliffe, who was John Buckley
Esq.'s tenant at Grotton, died in 1791, and William succeeded him on
this larger, 24 acre farm, right next door to his father and cousin at
Grottonhead. The vacancy he left at Thornlee was now an opportunity
that would be taken up by his cousin, our ancestor John Shaw.

Hugh the Elder's second son, John Shaw of Lane (1764-1838),
was just two weeks older than our ancestor, John Shaw of Thornlee. At
the time when our ancestor John was moving to Thornlee, John the son
of Hugh the Elder was a tenant at Lane, right next door. There were
two farms at Lane, one owned by the descendants of Henry Shawe, as
we have seen, and the other by a Robert Lees. John Shaw of Lane was
a tenant of Robert Lees in the period 1790-1799, occupying land that
bordered Thornlee. He had married Sarah Andrew from Knowles

Lane, a farm about 300 yards west of Thornlee, just across the county boundary into Ashton. John and Sarah later moved to live at Knowles Lane until his death in 1838. They had nine children, but buried five of them during their lifetime at St Anne's Lydgate, where many of the family's names are recorded on a gravestone.

Hugh the Elder's third son, called Thomas Shaw (1775-1853), occupied the second largest tenancy at Grottonhead from 1824 onwards. At this stage, the entire Grottonhead lands of 74 acres were occupied by Hugh Shaw (1754-1831) and Thomas Shaw (1775-1853), sons respectively of the brothers William and Hugh Shaw. Thomas later moved to Springhead, where he died in 1853, his will describing him as 'a farmer late of Grotton-head'. The sole executor of his will was his nephew, yet another Hugh Shaw (1786-1877), one of two surviving sons of his brother John Shaw of Lane. To this nephew he bequeathed 'the Clock that was my Fathers, as a mark of my esteem, and as a remembrance of His Grandfather.' The reference to 'my father' and 'his grandfather' is to Hugh Shaw of Grottonhead who had died in 1814.

There was a now a very large cluster of Shaws, all living within half a mile of each other in this part of Quick Mere. Many were tenants on the Buckley family estate, and all could trace their ancestry back to Boarshurst in the 16th and 17th centuries.

Our ancestor John Shaw's move, from Golburnclough and Ryetop to the Buckley tenancy of Thornlee, was therefore in no way random, but part of a migratory pattern, and an opportunity presented by extended family networks. Although by now John was quite a distant relation of the descendants of Gyles Shawe of Boarshurst, he had been born on their estate at Fur Lane, they were close neighbours while he was growing up at Golburnclough, and he would have known them well. He was, however, closely related to the Shaws of Grottonhead, and when he moved to Thornlee, it was to occupy a tenancy being vacated by his cousin William (son of Hugh Shaw the Elder). John and this William were just three years apart in age, while he was exactly the same age as Hugh the Elder's second son, his namesake and neighbour John Shaw of Lane. All three were great-great-grandsons of the William Shaw of Lower House who had died in 1701. Family networks mattered.

*****

Writing in the 1820s, James Butterworth describes 'an ancient though small village called Thornley (ie the field of thorns)…pleasantly seated in the midst of rich meadow land.'[11] Land Tax records show that, in 1793, our ancestor John Shaw occupied a house and land at Thornlee, paying land tax of 2s.6d. The landowner was John Buckley Esq.[12]

A survey of the Thornlee tenancy, drawn up for the landowner in 1779, records a farm comprising 11½ acres of land: 4¼ acres in Saddleworth and 7¼ acres in Ashton parish, Lancashire, with the county boundary line running between the Meadow and the Roundfield.[13]

Today, the settlement of Grotton has greatly expanded to encompass the previously distinct hamlets of Thornlee and Lane, but there are echoes of the past. At the southern edges of Grotton, streets bear the names Coverhill Road, Thornley Park Drive and Thornley Close; Thornley Lane still leads to Knowles Lane Farm, stone buildings that are now Grade II listed, where John Shaw's namesake and cousin spent his later years. At Thornlee, our ancestor John Shaw's house, garden and large meadow have been replaced by modern housing. But, his arable fields are open ground, if uncultivated, while beyond them rise the steep slopes of Shaker Hill, once grazing land but now overgrown.

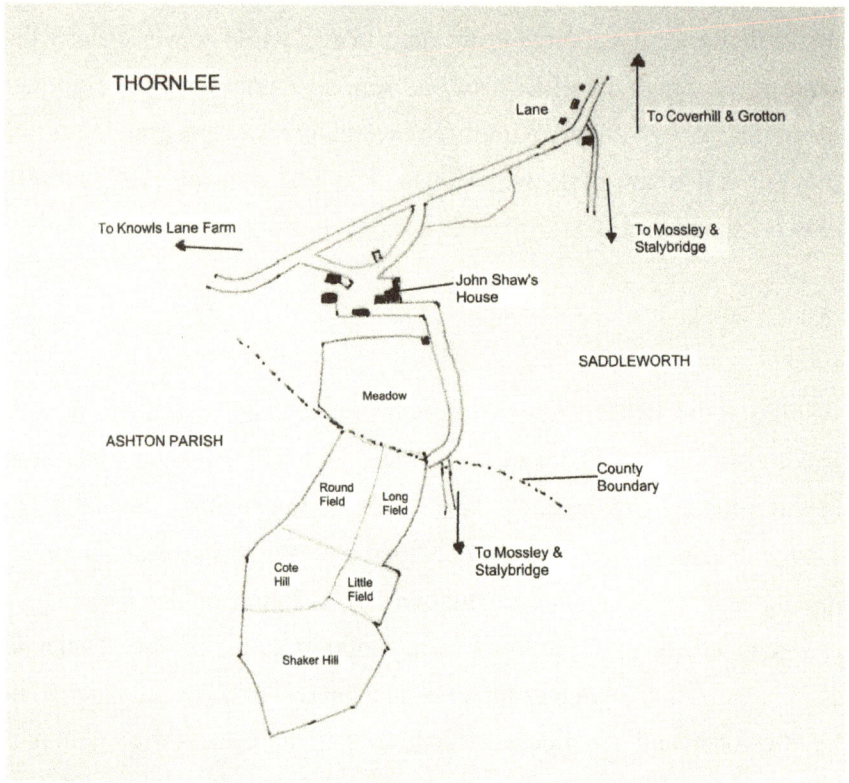

Thornlee: 1779

Saddleworth	A	R	P	Ashton	A	R	P*
1. House	0	0	0	5. Roundfield	1	2	0
2. Green	0	2	20	6. Longfield	1	0	25
3. Park	0	3	29	7. Littlefield	0	2	29
4. Meadow	2	3	08	8. Cotehill	1	0	29
				9. Shakerhill	2	3	03
Total	4	1	17		7	1	06

*1 Acre = 4 Roods; 1 Rood = 40 Perches

163

The Buckleys, like many a wealthy family, often found themselves short of ready money. They attempted to sell the farm at Thornlee on at least three occasions: in 1794 and in 1819, when the occupier was John Shaw, and again in December 1821, after John's death, when the occupier was 'Mrs Shaw' (ie Mally). On 11 February 1794, the Manchester Mercury carried an advertisement of five 'Farms to be Let', that is, to be sold with tenants in occupation. Three were in Saddleworth, at Grottonhead, Loadhill Platting and Thornlee:

'Lot 3rd. A Messuage and Tenement called THORNLEE situate in Saddleworth aforesaid, together with 11½ statute Acres of arable, meadow and pasture land, now in the possession of John Shaw, as tenant thereof... NB The above tenements are situated in a populous country, upon good turnpike roads, and are very desirable situations for clothiers...The respective tenants will shew the premises, and further particulars may be had, by applying to Hugh Shaw the Elder of Grottonhead, or to Mr Watson attorney at Stockport.'[14]

As well as managing 11½ acres of land, the family worked as weavers, and there would have been other wage-earning opportunities too in the growing economy of western Saddleworth, quite possibly at Hugh Shaw's textile business. John died at the very start of 1821. He had lived 28 years in Thornlee, a short walk from the new church of St Anne's at Lydgate, where four of his children had been baptised. Yet, despite the convenience of St Anne's, as well as the growing appeal of non-conformism, he wanted to be buried at St Chad's, where he had himself been baptised and married, and where his parents and grandparents lay. On 5 January 1821 he was taken the four miles or so to St Chad's Church for burial. He was a month short of his 57th birthday. The burial register records: 'John Shaw, age 56, of Thornlee Brook'.[15]

This record helpfully includes the place where John lived and his age, details which enable us to confirm with certainty that he was indeed the eldest son of William and Betty of Golburnclough. Only two other children in Saddleworth were baptised with the name John Shaw between January 1764 and January 1765, meaning that they would be 56 years old in January 1821. One, baptised on 26 January 1764, was John Shaw of Lane, son of Hugh and Mary Shaw of Grottonhead, who married Sarah Andrew from Knowles Lane in Ashton and died there in 1838. The second, born at Fur Lane, was the seventh child of the estate owner, Giles Shaw (1726-1800) and his wife Hannah: this John died in December 1818 aged 54 ('in his 55th year').

After John Shaw of Thornlee's death, the lease of the house and land passed to his widow Mally, named on land tax records as 'Widow Shaw'. Mally remained in Thornlee at least until 1832, when the land tax records for the township of Quick cease. At that time she was paying rent of £10 per annum. There appears to be no record of her death. She was perhaps buried at Providence Chapel, the family having turned to non-conformism in the 1820s and 1830s, but there are no chapel burial records for this period.

John was the last of our branch of the Shaw family to farm the land, the last to weave woollen cloth on his own looms, the last to be buried at St Chad's and indeed the last to be named John. He died six years after the battle of Waterloo; two years after his son Samuel had enlisted in the army; and 17 months after the Peterloo Massacre.

This was a time of enormous social and economic transformation; of rapid urbanisation and new forms of employment; of resurgent evangelical religion and widening access to education; of burgeoning political awareness, increasing mobility and broadening horizons. The changing times brought opportunities for those who could take advantage of them.

*****

This was the environment in which John and Mally's seven children grew up. Three were baptised in St Chad's and the last four in the new hill-top chapel of Lydgate St Anne. The two eldest daughters, Sally (1790 -) and Betty (1792-1829), were both born at Ryetop and named after John's two youngest sisters. John signed both of their marriage certificates, in 1810 and 1815 respectively. The remaining five children were all born at Thornlee. One of these, our ancestor Stephen, is the focus of the next chapter. But here, we will touch briefly on the lives of three children, Thomas, Edna and Samuel.

Thomas (1794-) was John and Mally's first child to be born in Thornlee, although he was still baptised at St Chad. He married Betty Buckley on 26 March 1818 at St Chad's Rochdale, the mother church and namesake of the Saddleworth chapel. He was working as a 'cotton weaver' in Lees when his first two children, Thomas and Ann, were baptised in 1820 and 1822; but he had moved back to Thornlee by 3 April 1825, when his third child, Mary Ann, was baptised in the Independent Providence Chapel at Springhead.[16] This is the first reference in the family to cotton, the first reference to non-conformism, and the first baptism to give a child more than one name. Thomas was still at Thornlee in 1832-1836, the period when his mother Mally probably died. His occupation was now recorded as 'labourer', and by the census of 1841, when he had left Thornlee, he was working as a Carter: the opportunities of the industrial revolution appear to have passed him by.[17]

Edna (1796 -1875) was baptised in 1796, at nearby Lydgate St Anne that had opened just eight years earlier, one of several new churches to be built around this time to cater for the growing population. In 1824, at the late age of 28, she married John Broadbent, a 25 year old cotton spinner from Clerks near Uppermill. They had some ten children. The first was baptised at Lydgate in 1825, but thereafter all were baptised at the Zion Methodist Connexion Chapel in Lees, marking the date at which they, like Thomas, turned to non-conformism. For Edna's nephew, our our ancestor Eli, education at the Zion British School would be the stepping stone for his career, as we shall see in chapter 19, and Edna was surely instrumental in helping him enrol.

The Zion Chapel baptism register, strikingly neat and orderly in contrast to the scrawled records of Providence Chapel, lists nine of Edna's children: these include two Johns, an Edna and twins Benjamin and Joseph, noted as her 6th and 7th children. The mother's parentage is also recorded, here as 'daughter of John Shaw Clothier of Thorn Lee in the parish of Ashton under line', and there as 'daughter of John Shaw of Thorn Lee, Saddleworth, in the county of Yorkshire'.

Only four children remained with them by the census of 1841, one of whom, Samuel, is later described as 'a cripple'. Also in the census of 1841 and 1851 is Mary Ann Shaw, the daughter of Edna's brother Thomas, seemingly employed by Edna to help with her burgeoning parental responsibilities. No longer tied to the land, Edna and her husband John lived in Lees, Mossley, Lydgate and finally Uppermill, where John died on 29 May 1795, and Edna followed just six days later, aged 79.

Samuel (1798- 1868), the closest in age to our ancestor Stephen Shaw, lived an interesting and varied life. Baptised in Lydgate Chapel on 18 November 1798 - 'Samuel, son of John Shaw of Thornlee, Clothier, by Mally' - he made a decisive break with Saddleworth. On 16 September 1817, at the age of 18, he enlisted as a Private in the Second Dragoons (Royal Scots Greys). He may have been inspired by the victory at Waterloo in 1815, where the Second Dragoons had

played a prominent part, or perhaps by the prospect of regular pay at
'1s.3d. per diem' (about £5.15s. per quarter).[18]

The Second Dragoon's duties, in this post-war period, were defined
as 'Cavalry at Home'. Samuel was initially stationed at Piershill
Barracks near Edinburgh, but he moved regularly over the next ten
years, spending much of his time in Ireland, at Caher, Limerick,
Dundalk and Carrick on Suir, with shorter stays in Scotland, at Crieff
and Piershill, and in England at Birmingham, Coventry, Nottingham,
Manchester and Ipswich. Accommodation was in barracks, in camp or
more often 'billeted on Innkeepers'. His tours in Ireland were
characterised by route marches (up to 16 days in a quarter), occasional
'Escort Duty' and bouts of sickness. On a return tour to Ireland in late
1826 he spent 8 days in a regimental hospital and a further 24 days in
the spring of 1827. He was eventually deemed unfit for service and
discharged on 23 May 1827.

By then Samuel had a wife, which might have had something to do
with his propensity for sickness absences. She was Martha Wilde
(1800-1862), and he had married her on 5 October 1825 in the Church
of St Mary, St Denys and St George, which would become Manchester
Cathedral in 1847. The marriage certificate records his occupation as
'Private Second Dragoons'. He had obtained an education, and census
returns show that after leaving the Dragoons he became a book-keeper,
then a cashier, living in Chorlton-upon-Medlock in south Manchester.

Samuel and Martha had just one child, a daughter named Sarah
Jane (1835-1866). She was close in age to her cousin, our ancestor Eli
Shaw, who was the son of Samuel's younger brother Stephen. In 1859,
at St John's Parish Church Manchester, Sarah Jane married Thomas
Hayes (1829-1872), an engraver from Staffordshire.[19] A son, Frank
Hayes, was born in 1860, and the following year the census shows all
five sharing a house in Chorlton: Samuel and Martha, Sarah Jane,
Thomas Hayes and Frank.

Circumstances soon changed. In 1862 Samuel's wife Martha died, followed by his daughter Sarah Jane in 1866. Samuel now moved out of the city to the more wholesome environment of Cheadle in Cheshire, leaving Frank in the care of his father and a housekeeper in Chorlton. Samuel died in Cheadle in August 1868, aged 69, his will describing him as: 'Samuel Shaw formerly of the City of Manchester, Cashier, but late of Cheadle in the county of Chester, Gentleman.' It was proved 'by the oaths of his nephew Eli Shaw of 69 Stockport Road, Ashton-under-Lyne in the county of Lancaster, Schoolmaster, and Thomas Hayes of 33 Clare Street Chorlton-upon-Medlock in the city aforesaid, Engraver, two of the Executors.' Samuel's estate was valued at 'less than £3000', and his intent was to bequeath almost all of this to his grandson, Frank Hayes, if and when he reached maturity at the age of 21.[20]

Although Samuel had lived away from his Saddleworth relatives for many years, on military service and then in Manchester, his family ties remained strong, especially with his nephew Eli, who, as an executor of his will, would have a further part to play in young Frank's life (see chapter 20).

The sixth child of John and Mally was Stephen (1801-1881). A child of the 19th century, he is the focus of our next chapter.

18 : A PROVIDENTIAL LIFE

Stephen Shaw (1801-1881) was born into the 19th century, and his life spanned eight decades of radical change in politics, religion, industry and education. Three years younger than his brother Samuel, he was baptised at St Anne's Lydgate on 8 February 1801: 'Stephen, son of John & Mally Shaw, of Thornlee'. He later married Mary Eastwood on 24 January 1826, in the fine parish church of St Michael and All Angels, Ashton-under-Lyne. He was almost 25 years old, and Mary 18. He signed his own name, while Mary marked hers with a cross. (Genealogical Table 1C)

Mary was the daughter of Joseph Eastwood, and had been born and brought up in nearby Lees. The families knew each other: Land tax records in the 1790s and early 1800s show Joseph Eastwood renting a house and land in the close vicinity of Thornlee.

Lees lay within Ashton parish, and the parish church of St Michael & All Angels was also the church where Mary's parents had married in 1804.[1] However, both families were now turning to non-conformism. Several of Mary Eastwood's siblings had been baptised at the newly founded Providence Chapel in Springhead, from as early as 1812, while Stephen's siblings, Thomas and Edna, each had children baptised in non-conformist chapels in 1825 and 1827 respectively.[2]

Non-conformist chapels were allowed to baptise children, but not yet to conduct marriage ceremonies. That would soon change in the face of a vibrant popular movement. The Test Act, which prevented non-conformists from occupying public or political positions, was repealed in 1828, and in 1837 non-conformist chapels were granted the right to conduct marriage ceremonies. Meanwhile, Stephen and Mary had to marry in an Anglican church.

Mary's father Joseph had married his first wife, Rachel, in St Michael's Ashton in 1797, but she had died in 1803, leaving him with a young child. He re-married the next year, to Sarah Bradbury, and together they had nine further children: Mary was the second of these, born in 1807 and baptised in the church of Hey St John the Baptist. The 1841 census records the Eastwood family still living in Lees, and Joseph working as a cotton waste spinner – an example of a recycling business from an earlier age.

Stephen and Mary's first child, Daniel, was born on 27 July 1829 and baptised on 13 September at the Providence Independent Chapel, Springhead, which would play an important part in the family's life, as we see later in the chapter. The register records Stephen and Mary now living close to Springhead, in Austerlands, which in 1822 is described as having two vital institutions: 'a hamlet with a large cotton factory and one public house 3½ miles from Oldham'.[3] The hamlet was growing quickly, and by 1841 it had become a centre for cotton spinning, which accounted for two-thirds of local employment.

Entries in a family bible tell us that by 1839, when their son Eli was born, Stephen and Mary had moved the short distance to Woodbrook, equidistant between Springhead and Austerlands, and a quarter mile from each. The census of 1841 shows Stephen and Mary living there with four children, Daniel having apparently died in infancy. Mary is recorded as a housewife: her children were young, but Stephen's income was sufficient for her not to have to work. Their children did not work either, until they were at least 10 or 11 years old, but they did go to school. In 1851 their daughter Sarah Jane aged 7 was recorded as a scholar; Eli, aged 12, worked as a power loom weaver, while also obtaining an education, probably at night school and Sunday school classes for working children.

In 1822, Woodbrook had been described as 'a small cotton manufacturing hamlet', but by the 1840s its population had grown to over 200.[4] The village was dominated by the cotton mill of John Robinson & Sons, which employed 94 people in 1834 and 121 in 1851.[5] In 1841, some 78% of all Woodbrook residents in employment worked in the cotton industry. All but three of these were cotton operatives of one kind or another – spinners, piecers, carders, tenters, pickers, rovers, twisters... Some of these roles, piecers for example, were often carried out by the nimble hands of children, working alongside their parents who operated the looms.

Other employments in Woodbrook included: beer seller, outdoor labourer, washer woman, stone cutter, slater/sawyer, dressmaker, woollen weaver, housework, errand boy/girl, farmer and schoolmaster. The last is significant: elementary education was now widespread. In 1841, the small settlement of Woodbrook (population 236) included one schoolmaster. Neighbouring Austerlands (population 360) had two schoolmasters.

Three roles in Woodbrook stand apart from the rest in 1841: John Robinson, mill owner; his son Thomas Robinson, book-keeper; and Stephen Shaw, warehouseman. In the 1851 census, Stephen's entry immediately follows that of John Robinson and his family. John Robinson was typical of many cotton mill proprietors in the early Victorian decades. He was relatively wealthy, educated, worked his entire life in textiles, and lived close to the mill which he owned and would pass to his son at his death. He was committed to his local area and was non-conformist in religion. It is reckoned that that as many cotton mill owners in Lancashire were non-conformist as Anglican.[6] John Robinson had been a strong supporter and benefactor of Providence Chapel at nearby Springhead since its foundation in 1807, and his family would continue to support the chapel over three generations.

Architect's sketch of Providence Chapel and
Sabbath Day School, 1855.

In Providence Chapel, Stephen shared a common commitment
with the Robinsons. Churches have always been places that facilitate
connections, temporal as well as spiritual. This was no doubt the case
at St Chad's, the only church in Saddleworth for more than five
centuries, but it was even more so in non-conformist chapels. With its
egalitarian ethos, encouragement of enterprise and industry, and
commitment to the improvement of both the individual and the
community, non-conformism was particularly good at fostering
employment connections. As one historian puts it, chapel was 'a place
where diligent young men could catch the eye of an employer and so
gain more desirable situations.'[7] It can be no coincidence that Stephen
obtained the role of warehouseman in the Robinsons' mill at
Woodbrook, while both families attended the same chapel.

The role of the warehouseman was to oversee the storage of the
raw cotton as it waited for treatment and spinning; to oversee the

packing of the spun cotton ready for transport to market; and to carry out stock-taking. It was a role that required a level of education and an ability to oversee and manage activity. There was no other warehouseman in Woodbrook.

Cotton spinning was expanding rapidly in the western part of Saddleworth, adjoining Ashton and Oldham, and settlements of terraced housing for workers sprang up around the mills. By contrast, in the northern and eastern parts of Saddleworth (Lordsmere and Friarmere) woollen weaving tended to remain dominant, as the examples below show.

1841	Working Population	Employed in Wool	Employed in Cotton	Warehousemen
Austerlands	172	3 (2%)	113 (66%)	2
Uppermill	381	215 (56%)	12 (3%)	0
Woodbrook	106	3 (3%)	83 (78%)	1

In the 1850s, Stephen's family moved a mile further west to Lees, in Ashton parish and the county of Lancashire. Mary had relatives there, of course, but another draw was the education of their only son, Eli. An intelligent and motivated scholar, Eli had gained a place at the Zion British School, helped we assume by his aunt Edna, whose own children had been baptised at the Zion Methodist chapel in Lees. Eli was later selected to become a 'Pupil Teacher', a stepping stone to a qualified teaching role. Education provided by non-conformist chapels was now an important means of social and economic advancement.

The census of 1861 records Stephen and Mary living in Warrington Street, Lees, sharing the house with their three unmarried children, Hannah, Sarah Jane and eight year old Mary Emma, and also their married daughter, Edna, with her husband Johnson Winterbottom and one year old daughter. Eli now lived away from home, working as an assistant master in a school in Rochdale, but around the corner, in

Princess Street, lived one of Mary's younger sisters, Mally Eastwood, with her husband James Wild and their family. Family networks remained tight in an industrial age.

At the age of 60, Stephen had given up paid employment in a cotton mill, turning instead to trade, as a cotton waste dealer. The cotton spinning process left quantities of waste cotton material, which could be recycled and used for a variety of other products. In 1841 Stephen's father-in-law, Joseph Eastwood, had been working as a 'cotton waste spinner', and there were markets for cotton waste. Stephen had a lifetime's experience of the cotton industry and he was well networked in Lees and the surrounding area.

The cotton industry was booming, but a shock lay just ahead. In April 1861, the American Civil War broke out, interrupting the supply of cotton to England. Most mills closed. Contemporary accounts describe the tall mill chimney smokeless, and streets without the usual clatter of carts and clogs.[8] There was a surge in unemployment and destitution: it was known as the Cotton Famine. There was rioting too, notably in Stalybridge, directed against the owners of mills that had closed.

Despite this, in a sign of growing political awareness, Lancashire cotton workers supported the abolition of slavery and the Union blockade of Confederate cotton-growing states. President Abraham Lincoln sent a letter in January 1863, thanking the Lancashire cotton workers for their support, describing it as 'an instance of sublime Christian heroism, which has not been surpassed in any age or in any country.'[9] A statue of Lincoln was later erected in Manchester, dedicated to the support of the working people for the abolition of slavery.

The Cotton Famine had other consequences too, as communities rallied to provide support. Relief centres provided food, clogs and clothing. There was an abundance of private charity. The Minister at Providence Chapel, whose salary was funded by pew rents, worked without pay until times improved. At the Sunday School, an adult class was opened for unemployed males over 15, who received 4 pence for each half day of study. Local authorities were empowered to borrow in order to create employment by investing in local improvement schemes.

The interruption of raw cotton imports also led to economic diversification away from the over-reliance on cotton spinning. New enterprises emerged. By 1861, Stephen Shaw no longer worked in a cotton mill, but was self-employed as a Cotton Waste Dealer, and so less impacted by the mill closures. Shortly afterwards, he was working in coal, responding to the growing demand for fuel from houses and businesses in the Lees area.

By 1871, Stephen and Mary had moved a few yards to live at 3 Spring Lane, Lees, a terraced house which still stands, well cared for, today. Only two children shared the house with them now – Sarah Jane, a 27 year old Cotton Weaver, and the youngest daughter Mary Emma, now an 18 year old Cotton Creeler. Their eldest daughter Edna lived just around the corner in Catherine Street.

The brothers Johnson and Hugh Winterbottom from Lees had married Stephen's daughters, Edna and Hannah respectively. Both brothers turned away from weaving and spinning after the Cotton Famine. Hugh was already a coal merchant in Lees: the company he founded would continue for a further seven decades.[10] Johnson and Edna now moved to Miles Platting in Manchester where he too set up his own coal business.

At the start of the 19th century two local evangelists, John Buckley and Joseph Winterbottom, started preaching in a field at Grotton Hollow, Springhead. They attracted a group of followers, and in 1806/7 built a chapel there at the bottom of Radcliffe Street, which they named 'Providence Chapel'.[11] It was a small, barn-like building, three windows long, but it attracted a packed congregation. A survey of religious attendance in Saddleworth records that on Sunday 30 March

1851, 272 people attended morning service at Providence Chapel and 388 in the afternoon.[12]

In 1854/5 the old chapel was demolished and a new one built just above it on the eastern side of Radcliffe Street, designed to seat 900 people. The corner stone of the new building was laid in July 1854, at a ceremony involving a large number of spectators. Also present were Ministers from other Independent chapels, including Rev William Thomas of Ryecroft Chapel, Ashton-under-Lyne, who was the first Minister of Ryecroft Chapel and the predecessor of Thomas Green (See Chapter 19). The new Providence Chapel would last over 115 years, before being demolished in 1969.

A 'Sabbath and Day School' had been founded in 1818, and by 1837 it was providing education for 300 scholars. In December 1861 this was replaced with an imposing new schoolroom on the western side of Radcliffe Street, that still stands today. The schoolrooms were built to accommodate 800 students and, unlike the candle-lit chapel, were 'brightly illuminated with gas'.

After the demolition of Providence Chapel in 1969, an extension was added onto the western end of the school building: this functions today as the Springhead Congregationalist Church.

The site of the old Providence Chapel is now a flat, grassy area, opposite the Sunday School. The main part of the graveyard, largely overgrown, lies to the east and south, on the Grotton Hollow side of the old chapel. Stephen and Mary Shaw are buried there. So too is their daughter Edna with her husband Johnson Winterbottom and daughter Matilda, as well as Mary's parents Joseph and Sarah Eastwood. Over 150 graves and inscriptions are recorded, but only about five gravestones are visible today. Remarkably, one of these, still standing, marks the grave of Stephen and Mary.

Stephen died on 11 February 1881 at the age of 80. The death certificate records that he was a coal dealer, and the cause of death was attributed to old age. His youngest daughter Mary Emma was present at his death. He was buried close to the chapel wall, on the eastern, Grotton Hollow side of Providence Chapel. He had worshipped at Providence Chapel almost all of his adult life. His marriage had lasted 55 years, and his widow Mary was buried in the same grave the next year. The inscription on their gravestone reads:

'In Affectionate Remembrance of STEPHEN SHAW of Spring Lane Lees who departed this Life February 11th 1881 in the 81st Year of his Age Also his beloved Wife Mary who departed this Life December 10th 1882 in the 75th Year of her Age'[13]

Stephen and Mary were buried in the grave next to that of their grand-daughter Matilda, who had died aged seven in 1867: she would be joined there later by her parents Edna (d. 1899) and Johnson Winterbottom (d.1901).

Stephen's father John had made a radical shift by moving from the deeply rural part of Lords Mere, where his ancestors had lived for many generations, to the west of Saddleworth, closer to the burgeoning markets of Ashton, Oldham and Manchester. But it was his sons Stephen and Samuel who really broke the mould, leaving behind the pattern of subsistence farming and domestic woollen manufacture that had characterised previous generations. For two decades he worked as a warehouseman in a cotton mill, before later venturing into trading, in cotton waste and then coal. He broke with the Church of England to adopt non-conformism. His own education enabled him to embrace new forms of employment and lifestyle, while he supported his son Eli through the best local school, and thence to a career in education. He was part of a new age.

*****

In the late 1850s, a new technological innovation brought photographs to the living rooms of ordinary people. Ambrotype photography, which produced positive images on glass plate, proved popular and affordable. In 1858, Stephen and his family posed for a professional photographer from Manchester. This was the first ever photograph in the family, and it was not a frivolous occasion. There would have been only one take of the photograph: so, there should be no blinking, and no suspicion of a smile either. Everyone was dressed in their Sunday best, their hair neat and tidy, and the girls have identical, immaculate centre partings.

Stephen, aged 57, a proud father with a confident air, has a good head of hair, if receding a little, with greying sideburns fashionably shaped towards his chin. He sits beside his wife Mary, who is of matronly demeanour. Their five older children stand behind them, ranged in order of age, with Eli in the centre. Little five year old Mary Emma stands at the front between her parents. Eli, aged 19 and now employed as a teacher, is a tall, good-looking young man, with elegant hands and clean-shaven jaw, in contrast to his later bushy Victorian beard: he fixes the camera with a stare of youthful intensity.

The photograph recorded the family at a moment of transition. Eli had just left home to take up a teaching job in Rochdale, while Matilda and Edna were both poised to marry at the end of the summer. The future, as so often, diverged from their plans. Life remained uncertain: Stephen and Mary had seven children, born over the space of 24 years, but they buried three during their lifetimes.

For those that survived, we can see that prosperity was generally increasing, and employment opportunities widening, especially for those of entrepreneurial temperament. A middle class was emerging, not rich in capital, but educated and increasingly empowered.

Stephen and Mary Shaw in about 1858. Back Row left to right:
Sarah Jane, Hannah, Eli, Matilda, Edna; Front: Mary Emma.

Stephen and Mary's first child, Daniel was born in Austerlands on 27 July 1829, and baptised, with a name resonant of the Old Testament name, in Providence Independent Chapel Springhead, on 13 September 1829 – the first definitive evidence of the family's attendance at Providence Chapel. Little Daniel must have died in early childhood, though there is no record. Their second son, Eli, is the subject of chapters 19 and 20: the next paragraphs cover the lives of their five daughters.

Edna: (1832 – 1899), the eldest daughter, was named after Stephen's sister, who lived in Lees and attended the Zion Methodist New Connexion Chapel. The young Edna married Johnson Winterbottom in Saddleworth in the autumn of 1858: he too had been baptised at Providence Chapel. Three male children lived to adulthood, Frederick, John Hampden and Harold, but their daughter Matilda died aged seven.

Johnson Winterbottom, coal merchant of Miles Platting,
and his wife Edna, daughter of Stephen Shaw, 1870s.

Edna and Johnson were in fact not so very distant relations. The maiden name of Johnson Winterbottom's mother was Ann Shaw: she and Stephen were both direct descendants of William Shaw of Lower House (c.1653-1701). Ann's great-grand-father was William Shaw's youngest son Hugh, who had left Lower House in 1713, founding a prolific line of Shaws at Halls (see Table 8 and pages 125-6). She was born at Halls in 1802, just one year after Stephen Shaw's birth at Thornlee.

Edna and Johnson lived in Lees, initially staying with Stephen and Mary in Warrington Street, before moving round the corner to Catherine Street. The 19th century saw a strong demand for coal in local homes and businesses. By 1871, Johnson's younger brother Hugh had already become a coal merchant, and soon afterwards Johnson also moved into the coal business, establishing a Coal Yard in Newton Heath and then Miles Platting. His three sons worked in the family business, initially as Coal Carters, and all three boys married in the Congregational Church, Oldham Road.[14]

Edna died in Miles Platting in 1899, and Johnson two years later while on a trip to Whitby: they were both buried at Providence Chapel, Springhead, in the same grave as their young daughter Matilda, and beside the grave of Stephen and Mary. Their gravestone is no longer visible, but contained the inscription: 'Life's race well run; Life's work well done. Then comes rest.'[15]

Hannah (1841 – 1904), as a 20 year old in Lees, worked as a cotton weaver, while living with her parents in a house shared with Edna and Johnson Winterbottom. Johnson's younger brother, Hugh, was evidently a regular visitor, for in 1865, he and Hannah were married. They raised four children, three of whom were given names that resonated strongly in Hannah's family: Samuel Shaw Winterbottom (b.1866), Stephen (b.1869), Albert (b.1871) and Mary (b.1873).

Hugh Winterbottom, coal merchant of Lees,
and his wife Hannah Shaw, sister of his brother's wife Edna, 1870s.

By 1871, Hugh was working as a coal merchant and, in 1875, he established a company that was based at 55, St John Street, Lees. Commercial directories in the 1870s record Winterbottom Brothers & Co. Ltd with premises at Lees, Mossley, Grotton, Gorton, Openshaw, Delph, and the railway stations at Saddleworth and Oldham. Hugh's father-in-law Stephen Shaw became a director, as in due course did Hugh's three sons. After Stephen's death in 1881, Hugh and Hannah moved into his house at 3 Spring Lane, where his widow Mary lived for one more year. Hugh and Hannah then remained in the house for over 30 years, until Hannah's death in 1904.[16] At the age of 65, Hugh remarried to 51 year old Betty Kershaw, moving into 5, Spring Lane. He died, aged 78 in August 1920, at his son Albert's house, Wellfield House, Lees, leaving almost £4,000 to his coal merchant sons Samuel and Albert.[17]

Samuel Winterbottom died in 1933, but the business was continued by his brother Albert, with Albert's son Norman, Samuel's widow Martha and her son Harold. Company assets in 1933 included railway wagons, motor wagons, horses, carts, lorries, coal scales, bags and tools as well as several plots of land and buildings. The company was finally dissolved by 1948.[18]

Matilda (1835–1859), like her siblings, went to work in a cotton mill in her childhood. In 1851 she was employed as a 'tenter', which involved stretching milled cloth on a frame, so that it dried without shrinking. On 22 August 1858, at the age of 23, she married Samuel Standring in St Michael's Parish Church Ashton. He worked in a cotton mill, first as a cotton twister (operating a machine to twist yarns and threads together) and later as a 'self actor minder'. He had been born in Saddleworth, but had lived most of his life with his parents in Knott Lanes or Lees. They were married for just seven months: Matilda had contracted tuberculosis and died on 28 March 1859. She was buried in St Thomas's Leesfield Cemetery on 2 April.[19] Two months later, Matilda's sister Edna gave birth to her first child: she named the baby girl Matilda.

While Matilda was only 24 years old at the time of her death, she was nevertheless one of the older burials in the cemetery that year. The Leesfield Burial Register notes the age of each person buried, and gives us a snapshot of the still appalling child mortality at the time. In the first four months of 1859, from 5 January to 8 May, there were 43 burials: No fewer than 31 of these were of children under the age of 10.

Sarah Jane (1844 – 1877) was Stephen and Mary's sixth child. As the population continued to grow rapidly, a single Christian name was no longer sufficient to distinguish people with the same surname, and the fashion for giving children two Christian names now reached Saddleworth. In 1835, Samuel Shaw's daughter had been baptised Sarah Jane in Manchester: Stephen and Mary now gave their latest daughter the same names. She worked as a cotton weaver and then as a cotton creeler in Lees, winding thread onto bobbins. In 1871, at the age of 27, she married James Dyson Edwards from Lees, but she died following childbirth six years later, succumbing to a 35 day long puerperal fever (also known as childbed fever).[20] Her her baby girl survived and was baptised Sarah Ann, while her husband remarried the next year. Sarah Jane was the third of Stephen and Mary's children to die in their lifetime.

Mary Emma (1853 – 1917) was born nine years after her nearest sibling Sarah Jane, when her father Stephen was aged 52 and her mother Mary 46. She lived her whole life in the Lees and Springhead area and was recorded as present at her father's death in 1881. She too worked as a cotton creeler, before marrying at the age of 21. Her husband was Robert Wilde (1849-1913), who had been born in 'Thornley, Lees', and worked as a book-keeper and later a cotton broker's agent. Robert's elder brother, John Wilde (1838-1917), a notable product of Springhead Sabbath School, had become a Congregationalist Minister, who served for 54 years at Stainland near Halifax.

Mary Emma died four years after her husband Robert, in October 1917 at their home, 161 Oldham Road, Springhead. She left just £41.11s. to Harry, the eldest of their three children. Harry Wilde became a builder's merchant who, in the 1930s, served his local community as a councillor and then chairman of the Springhead Urban and District Council that had formed in 1895. On his death in 1939, he was was buried in the same grave as his grandparents, Stephen and Mary Shaw, at Providence Chapel.[21]

Stephen Shaw made a defining move into non-conformism, which shaped his own values and those of future generations. In a now industrialised world, he moved with the rapidly changing times, from farming and weaving to cotton and coal, as an employee and as a self-employed trader. And two of his daughters helped run successful coal businesses. But it was his only surviving son, Eli (1839-1898), who most dramatically embraced the opportunities offered by non-conformism, education and the industrial revolution. His move to Ashton in the mid-19th century signalled a new phase in the family of modernity, confidence, community spirit and prosperity. His impressive life is the subject of the next two chapters.

VI ASHTON-UNDER-LYNE (1860-1960)

19 : 'A CONSCIENTIOUS AND HIGH-PRINCIPLED MAN'

At the dawn of the 19th century, cotton was becoming the economic king, and Ashton was booming. It had been a small place, located on the north bank of the River Tame that flows from Denshaw Moor in Saddleworth, joining with the River Goyt near Stockport to form the River Mersey. Its name denotes a town ('tun') enclosed by ash trees, but the origin of the adjunct 'under-Lyne' is less certain. In 1422, the rent role of Sir John Assheton, who held the Manor of Assheton, refers to 'sub-lima', while an earlier survey of Manchester refers to 'subter-lineam'. Some have suggested that the term indicates proximity to an administrative boundary, but it is generally taken to describe the town's geographical location, below the line of the Pennine hills, which of course divide Lancashire from Yorkshire.[1]

In the 12th century, Ashton was a manor within the Barony of Manchester, held held by a family who, true to their Norman heritage, adopted the name of their manor as their own surname, calling themselves de Eston, and later de Assheton. The town was granted a royal charter in 1414, which enabled it to hold a fair twice a year and a market every Monday.[2] The manor of Assheton bordered both Saddleworth and Staley, and there were many connections between them, including inter-marriage between the two families in the 15th century. The successors to the two manors, the Booths and the Earl of

Stamford, would later hold lands in Quick Mere, Saddleworth, as well as in Ashton and Stalybridge.

By 1700, the population of Ashton was still only 550 but, with the advent of cotton, the town now drew in migrants from Lancashire, Yorkshire, Cheshire, Derbyshire, Staffordshire and beyond. The migrants worked in the cotton mills but also in a host of trades and professions, such as butchers, drapers, monumental masons, printers, architects, photographers, teachers, mill secretaries and more, who formed an emerging middle class. By 1861, the population had reached 34,886, briefly pausing for breath in the Cotton Famine years, before reaching a peak of 51,573 in 1931. Almost overnight, a small market town had transformed into a large mill town, sitting at the convergence of new canals and later railways.

Ashton Town Hall, a symbol of civic pride and purpose, built in 1840 and enlarged in 1878. Two Russian guns beside the steps had been captured in the Crimean War and gifted to the town in 1858, through the auspices of the then Mayor, Hugh Mason.

This was the rapidly developing, confident town that Stephen and his children knew in the 19th century. It was a period when fine landmark buildings were erected, symbols of civic pride and purpose that defined the town. These included the town hall (1840), the covered market (1829 and re-built 1861), the swimming baths (1870), St. Peter's Church (1821), the new Albion Congregationalist Church (1890), all now listed Grade II* or II. Over a period of 67 years (1821-1888), there was also extensive restoration of the ancient parish church of St. Michael & All Angels, now Grade I listed. Ashton's first ever public park, Stamford Park, opened in 1873, following years of campaigning and fundraising. Over 60,000 people attended the inauguration by the Earl of Stamford. This was the town's heyday. But the boom would last little more than a century. By the 1920s, the overseas cotton market was beginning to decline, and Ashton's principal industry would decline with it.

*****

Eli Shaw (1839 – 1898) was an extraordinary man, whose life was transformed by education. He was born in Woodbrook, in Quick Mere, on 30 January 1839, but his adult life would be lived in Ashton.[3] After the death in childhood of Daniel, he was Stephen and Mary's only son, alongside five daughters. The name Eli, like Daniel, reflects the strong Old Testament tenor of non-conformism; it was also the name of his mother's youngest brother, Ely Eastwood, born in 1815. At the age of 12, Eli, like his older siblings, was working in a cotton mill, where he was a power loom worker. However, he took full advantage of the educational opportunities now available, in Sunday Schools and Day Schools.

The Sunday School Movement had begun in 1780, when Robert Raikes founded the first school in Gloucester, and it spread with extraordinary speed: Sunday School attendance nationwide had reached half a million by 1818, and at least 5 million by 1900, before declining in the 20th century. The schools provided a mixture of religious and secular education, encouraging Christian values and future church membership on the one hand, while teaching 'utilitarian skills such as reading and writing, and less tangible social skills such as manners, punctuality and self-discipline', on the other. Non-conformist Sunday Schools tended to target the least educated and most secularized sectors of the population, such as children employed in factories, and the demand was intense.[4] In Springhead, a purpose built Sunday School had started at Providence Chapel in 1818, and by 1837 over 300 children were in regular attendance.[5]

The Factory Act of 1833 restricted hours of child labour in factories, and stipulated that children so employed should receive at least two hours of schooling per day. The legislation now gave state encouragement to the education of children, and also to the employment of teachers: as we have seen, in 1841 one schoolteacher lived in the small hamlet of Woodbrook, while two lived in Austerlands. In 1843, a further Act of Parliament legislated that children should not work more than half time, and should attend at least three hours of school per day. The Government also allocated funding to support schools: to the National Society for Church of England Schools (founded 1811); and to the British and Foreign Schools Society (founded 1808) for non-conformist schools. The latter category came to be known as 'British Schools'.

These so-called Factory Schools were of varying quality. Leonard Horner, Inspector of Factories, carried out inspections of 427 factory schools in Lancashire in the period 1848-1850, and in summary his findings were:

76:    Efficient
26:    Tolerably good
146:   Greatly inferior to these

112: So low in quality that the term indifferent is better than they deserve

46: Not only of no value, but positively mischievous as deceptions and a fraud upon the ignorant parents who pay the school fees[6]

Despite this unpromising context, a school in Lees received exceptionally high praise from Mr Horner. This was the Zion British School, founded in 1844 by the Methodist New Connexion, with influential support from two local mill owners. It was here that Eli Shaw discovered his lifelong passion for education.[7]

ZION BRITISH TRAINING SCHOOLS, LEES,
For Boys and Girls.

UNDER THE MANAGEMENT OF A COMMITTEE OF GENTLEMEN.

Superintended by Mr. George Atkins,

WHO IS ASSISTED BY EIGHT WELL-TRAINED PUPIL-TEACHERS.

COURSE OF INSTRUCTION.

1 Reading.
2 Spelling.
3 Writing (from Copies and Dictation.)
4 Arithmetic (Written and Mental.)
5 Geography (Physical, Political, & Historical.)
6 Grammar, including the Analysis of Sentences.
7 History (English and Scripture.)
8 Mensuration.
9 Algebra.
10 Geometry.
11 Mechanics.
12 Collective Lessons on various subjects.

The Girls are also instructed in Plain and Ornamental Needlework, Knitting, &c.

The Schools are supplied with a good Library, (which has lately been greatly enlarged), free; for the use of the more advanced Scholars.

Extracts from the Reports on the above named Schools, made by Her Majesty's Inspectors, L. Horner, Esq. and J. D. Morell, Esq.

Prospectus for the highly rated Zion British School Lees, 1850, where Eli studied and was appointed a Pupil-Teacher.

Founded in 1844, in rooms adjoining the Zion Chapel, the Zion Lees British School rapidly established a reputation for excellence.

A succession of glowing reports by school inspectors during the 1850s inspired a long article on the front page of the Oldham Chronicle of 7 April 1860, which began: 'The people of Lees have a right to be proud of their British School, for it has justly earned its title, not simply in its primary signification as connected with the British and Foreign School Society, but because it has long ago established its reputation throughout England as one of the best, if not *the* best, school of its class in the Empire.'

This was quite a claim, but even HM Inspector of Schools, Mr Morrell, commented: 'The school at Lees is without exception one of the most vigorous and stimulating which I have yet met with.'

Not only did the parents have to pay school fees, but controversially, they were asked to buy their children's books as well. At first this met with objections, but by 1851 the Manchester Spectator commented that 'the parents now supply their children's school books most readily.'

Despite its name, the school was non-sectarian in approach, albeit still Christian. The teachers and pupil-teachers were not required to hold particular beliefs, and in 1860 it was recorded that 'six attend Zion Chapel Lees, four attend the Established Church, two are Congregationalist, one Baptist and one Moravian.'

In 1853 there were 410 scholars: 250 day scholars and 160 half-timers or factory children. The system of education was a combination of the 'monitorial and sectional' approaches. 'The whole school is divided into two portions, which are taught in two distinct rooms. Each portion is again divided into four classes, the average number being 51 in each class in the books, and about 45 in actual attendances... The plan [involves] dividing each section into small groups of five or six, over each of which is placed a trained monitor, while the whole section is superintended by a pupil teacher to ensure the monitor doing their part carefully and industrially.'

As a teenager in the 1850s, Eli was elevated to the role of 'Pupil-teacher'. This was a role for 'intellectually promising youths' aged 13-18, selected to teach in elementary schools, while also receiving secondary education from the head of the school and training for a career as a teacher. Pupil-teachers had an important, paid role. By 1860, when the number of pupils had risen to 485, the school had 6 teachers, 8 pupil-teachers (5 male and three female) and about 40 trained but unpaid monitors. We should note the active participation of girls and women as both pupils and teachers: non-conformism tended to be egalitarian in both religion and social development.

Pupil-teachers took responsibility for teaching a class of around 50 scholars, under the guidance of a school master/mistress. They oversaw about eight monitors and helped maintain discipline in a large room containing some 200 children. They served an apprenticeship which typically led to a career in education, though it also had wider application. There must have been strong competition for pupil-teacher apprenticeships. The Oldham Chronicle reports that, by 1860, 'eleven pupil teachers have completed their term of apprenticeship and of this number seven are engaged in the work of education.' Of the other four, one had 'retired from the profession in consequence of declining health', while three 'occupy important situations unconnected with scholastic pursuits'. Eli was one of the seven to have completed his apprenticeship, and to pursue a career in education.

The Superintendent of the school for its first fourteen years was a Mr George Atkins. He attributed the success of the school to the quality of its teachers: 'There were no better masters, no better mistresses and no better pupil-teachers to be found'. Yet he too came in for high praise: 'Mr Atkins is very vigorous and active in discipline...the whole system and spirit of the school is active, energetic and stimulating to the mind.' Mr Atkins was very clearly a role model for Eli, about whom similar words would be written when he was headmaster of Ryecroft British School.

In 1861, aged 22, Eli was employed as Assistant Master in an elementary school at 3 Whitehall Street, Rochdale. The census records that neighbours of the school included a Roman Catholic Priest 'stationed in Rochdale', solicitors' offices, a picture frame maker, a milliner, a coal miner, an old clothes dealer and a 'bleeder with leeches'. Residents of the school included Eli, one other Assistant Master from 'Devonshire', the Schoolmaster and his 70 year old mother from Berkshire, a 20 year old cook/domestic servant from Scotland and a 16 year old general servant from Manchester. Six children boarded at the school, ranging in age from 9 to 14. The youngest was the Schoolmaster's nephew from 'Somersetshire', and others came from Shipley, Bacup, Manchester, Darlington and Saddleworth. There would not have been such mobility and diversity even one generation earlier. The census records that there was also a stable at the address, but that this was 'unoccupied'.

*****

In 1863, Eli moved to Ashton under Lyne, and on 11 February 1865 he was formally admitted to Ryecroft Chapel as a member. The following year, on 2 May, he was married there to Mary Ann Hulme, she becoming a church member on 20 June 1869.[8] A non-conformist wedding was not an option that had been open to Eli's father, Stephen.

For 33 years, until his death in 1898, Eli was a schoolteacher and then Headmaster of Ryecroft Day School, and Superintendent of Ryecroft Sunday School. In 1866, he also took charge of the Young Men's Class, which provided education in literacy and numeracy, as well as a grounding in Christian morality and development in community leadership. He cannot have had much spare time, yet in 1880, to add to his responsibilities, he was elected a Deacon of the church, and then Church Secretary, while also chairing the Church's

Home and Foreign Missionary Society. In his later years, he also became a magistrate and a town councillor. Ashton would be Eli and Mary Ann's home for the rest of their lives, and Ryecroft was Eli's vocation. They lived initially at 69 Stockport Road, very close to Ryecroft, later moving to Mona House at 124 Stockport Road, and later again to 119 Wellington Road..

Ryecroft Independent Chapel had been founded by members of the Congregationalist Albion Chapel, which was struggling to cope with increased demand for sittings as a result of the rapid development of the west end of Ashton. Albion Chapel, off Crickets' Lane in the narrower streets of the old town, had become 'inconveniently crowded' because 'the demand for pews was so great'. The 'large and elegant' school rooms at Ryecroft opened first in 1847, designed to accommodate 1000 pupils. The church opened six years later, on 8 June 1853. It had cost £5000 to build and was entirely free from debt.[9] The buildings were located in the Ryecroft area of Ashton, on Stockport Road, adjacent to William Street at the side and Bollington Street at the back. The site contained the church on the left, the Sunday school on the right and office rooms at the back. The buildings, in the 'Old English style of architecture', were regarded as 'among the finest in the Parish and ... a beautiful ornament to the West End of the town'.

They joined two other prominent buildings recently constructed in the area. Ryecroft Mills, just north of the chapel, had been built in the 1830s by Abel Buckley, who came from a mill-owning family. A committed Congregationalist and member of Albion Chapel, he strongly supported the development of the new chapel and school at Ryecroft, and it was he who laid the foundation stone of the chapel in 1852. A Liberal in politics, he became Ashton's first mayor in 1847, while his son, another Abel, later became Liberal MP for Prestwich.

Just to the south of the new chapel, by the Ashton canal, were the Oxford Mills, constructed in the mid-1840s by Thomas Mason, whose son Hugh would become sole owner in 1860. The Masons too were members of Albion Chapel and Liberal in politics. Hugh married Abel Buckley's daughter Sarah in 1846, was an early school superintendent at the new Ryecroft school, and later became Mayor of Ashton and a Liberal MP.

Non-conformist and Liberal networks, often championed by such Cotton Kings, were influential. They also created opportunities. In the 1840s, Stephen Shaw's attendance at Providence Chapel surely helped him acquire the role of warehouseman in the Robinsons' cotton mill at Woodbrook. Now Eli's connections with Providence Chapel and Zion British School would not only have alerted him to a teaching opportunity in Ashton, but would also have commended him to the school and church authorities in Albion and Ryecroft. Connections between the chapels were strong too: we saw earlier that Ryecroft's first Minister, William Thomas, attended the ceremony to lay the corner stone of the new Providence Chapel in Springhead, in 1854, one year after Ryecroft Chapel had first opened its doors.

Centenary Medals of the Sunday School Movement, founded by Robert Raikes. By the 1880s, some 1000 children and adults were attending the Ryecroft Sunday Schools.

Ryecroft now thrived. A substantial and influential community hub, it comprised three distinct, but complementary, functions: the church, the day school and the impressively large Sunday School. Its scale, reach and social ambition were remarkable, not only feeding the new hunger for education, but aiming for a much wider social impact. An account in 1884 records:

'In connection with this church there has always been a day and Sunday school, the latter having now grown into a vigorous and powerful institution, numbering about 1,000 scholars and 80 teachers. The day school also, from the most feeble beginning, has developed into an influential department, and owes its success partly to the excellent committee of management, and the energy of the present headmaster Mr Eli Shaw whose efforts have been ably seconded by the two mistresses Misses Simister and Fullerton. Mr Shaw has been at Ryecroft twenty-one years. According to length of service he is the oldest teacher in the town. Miss Simister has held her position as mistress of the infant school for 20 years. Twelve classrooms have been added to the original building, and a handsome lecture room calculated to seat about 200 people.'[10]

Ryecroft's own reports record that, in 1883, no fewer than 76 teachers and 'officers' were involved in Sunday School activities.[11] Sunday school classes took place in both mornings and afternoons and were regularly attended by 1007 children (459 boys and 548 girls). The Sunday School library held 1718 volumes, and during that year it issued 2957 loans. Nor was the Sunday School only for children. Sixty adult women attended a class for mothers, which included literacy, childcare and female health care, as well as providing a safe and supportive social venue. The 'First Class' of the Sunday School, which Eli led, was for adult working men. It taught literacy and numeracy, and beyond that aspired to develop community leaders of the future.

Nor was the work of the Sunday School restricted to Sundays. On a cold Saturday evening in February 1884, a tea party was held for children of the Sunday School, presided over by Eli Shaw. No fewer than 230 children sat down to tea in the upper school room, where they enjoyed a programme of entertainment, much of which was provided by the children themselves. This included: two pianoforte solos (one performed by Eli's 15 year old son Richard); four violin solos with pianoforte accompaniment; some tricks and legerdemain by one of the boys and numerous recitations by both girls and boys. Indeed the Ryecroft Sunday School Amateur Dramatic Society, which included adults, was widely celebrated, well into the 20th century, for its performances of dramas and pantomimes.

In February 1891, Eli completed 25 years in charge of the Young Men's Class and was presented with 'a splendid reading lamp' and a leather-bound copy of the newly published 'Parallel Bible' inscribed with the following:

'Presented to Mr Eli Shaw by the Past and Present Members of the Young Men's Class in appreciation of 25 years of continuous service in the Ryecroft Independent Sunday Schools, Ashton-under-lyne. February 14th 1891.' [12]

As the Ryecroft Minister Thomas Green quipped, with biblical wit, these were two lights: one to read by and the other, 'a light unto our path'. We have come a long way from the world of husbandmen and domestic weavers.

The ceremony included tea, violin and song recitals, poetry readings and more than a few speeches, liberally punctuated by cheers.

Mr Garratt, a scholar of the Young Men's Class under Eli's tuition for many years, and now proud to be one of its teachers, gave one of the speeches: 'There was a point about Mr Shaw which everyone must have noticed, and that had been an inspiration to many of them – his determined, persistent punctuality and regularity in attendance at the Sunday School. (Cheers)' In fact Eli believed that owing to his 'splendid health' over the last 25 years, he had only missed half a day from the day school 'through indisposition' and none at all from the Sunday School.

Eli Shaw seated centre, with teachers from Ryecroft School, c.1896. His son Richard, also a teacher, stands behind his father's left shoulder. Both Eli and Richard died in 1898.

Thomas Green, said that 'he had found in Mr Shaw one of the most faithful, one of the most thoroughly trustworthy and to be depended upon, one of the most patient ... conscientious and high-principled men that anybody had to work with. (Cheers) ... The influence Mr Shaw had had upon the teachers, as well as upon the class he had been connected with, had been quite incalculable. The whole institution owed a debt of gratitude to Mr Shaw which it could never repay. (Cheers)'

It is evident from Thomas Green's letter below that the Young Men's Class could be challenging to manage. Yet the students held Eli in high esteem and, at his funeral, members of the class carried his coffin into the church.

Eli's name appears in various records of the time, such as an attendance record of the General Conference of Non-Conformists in Birmingham in 1869 and the 1892 Report of the British and Foreign Schools, which identifies him as headmaster of the Ryecroft British School.

As a child I was taken to visit a man in his 90s who had been taught by Eli in both the Day School and the Sunday School. Eli, he said, 'was an excellent teacher, firm but fair'. When I asked what he meant by this, he recalled committing a misdemeanour in a Sunday School class and being punished with a rap over the palm. On the Monday morning, at the Day School assembly, he was called to the front and administered the same punishment again, 'for having committed a misdemeanour on the Sabbath'. He thought the punishment 'firm but fair', and recalled it with clarity and even fondness some 80 years later.

*****

Non-conformism was not discouraging of commercial activity, and later in life Eli became a member of the board of directors of the Harper Twist Co. Ltd. The company formed in 1873 with a capital of £30,000 and purchased the Harper Mill for £9,000, re-building and enlarging it after a fire in 1871. The mill was sited between Mossley Road and Queen Street, and was unusual for not being close to a canal.

It was five stories high and 22 windows in length. By 1884 it contained 33,880 mule spindles, increasing to 40,968 in 1891, and 43,000 by 1903.[13] Eli's eldest son George was company secretary and a member of the board of directors. The Harper Twist Company occupied the building until the mid-1920s, when cotton spinning ceased in the cotton slump. The building was subsequently used for other industrial purposes, before its recent conversion into apartments.

On 4 January 1895 Eli was created a Borough Magistrate, and in November 1897 he was elected Town Councillor for the St Peter's Ward in Ashton. He was also an active member of the Liberal Party and a member of the Ashton Liberal Council. His obituary describes him as 'a man of intelligence and culture, a fluent speaker and convincing as well as persuasive... an ardent politician, tenacious of his opinions, but just and tolerant of the opinions of others.'

One of Eli's long-standing friends was Hugh Mason, an archetypal non-conformist 'Cotton King', who served as a Liberal town councillor, then as Mayor of Ashton for three years from 1857, and later as Liberal MP for Ashton in 1880-1885. Hugh Mason was known for his philanthropic approach. This involved providing good quality housing for his employees at the New Oxford colony, as well as reading rooms, baths and other leisure facilities. During the Cotton Famine, he continued to employ workers at the Oxford Mills on full pay, at considerable financial loss to himself – one of just a handful of mill-owners to do so.[14] A Congregationalist, he was an active supporter of Albion Church and day schools, both of which benefited from his financial donations, and was also one of the first superintendents of Ryecroft School in 1847.[15] He died in 1886, and a large photograph is prominent in a family album compiled by Eli's son Charles shortly after Eli's death in 1898.[16]

Another public figure who was for many years a close colleague and friend of Eli, was the Rev Thomas Green, Minister of Ryecroft

Chapel for 41 years from 1856 until his death in December 1897. His photograph too is prominent in the family album. He had conducted the marriage ceremony for Eli and Mary Ann in 1866; he had baptised five of their six children (there is no baptism record for Edward, who died aged five weeks), and he had buried three of them. He had also buried Eli's wife Mary Ann after her sudden death in 1895.

According to a contemporary chronicler, Thomas Green 'has been most assiduous in his labours for the good, not only of the church over which he presides, but of the whole town ... There is hardly a society – social, political or religious – which has been originated for the benefit of the people with which his name has not been identified. ... His genial manners, combined with his superior culture and abilities, have raised him high in public esteem.'[17]

In November 1896, attempting to recuperate from illness by staying with his brother in Worthing, Thomas Green wrote a letter to Eli Shaw Esq., from one ageing friend to another. Its weariness reflects the darkening shadows of his own life, and perhaps also presages the future decline of Ryecroft:[18]

Melvell Green Esq

Havercroft
Worthing
Sussex
Friday Nov 27 1896

My dear friend,

I shall be very glad to hear from you if you can find a few minutes to write, both on things in particular and things in general.

I am glad to learn that your Richard* is reported to be better and I trust the report is authentic. May he go on till he is better than he ever was before. I always had a good opinion of Dr Smith professionally & I am bound to say my opinion has become still more to his credit by his recent dealings both with me & with Mary.

I think W. Baily's appointment to the superintendentship is as good as can be made considering how few are in the running. What a number of men there are at Ryecroft who have no hesitation in availing themselves of any self-sacrifice others may make for them & their families but who themselves do next to nothing.

I am of course curious to see how the election of Deacons and Deaconesses will go. I do not expect that the quota of either will be filled up. How is the Sunday afternoon Men's Class going on, & to what if any extent does it knock the Sunday School to pieces?

The weather here is very fine but cold – almost too cold for those who can walk but slowly.

I shall be glad on many accounts to be at home but I certainly do not feel much up to work just yet, & I like to believe that it will do neither Mr Craven* nor the folk in general any harm to be left together without the "old un" for a time.

Mary writes with me in ever warmest regards – ever sincerely yours

 Thos Green

(* Richard was Eli's son – see below. He did not recover from his illness, and died of tuberculosis one month after Eli in 1898. Thomas Green did not recover from his illness either: a funeral card records that he died on Wednesday 15th December 1897 and was buried in Dukinfield Cemetery on the following Tuesday. Mr Craven was Assistant Minister at Ryecroft and conducted the funeral services of both Thomas Green and Eli Shaw.)

****

Eli's wife, Mary Ann Hulme (1839-1895), had been born to a family of provision dealers, living above the grocery shop at 83 High Street, Lees. It was Mary Ann's grandfather, Thomas Hulme, who had first seized the opportunities arising from rapidly growing urban populations. The son of an illiterate weaver from Knott Lanes, Thomas completed an apprenticeship with a grocer in Manchester in 1805. He subsequently worked as a weaver in Oldham and an iron-turner in Lees until, at the age of 35, he started a grocery shop in Lees. Although he died only seven years later, in 1828, he had quickly built up a thriving business: his assets were worth £300 and included four 'messuages or dwelling houses' that provided rental income.[19] He left his estate to his wife Hannah for 12 years, and thereafter the messuages and rental income 'unto all my Children Then Liveing'. Four of his ten children had already died: it was a period of both high fertility and high infant mortality.

Thomas's eldest son, Richard Hulme, developed the family business further. When he died in 1862, his estate was valued at around £4,000.[20] The shop business was doing well: he left this to his wife, Mary Wrigley, who herself came from a family of provision dealers. He had also grown his father's property portfolio. He held five plots of leasehold land in Lees and Saddleworth, which he had developed and which were now occupied by two beerhouses, 16 cottages, a workshop, a stable and various 'other buildings'.

His will left instructions for these and other assets to be sold, with the proceeds invested in 'stocks, funds and securities', to be held in trust for the benefit of his six surviving children. His children would not be able to access the capital sum but should receive regular payments from dividends and interest. He explicitly instructed that his four daughters should receive payments from the trust fund 'for their sole and separate use, free from the debts, control and engagements of any husband with whom they may have intermarried'. Furthermore, when his children died, the trust fund should continue to make payments to their surviving adult children (his grandchildren).

Mary Ann's share of the trust continued beyond her death into the 20th century. In the early 1900s it owned some nine houses in Ashton, on Mossley Road and Margaret Street, which generated rental income for the beneficiaries, her sons George and Charles, and for Jennie, widow of her son Richard. In October 1914, at the start of World War I, the house at 306 Mossley Road was let to Albion Chapel for occupation by Belgian refugees, numbers of whom had sought refuge in Ashton. The trust was eventually closed in 1929 by Charles Shaw, who by then was Mary Ann's sole surviving child.[21]

After Richard Hulme's death, the shop in Lees was continued by his widow Mary until her death in 1886, when it passed to her three unmarried children. While her youngest son, John Edward, married late in life in 1892, and died in Springhead in 1905, it was her son Richard who continued the family business until 1900. Richard remained unmarried, but looked after his sister Hannah until he died in 1909. The eldest child, Hannah, described in the 1901 census as 'imbecile of feeble mind', helped in the shop and lived on until 1914. Donald Shaw recalled, as a young boy in the early 1900s, being taken by his father to visit his 'Auntie Hannah' in Lees, then the only survivor of her generation of Hulmes. Increasingly eccentric, she greeted the young boy with the unwelcoming words: 'What dosth' want? I an't na coal. I an't na bread.'

Eli, Mary Ann, and their children, remained close to the Hulmes of Lees, and the album compiled after Eli's death contains numerous photos of them. Eli was named as a trustee of the will of Mary Hulme in 1886,[22] the other trustees being her unmarried children, Richard, Hannah and John Edward Hulme. The two witnesses of the will were the brothers Johnson and Hugh Winterbottom, husbands of Eli's sisters Edna and Hannah respectively. Eli was visiting Richard and Hannah Hulme at 83 High Street Lees when he collapsed and died, in 1898.

Two of Mary Ann's sisters are of note. Elizabeth ('Lizzie) Hulme (1845-1927) married John Hirst, proprietor and editor of the Oldham Chronicle newspaper, which had been founded by his father Jonathan Hirst in 1854. The Hirst family were close neighbours of Stephen Shaw and the Hulmes, as well as prominent supporters of Providence Chapel for over three generations.[23] The modern-day Springhead Congregationalist Church contains a plaque in recognition of John Hirst's support. In 1898, Elizabeth Hirst was a witness to the will of Eli Shaw's son Richard, in the last days of his life, when her address was 3 Radcliffe Street Springhead, the house opposite to Providence Chapel.[24]

After John Hirst's death in 1917, his son Hubert continued to run the Oldham Chronicle and also to support Providence Chapel. The second son Henry (Harry) Hirst, though a lifelong Deacon of Providence Chapel, then moved to Rhos-on-Sea, in North Wales, with his wife Mollie. After Mollie died unexpectedly in 1920, Harry married Marian Smethurst. Marian was the daughter of William Sanderson Smethurst and niece of Sarah Helen Smethurst, who married Eli's son Charles Shaw. Harry Hirst was thus doubly related to the Shaw family: his mother was a Hulme and his second wife a Smethurst (see chapter 21). He remained a close friend of the family until his death in Rhos in 1965, Marian dying there five years later in 1970. The Oldham Chronicle continued to be run by the Hirst family, but circulation declined progressively after World War II, and it closed in 2017.

Another of Mary Ann's sisters, Sarah Hulme (1848-1924), married Joseph Ogden Lees, who had been adopted by Thomas and Fanny Lees as their grandson. He inherited wealth from his adoptive grandparents and went on to become a cotton mill manager. A record shows him travelling to New York in 1907.[25] When he died at Highfield House, Springhead in 1919, he left the large sum of £95,000. Sarah left a further £3,300 on her death in 1924.[26]

20 : THINGS FALL APART

Eli was a driving force in Ashton. He lived his life according to his principles and was a highly respected public figure. He was committed to education as a way of self-improvement and spent his entire adult life teaching others. He was equally committed to his church and wider community in Ashton, becoming a magistrate and town councillor. For the first time in this story, we meet a man who overtly strived to make the world a better place. He was a dedicated family man, and his obituary leaves evidence of a loving family life. But in three short years his world fell apart.

On 8 August 1895, Eli's wife Mary Ann had a sudden seizure and died: the death certificate suggests a stroke. Two years later, on 12 May 1897, Eli's son Alfred died with heart disease, aged just 21. Eli's second son, Richard, a music teacher, had by then contracted tuberculosis and was slipping towards his death in August 1898. And Eli's close colleague at Ryecroft for over thirty years, the Minister Thomas Green, also died in December 1897.

Eli's health suffered under these shocks. His obituary records that 'his robust health had visibly declined of late and ...his strength was very much impaired'. On 8 July 1898, Eli visited Lees: his sister Hannah Winterbottom lived in Spring Lane, and his youngest sister Mary Emma Wilde on Oldham Road, while his wife's siblings Richard and Hannah Hulme lived at 83, High Street, Lees.

His obituary records that: 'Feeling better on Friday, he ventured on a short journey to Lees, calling upon relatives there. After this he visited Mr and Miss Hulme, brother-in-law and sister-in-law. While there, he went into the yard, where he was suddenly stricken, fell down and died immediately of syncope. Dr Stansfield was summoned, but his life was extinct before he arrived.'[1]

Eli was buried in Dukinfield Cemetery in a grave that he had bought for his infant son Frank in 1879. That now also contained his wife Mary Ann and his son Alfred. Eli had drawn up his will in 1895, after his wife's death, signing it in his exceptionally clear and fluent style. His list of assets and possessions reflect the more affluent and sophisticated lifestyle that was possible in late Victorian Ashton. He bequeathed to his sons 'all my real and personal estate, loans, policies of insurance, shares, household furniture, plate, pictures, jewelry and whatsoever I possess'. His estate was valued at £2,631 and his will also refers to freehold and leasehold properties, which were to be retained unsold by his sons George and Charles. The family's prosperity had grown markedly through the economic changes of the 19th century and the emergence of a middle class.[2]

The Ashton Reporter printed a detailed obituary and account of Eli's funeral on 16 July 1898. A long list of family, friends and colleagues attended. The tributes to Eli's character commonly include words such as integrity, zeal, devotion to duty, energy. Messages attached to the many wreaths expressed deep sorrow and sympathy, but perhaps the most touching message, attached to a wreath from his son, read simply 'Charlie'.

Soon after Eli's death, his son Charles, our ancestor, compiled a photograph album of the family, their relatives and friends.[3] A large photo of Eli is on the first page. A number of the photographs carry the name of the photographer's company on the back. These are from a strikingly wide variety of locations, reflecting the family's now broader horizons as well as their new opportunities for holidays at the seaside: they include: Ashton, Oldham, Manchester, Miles Platting, Huddersfield, Bacup, Blackpool, Bury and the Isle of Man.

A plaque was erected in Ryecroft Church:

'In memory of Eli Shaw JP

Day School Master here and actively connected with the Ryecroft Church and Sunday School from 1865 to 1898.

A man of noble spirit and rare gifts, devoted to the service of God, the welfare of young people and the best interests of the community.

Scholars and friends unite in this testimony to the influence of a good life.'[4]

*****

Eli and Mary Ann's six children, born over a 20 year period, were all boys. They also adopted another boy, Frank Hayes. A month after Eli's own death, only two of these children were still alive. By good fortune, one of these survivors was our ancestor Charles (1871–1937), who will be the focus of the next chapter. But first we will look here at the lives of Eli's other children.

Three of Eli Shaw's four sons to live to adulthood. Left to right: George (1867-1923); Richard (1868-1898), Alfred (1875-1897).

George Hervey (1867–1923), the eldest son, spent his working life in the cotton industry in Ashton. In 1891, at the age of 24, he was the secretary and salesman of the Harper Twist cotton mill, one of some 34 cotton mills in Ashton alone at that time. Ten years later he was the Manager and by the time of his son's marriage in 1923 he was a Director.[5] In 1893 he married Mary Jane Bradbury, (known in the family as Jinnie), the daughter of a draper, her parents having moved to Ashton before her birth from Derbyshire and Barnsley. In 1895, Jinnie's father, Joe Bradbury, was a witness to Eli Shaw's will.

For most of their married life, George and Jinnie lived at Daisy Bank, 194 Oldham Road, Ashton. As living standards improved, so house names had become fashionable in Ashton. While George would live at 'Daisy Bank', 174 Oldham Road, his father Eli had lived at 'Mona House' on Stockport Road, and his brother Charles would move to live at 'Aingarth', 157 Henrietta Street. Other house names significant for the family would be 'Hawthorn Bank' in Zetland Street, and 'Craigmore' and 'Sorrento' in Kings Road.

George and Jinnie had two children, a small family by the standards of recent generations. Their first child, Dorris Mary, was born on 2 March 1894 and baptised at Ryecroft on 13 May by Rev. Thomas Green. Unfortunately, Dorris contracted tuberculosis, which spread to her kidneys, and she died from this wasting illness on 10 November 1917 at the age of just 23. She was old enough to have a little money of her own, and, touchingly, she left £23. 4s. 11d. to her father.

Their second child, a son named Herbert Eli, was born in 1899, a year after Eli Shaw's death. Turning 18 years old in 1917, the year his sister died, Herbert was conscripted for armed service in World War I. His parents must have feared losing their second child too, but Herbert survived the war, serving in the Duke of Cornwall's Light Infantry (Reg.No.30142) and receiving the British War Medal and the Victory

Medal. His name was listed on a memorial plaque at Ryecroft for church members who had served in World War I.[6]

By the 1920s, George had developed arterial sclerosis, and was in poor health. Herbert's wedding was perhaps timed with this in mind. He married Dorothy Dean in Manchester Cathedral on 7 November 1923. His father George signed the marriage certificate as a witness, but died just a month later, on 9 December, at the age of 56.He left £2,174 to his widow, Mary Jane,[7] who subsequently lived with her son and daughter-in-law until her own death in 1943.

Herbert Eli and Dorothy lived in Stalybridge, where he too worked in the cotton industry, as a salesman for a cotton manufacturing company. Their only child, named Norma Hillary Mepham after her marriage, moved out of industrial Ashton to Thornton Cleveleys on the Lancashire coast near Blackpool and Lytham St Annes. As we shall see below, she would not be the first or last family member to move out of Ashton to an environment less polluted and to a town less reliant on a now declining cotton industry. Meanwhile, Herbert Eli died in Ancoats Hospital Manchester in 1956, at almost the same age as his father.[8]

*****

Richard Henry (1868 – 1898), born on 29 December 1868 at 69 Stockport Road, was named after his mother's brother and father in Lees, who were both called Richard Hulme. Within the family, his pet name was "Dickie". Richard followed his father into education, and in 1891, at the age of 22, he was an elementary school teacher at Ryecroft, where his father was headmaster.

Music had become an important part of the upbringing of Eli's children. The family subscribed to publications of music for 'Jeunes Pianistes', binding them into a single volume. Many of the pieces were for four hands: George, Richard and Charles all played the piano in their younger years. But it was Richard who excelled. For his 23rd birthday in 1891, he was given a copy of Mendelssohn's 'Lieder Ohne Worte', purchased from Sladin Brothers Music Warehouse in Ashton. This is a challenging piece, but he was an accomplished pianist. He also played the organ at Ryecroft Church, the harmoniums at smaller church gatherings, and he taught music too. Apart from music, he was also said to be a fine swimmer. These are the first known references to music and sport in the family: cultural horizons had broadened, and there was pride in Richard's achievements.

On 2 June 1897, the resignation of Mr Richard Henry Shaw, as organist at the Wednesday evening meeting, was accepted with regret by the Ryecroft Church members. The Assistant Minister Mr Craven was asked to write a letter expressing the thanks of the Church for Richard's honourable service in the role over many years. The letter expressed 'cordial and hearty thanks ... and high appreciation of the faithfulness, zeal and ability with which he has at all times discharged the duties of an important office in an important meeting.' The letter also congratulated Richard on his new appointment at the Abney Congregational Church in Mossley, known for its strong musical tradition, and 'the commencement of what the church hopes will be a long and successful public musical career.'[9]

A month later, Richard married Jane Ellen Brown, known in the family as Jennie (perhaps to complement George's wife Jinnie). She was the eldest of the four children of William Brown, a letter press printer and stationery master in Ashton. Brown's printers and stationers would remain a successful business in Ashton for several generations. Richard and Jennie had long been friends, and on the same day in January 1894, Richard, Jennie and her younger sister Annie Brown were jointly admitted as Members of Ryecroft Church.[10] On 15 April 1898, a male child was born: he was named Alfred, after Richard's younger brother who had died just 11 months earlier, in May 1897.

Richard's future looked to be set fair. Yet, how often in this history was early promise cut short? We know from Rev Thomas Green's letter in November 1896 that Richard had been unwell: this was the early onset of tuberculosis. Just a year after taking up his new post in Mossley and marrying his wife Jennie, four months after the birth of their child Alfred, one month after the sudden death of his father Eli, and two weeks after preparing his own will, Richard died on 11 August 1898, at the age of 29. His wife Jennie had attended Eli's funeral in July, but Richard himself had been too ill to attend. Jennie's sister Annie was present at Richard's death, at the Trinity Square nursing home in Ashton. His death certificate records his occupation as 'Professor of Music'. He was buried at Dukinfield Cemetery on 13 August, and his gravestone reads: 'Richard Shaw Musician'.[11]

Jennie did not remain long in Ashton. A 29 year old widow with a four month old child, she must have felt an urge to find new pastures. She also benefited from Richard's inheritance and his share of the Hulme family trust fund, which enabled her to live independently and provide for her son Alfred.[12] In December 1901, when Jennie was 31 and her sister Annie 26, the two moved together to Lytham St Anne's on the Lancashire coast.[13] Ten years later, they were joined by their youngest sister Alice Brown. Young Alfred had no father, but was raised in this seaside town by his mother, his aunt Annie, and in his teenage years by his maiden aunt Alice too.[14]

In 1921, Annie moved away from Lytham, marrying Richard Nowell, from Ashton, who in the First World War had served as a Lt Colonel in the Manchester Regiment. She was 47 and he 41. They lived in Devon, breeding cattle, until in 1953, when at their respective ages of 79 and 73, they emigrated to Brazil. Richard died there five years later, and Annie returned to Lytham, where she remained until her own death in 1973, five days short of her 99th birthday.

In 1925, Alfred also left Lytham to join an accountancy firm. He eventually married in 1936; but he was now 38, and his wife Winifrid Ogden was 39 – on the late side for starting a family. Alfred's work now took him to Bristol, and this is where he and Winnie lived until his death in December 1972. He was a gentle, softly spoken man, much as his father Richard appears to have been. He died four years after his mother, and one year before his aunt Annie, to both of whom he was so close.

Jennie may have left Ashton, but she kept in touch with her Shaw relations there. In 1933, she returned to Ashton to attend the wedding of Donald Shaw, son of Richard's only surviving brother Charles. And in 1937, she attended the funeral of Charles Shaw at Ryecroft. She was briefly joined in Lytham by her brother Sidney: he had continued the family business in Ashton, although living in Wilmslow, Cheshire, in a house which he named "Ryecroft". However, after Sidney's death in 1954, and that of her sister and companion Alice in 1956, Jennie moved moved to Bristol to live with her son Alfred. She died in a nursing home in Clevedon in 1966, at the age of 96. She had never re-married.

*****

Alfred (1875–1897) was born on 8 July 1875 and became a Clerk to a Merchant by the age of 15. Unfortunately, his promise was short-lived: he died on 12 May 1897 and was buried beside his younger brother Frank, and his mother Mary Ann, in the grave his father had bought in 1879. He was 21. Just two years spanned the deaths of Alfred's mother, his brother Richard and himself. Eli would follow a year later.

*****

Two other children had died earlier in infancy: Edward, at just 5 weeks in 1872, and Frank, just before his second birthday in 1879. Eli had bought a grave for Frank in the 'Dissenters' Part' of the recently opened municipal cemetery at Dukinfield. It would later receive Eli's wife Mary Ann, his son Alfred and Eli himself.[15]

We saw in chapter 17 that Frank Hayes (1860-1877) was the only grandchild of Eli's uncle Samuel Shaw, the son of his only daughter Sarah Jane. In 1861 Samuel and his wife Martha, Thomas Hayes, his wife Sarah Jane and the seven month old Frank were all sharing a house at 73 Booth Street West, in Chorlton-upon Medlock, Manchester. But the next decade was riven by pestilence. Young Frank's grandmother Martha died in 1862 and his mother Sarah Jane in 1866. Samuel now moved to Cheadle, leaving Frank in Chorlton, with his father Thomas Hayes and a housekeeper. Samuel himself then died in 1868, and four years later, in 1872, so too did Frank's father.

The 12 year old Frank Hayes was now an orphan. Eli had been close to his uncle Samuel (Frank's grandfather) and to his cousin Sarah Jane (Frank's mother). He was also the only remaining executor of Samuel's will, which left all his estate to Frank, if or when he attained maturity at the age of 21. Eli and Mary Ann now stepped forward to adopt the young boy, taking him into their house in Ashton, just as John Shaw of Lower House in Boarshurst had adopted his nephews, William and John, in 1657. Frank attended Ryecroft British School, where Eli was the Headmaster, and by 1877 he had become a Pupil Teacher, just as Eli had done at the Zion British School in Lees. A career in education beckoned, as did the prospect of inheriting his grandfather's estate.

Unfortunately, much like the 17 year old Thomas Hawkyard in the previous century, Frank did not live long enough to pursue his profession, or to receive his inheritance. On 1 November 1877, at the age of 17, he died of typhoid at Eli and Mary Ann's house on Stockport Road, Ashton. They arranged for him to be buried at St Mary's Prestwich, where his parents and grandparents all lay. Frank's estate was valued at 'under £100', and this was granted to his uncle George Hayes of Audley in Staffordshire.[16] Samuel's will had stipulated that, in the event of Frank dying before he reached maturity, the estate should be distributed equally between the children of all Samuel's brothers and sisters: by now, these were quite numerous.

Six weeks before Frank Hayes' death, Eli and Mary Ann's youngest child was born on 21 September 1877. They named him Frank. Unfortunately, his life was even shorter.

The 19th century brought rapid advances in education, technology and prosperity, but disease could still destroy families, as in earlier generations. Eli was a man of his time. His faith was strong, his energy levels high, his health robust. He was committed to his community and was held in high regard. He achieved much in his life. But in his last years, he witnessed death cutting a swathe though his family and destroying the aspirations of many of his children.

21 : A MODERN LIFE

Charles Shaw in his mid 20s. c.1897.

In the space of three years, our ancestor Charles Shaw (1871-1937) had lost both his parents and two of his three surviving brothers (Richard and Alfred). Only he and George were now left from Eli's large family.

Charles had been born on 27 March 1871 in Lees: his mother, Mary Ann, had returned to 83 High Street, Lees to stay with her own mother, Mary Hulme, during her confinement.[1] Thereafter Charles lived his whole life in Ashton, though he maintained close contact with his relatives in Lees and Saddleworth, the Hulmes and the Hirsts, the Winterbottoms and the Wildes.

In 1891, at the age of 20, he was working as a Clerk to a Shipping Agent, and two years later, in December 1893, he joined the Manchester Ship Canal Company, which would be his employer for the rest of his life. The Ship Canal first opened to traffic one month later, on 1 January 1894, and was formally opened by Queen Victoria in May 1894.[2] Charles worked his way up in the company. By 1901, he was an Audit Clerk, ten years later Assistant Cashier, and later Chief Cashier. A recognisably modern man, he commuted daily by train from Ashton Charlestown Station to Manchester.

On 23 March 1899, seven months after his father's death and four days before his 28th birthday, Charles married. His wife was Sarah Helen Smethurst (1874-1949). Known as Helen, she was the fifth child of Samuel Smethurst JP and his wife Helen.

Samuel Smethurst was from an Oldham family of cotton spinners. His life journey bore many similarities to that of Eli. Born in 1840, one year after Eli, he joined the Methodist New Connexion church and gained an education. Moving to Ashton in the 1870s, he worked his way up from cotton spinner, to 'overlooker operative cotton spinner' and then, for the last decades of his life, to cotton mill manager. Like Eli, he also became a magistrate. His eldest son, William Sanderson Smethurst (the father of Marian Smethurst, who married Harry Hirst), had also become a cotton mill manager, as Eli's eldest son George would do.

Charles and Helen Shaw's family was small, compared to those of previous generations. Dorothy Madge, born in 1900, was named after Helen's younger sister Madge, who had died in 1894 at the age of 18. Donald Smethurst Shaw, born on 21 February 1904, was given his mother's maiden name as a second name, the first time this had occurred in the family. They lived in Ashton, first at Layard Street, then for two decades at 211 Portland Street, before moving to Catherine Street and finally to "Aingarth" in Henrietta Street, their home until Charles's death in 1937.

Like his father, Charles was very active in a wide range of social activities. He too was a committed Liberal in Ashton, for over forty years. He was a long-standing member of the Central Liberal Club, and of the Executive Committees of the Ashton Liberal Association, where he was also President. After Lloyd George's coalition government of national unity in the First World War, the Liberal Party fell on hard times, but Charles was 'always urging that, with more enthusiasm and drive, Liberalism was bound once more to come to the front' (a forecast yet to be realised).[3] There were limits, however: his obituary records that 'in earlier years he never spared his energies at election times, but consistently refused invitations to contest wards in the Liberal interest'.

Sport had become an important part of social life in the later 19th century. It was seen as a way of enjoying the greater leisure time now available, but was also explicitly promoted to improve health and fitness in these more urban times, and to counter social problems such as alcohol abuse. Football clubs sprang up: Ashton United in 1878, Newton Heath in the same year (becoming Manchester United in 1902), St Mark's West Gorton in 1880 (becoming Manchester City from 1894) and Oldham Athletic in 1895.

Charles was a member of Ashton Cricket Club, which had been founded as early as 1857. He was a founding member of Ashton Lacrosse Club, playing in its first match in 1896, and becoming a Vice-President of the club. He was also a member of the Ashton Golf Club from its inception in 1913: he and Helen attended the opening ceremony on 12 March, where the guest of honour was Sir Max Aitken MP, the future Lord Beaverbrook.[4] His enthusiasm for sports, and for lacrosse in particular, was passed down to the next two generations.

The first Ashton Lacrosse Team of 1896/7.
Charles Shaw, far right, back row, was a founding member.
On the day this photo was taken he was injured and unable to play.

Charles, like his father Eli, was active in Ryecroft Independent Church, where he was elected Deacon in 1910 and Church Secretary in 1928.[5] He was also involved in Sunday School work and taught the Young Men's Class for many years, as his father had done. He was a trustee of the Ryecroft Church, the Ryecroft School and the Bridge Street School. He was treasurer of the Ashton and District Congregational Association at the time of his death, having previously been its Chairman.

Yet with hindsight, we can see that Charles and the other Church Trustees were managing a period of decline at Ryecroft. Successive Acts of Parliament from 1870 onwards encouraged more state education, restricted child employment and steadily increased the age for compulsory child education. All these changes may have been positive, but they progressively weakened the pioneering roles of the Ryecroft Day School and Sunday Schools.

The passing years also began to erode the infrastructure at Ryecroft. Soon the once admired school buildings would be deemed inadequate for modern educational requirements. In 1904 an H M Inspector's report recommended widespread improvements to the school rooms, including: the flooring, ventilation, lighting, cloakrooms, a narrow and steep staircase, upstairs heating, levelling of the yard and subdivision of the large main room to provide additional classes. On 1 July 1908 the school, with its 633 Infant and Middle School pupils, formally transferred to the Ashton Local Education Authority as a provided school, now known as 'Ryecroft Council School', pending construction of a new school. It took 25 more years for the promised new school buildings to be completed, at which point, on 3 September 1933, the school at Ryecroft closed its doors for the last time, now used only for church meetings and Sunday School classes.[6]

An era of confident and ambitious community service was approaching its end. Ryecroft Church, that 'ornament to the west end of the town', would later be found to have widespread dry rot, and it had to be demolished in 1967. A closing service was held on Sunday 4 June 1967, and the membership, now reduced in number, joined Albion church, whence the first members of the church had come 120 years before.

At the end of 1931 Charles prepared his will and wrote a letter for his children. The shock of losing both his parents and two brothers so suddenly in the 1890s had left its mark, and he anticipated that he too might die suddenly.[7] So it transpired. On 11 July 1937, he underwent a planned operation at the High Elms Nursing Home, Victoria Park, Manchester. He had postponed the operation until retirement, proud of the fact that in his long career with 'the Canal Company' he had not missed a day's work through sickness (just as his father Eli had taken pride in having missed only a half day of work in his entire life 'through indisposition'). He would have been the first of our ancestors formally to retire from work. But he died under the anaesthetic. His work colleagues had brought a presentation to make to him, but were too late to offer 'this expression of their esteem'.

A meeting of Church Members on 28 July stood in silence to mark his passing and recorded that 'the church had sustained an irreparable loss'. No one had anticipated the tragic outcome of his illness, and 'the blow to the church and his friends was one they would feel very deeply.'[8] A lengthy obituary in the Ashton Reporter observed that 'his advice and influence would be sorely missed'.

The funeral service took place at Ryecroft Church. Among the family mourners listed in the obituary, many were widows, reflecting just how many of Charles and Helen's close relatives had died in the recent preceding years. After his brother George's death in 1923, Charles was the only surviving child of Eli and Mary Ann Shaw's six children. Similarly, in 1937, of the six children born to Samuel and Mary Smethurst, only Helen and her brother Sam were still alive. However, the wide diversity of mourners is indicative of just how deeply Charles was immersed in his community, in its commerce, politics, faith, leisure and public service.

Family mourners included:

- Mrs Shaw – Charles' widow Helen, who would live on in Ashton until her death in 1949;
- Their son Donald, with his wife Marion and her mother Clarissa Hewitt;
- Their daughter Madge with her husband Harold Vick;

- Sarah Jane Shaw (Jinnie), widow of Charles' brother George, and their son Herbert Eli;
- Jane Ellen Shaw (Jennie), widow of Charles' brother Richard;
- Children of Elizabeth Hulme, who had married John Hirst: Harry Hirst and his wife Marian (nee Smethurst); and Hubert Hirst's widow, Jane;
- William and George Lees, children of Sarah Hulme, who had married Joseph Ogden Lees;
- A number of relatives of Charles' wife Helen Smethurst – her brother Sam (who would die in May 1938); Noel the son of her brother Joseph Smethurst; May the widow of her brother John Smethurst; Lizzie the widow of her brother William Sanderson Smethurst, now of Colwyn Bay, whose daughter Marian had married Harry Hirst.

Other mourners included:

- A Director and the Secretary of the Manchester Ship Canal Company and a large number of Charles' colleagues;
- A large group of Ashton Town Councillors;
- Senior members of the Ryecroft Independent Church, the Young Men's Class and the Ashton Congregational Association; members of the Albion Congregational Church, the Bridge Street Church and the Ashton Auxiliary of the London Missionary Society;
- Representatives of the Ashton Liberal Club and the Mossley Division Liberal Association.

The funeral service was followed by cremation at South Manchester Crematorium. In a letter to his children, Donald and Madge, Charles had asked for his ashes to be scattered, adding: 'I do not believe in graves and headstones.'[9]

Charles Shaw and his wife Helen Smethurst, with children Madge
(left) and Donald (right), c. 1920.

*****

Charles and Helen Shaw's daughter, Helen Madge (1900-1969), known
in the family as Madge, was born in.Ashton in 1900. She married
Harold Vick in Ryecroft church in November 1930. He was from
Leeds, and had been staying with the family as a lodger. They moved
to Cheadle Hulme, where they had two children: Helen Madge (1931-
2016), known as Helen, and Dorothy, known as Wendy, (1932-2010).
During World War II, Harold served in the Royal Air Force. He
survived the war, but died ten years later in 1955. Madge did not
re-marry and remained in Cheadle Hulme until her death in 1969.

Charles's only son, Donald Smethurst Shaw (1904-1982) was born
in Ashton on 21 February 1904. He went on to study at Manchester

Grammar School, where he was a student during the First World War. A letter to parents from the Headmaster, dated 25 March 1918, informed them that the school would only provide vegetarian meals because of food rationing, but that 'we will do our best to make the meal as nutritious and appetising as we can'. There was rationing, and students were advised not to 'surrender any of their meat coupons for school purposes.'[10]

Donald Shaw, seated fourth from right on the front row, next to the Headmaster of Manchester Grammar School, 1918.

Donald's childhood memories included 'knocker-uppers', who would use a long pole to tap on bedroom windows and wake up mill-workers, who typically did not have watches or clocks. He recalled how families would spread straw in the cobbled street outside their house, to dampen the noise of passing carts, if a family member was ill or dying. He also recalled going with his father to Lees and Springhead, where they would visit relatives on the Hulme side of the family: his eccentric spinster aunt Hannah Hulme, the Hirsts, who owned the Oldham Chronicle, and the family of Joseph and Sarah Ogden Lees who lived at Highfield House. Eli's youngest sister Mary Emma Wilde also lived in Springhead until her death in 1917.

As a teenager, he learned poetry by heart and could recite it many years later. Among family papers, some of his own lines have survived, and he showed a talent for drawing. But his artistic attributes did not lend themselves to a career, and while a university degree had been a possibility, Donald's father believed in starting on the ground floor and working up from there, as he had done. So Donald went straight from school into employment. He could write well, and there was early talk of him working as a journalist for the Oldham Chronicle. But in January 1930, at the age of 25, Donald joined the newly formed Lancashire Cotton Corporation (LCC), where he would remain for over three decades.

The LCC was a state enterprise, established by the Bank of England to rescue the failing cotton industry in Lancashire. Many mills had closed and others were at risk. The LCC set out to rationalise the sector, using the most efficient mills to lower production costs and shutting down the least efficient ones. It acquired over 70 mills and retained less than half.

Donald became a senior manager responsible for cotton distribution. For most of his career he was based at the head office at Blackfriars House, on the corner of Deansgate and Blackfriars Street in Manchester, overlooking the slow moving River Irwell. During World War II, because of its strategic importance, the LCC headquarters were evacuated to Hopwood Hall in Middleton. In these war years, Donald volunteered as an Air Raid Warden and Flight Lieutenant in the RAF Reserves. In 1964, the rationalisation of the cotton industry in Lancashire was complete, and the LCC was taken over by the private textile company Courtaulds, where Donald worked until retirement a few years later.

Cotton was a global product, and in 1962 Donald undertook a tour of the Sudan, one of the major suppliers to Lancashire mills. After retirement he travelled to Bangkok to visit his eldest son who was stationed in the far east, returning via Cape Town. International travel, for work or enjoyment, had been unheard of in earlier generations.

In his youth, like his father, Donald was an enthusiastic lacrosse player. He was Acting Captain in 1932/3, when Ashton were champions of the North of England 2nd Division, achieving promotion to the 1st Division for the first time in their history. He remained a strong supporter of lacrosse in the north-west. He was President of the Ashton Lacrosse Club in 1949-1951, and in subsequent years was elected President of the Lancashire Lacrosse Association, the North of England Lacrosse Association, the Centurion Lacrosse Club and the English Lacrosse Union.[11]

A picturesque wedding: Donald Smethurst Shaw and
Marion Clarissa Shaw Hewitt, Ashton Parish Church, 1933.

On 5 September 1933 Donald married Marion Clarissa Shaw Hewitt at St Michael's Ashton, the same church where his great-grandfather Stephen had married in 1826. The wedding was described by the Ashton Reporter as 'one of the most picturesque nuptial ceremonies seen in Ashton'.[12]

Marion was the only daughter of Silas Hewitt, the son of a monumental mason, who, unlike his brothers, had different aspirations and trained as a pharmacist. After serving an apprenticeship in Shrewsbury, where he lodged in the house of a pharmaceutical chemist, he returned to Ashton, establishing 'The Avenue Pharmacy' on the corner of Market Avenue and Old Street.

From 1913 onwards, one of Silas's responsibilities was to pay regular visits to the Ladysmith Barracks in Ashton. Unfortunately, as World War I approached its end, many troops returning from the trenches brought with them the 'Flanders Flu' or 'Spanish flu', as it came to be known in countries other than Spain. The global pandemic killed an estimated 50 million people worldwide and about 250,000 in Britain. In early November 1918, at the height of the pandemic, Silas contracted influenza at the barracks and died at home a few days later.

Marion was just 10 years old in November 1918. She was brought up by her mother Clarissa, and her maternal grandparents Herbert and Mary Ann Shaw, to whom she owed her middle names of 'Clarissa Shaw'. Herbert came from a Staffordshire yeoman family, and had moved to Ashton in 1860 after he too had lost his own father at the age of ten.[13]

In a man's world, where women neither had a vote nor were encouraged to have a profession, Clarissa continued running the pharmacy, invested in property in Ashton and travelled widely in Europe and even North Africa. She was equally determined that her daughter should not be without a profession to fall back on, if ever she too were widowed. So Marion studied pharmacy in Manchester, passing her national exams in London in 1929, and working in the Avenue

Pharmacy until after her marriage. The pharmacy building was later sold to Boots the Chemist, and is now occupied by Yorkshire Bank.[14]

Marion's diaries reveal that she and Donald had a very wide circle of extended family, friends and acquaintances. They enjoyed an active social life in Ashton and Manchester: there were dances at the golf club and the lacrosse club, plays at the theatre, music concerts and sports events: Ashton hosted a wide range of cultural activities in these inter-war years. They frequently went for countryside walks with her pet dogs, Billy and Jumbo. A favourite route took them along Gorsey Lane (where Donald proposed), across the golf course to the 'waterworks' (now Knott Hill Nature Reserve), and occasionally beyond to Hartshead Pike. The commuter train to Manchester was a convenient meeting point in their courtship, as Marion studied and Donald worked in the city. On occasions she had the embarrassment of meeting her future father-in-law on the same platform.

Both families supported the match, though it was not without complications. As the report of the wedding noted: 'The bride is a very popular pharmacist and is a prominent member of the Parish Church.' Her family was Anglican and politically Conservative. Donald's family on the other hand was deeply rooted in Congregationalism, and actively Liberal in politics. Given the history of non-conformism in England, these were obstacles that required some compromise. The marriage took place at St Michael & All Angels Parish Church in Ashton, but on Sundays the family and children attended Ryecroft Independent Church. Donald remained an active member of Ryecroft, serving as Treasurer in the church, and teaching in the Sunday School as his father and grandfather had done. In 1956 he was awarded a 'Diploma of Honour for continuous and valuable services in the Sunday School cause during 35 years'.[15]

After their marriage, Donald and Marion lived at 'Craigmore', 345 Kings Road in Upper Hurst, Ashton. This was a 3-bedroom semi-detached house, which Marion's mother, Clarissa Hewitt, had bought for them as a wedding present, at a cost of £350. It was 100 yards down the road from 376 Kings Road, the stylish house which Clarissa had built in the early 1930s, and which she called 'Sorrento' after a visit to Italy. It was at Sorrento that their eldest child was born. After Clarissa's death in September 1954, the family moved into Sorrento, but soon decided, as many friends had already done, to relocate from Ashton. In the winter of 1959, they bought a house on the border of Cheshire and Derbyshire, with access to wonderful countryside.

For Donald, the move away from Ashton was a wrench: the town embodied five generations of family history. Indeed, for nearly 800 years, the family had lived in this part of the north-west, in Staley, Saddleworth and Ashton, an area scarcely five miles in diameter. Donald, like all previous generations, had stayed close to extended family networks. This was his 'country'.

Yet there were not really any living ties any more. No relatives were now living in Ashton, and his wide circle of friends had died or left. Like many a Lancashire town, Ashton was struggling to re-invent itself after the demise of the cotton industry.

All of Donald and Marion's four children had been baptised in Ryecroft. But now they were being drawn to the economic magnet of the South East of England, and would work further afield in continental Europe, North and East Africa, East Asia, India, South America and the Pacific. Of thirteen grand-children, eight would be born outside the United Kingdom. Congregationalism was in decline, and Ryecroft would soon be demolished. In another break with the past, Donald would later be accepted into the Church of England.

Donald died on 19 December 1982 and his ashes were interred at Dukinfield Cemetery. The grave had been purchased in 1918 by

Marion's grandfather, Herbert Shaw, for the burial of his pharmacist son-in-law, Silas Hewitt, and the impressive monument above the vault had been created by Silas's brothers, who were then running the Hewitt family monumental masonry business.[16] The grave overlooks the Tame Valley, once populated with numerous mill chimneys that powered the cotton industry and provided inspiration for the local artist L S Lowry, though now their number is now much diminished. Eastwards, beyond the Tame Valley, stands Hartshead Pike, and a little further lies Saddleworth, below the looming moors of the Pennines, where the family lived for 600 years.

After the death of his father, and his cousins Herbert Eli and Alfred, Donald had become the sole direct male descendant of Stephen Shaw. By this slender thread hung a family's connection to the past. It proved sufficient for his children to continue the Shaw name – not, perhaps, in Ashton or Saddleworth, but here are their roots.

BIBLIOGRAPHY

a) Primary Sources

- Archives
- Ancestry.co.uk
- The British Library
- Brotherton Library Special Collections, University of Leeds
- General Record Office
- District Probate Registry
- Lancashire Record Office (LRO)
- The National Archives (TNA)
- Nottinghamshire Archives
- Oldham Local Studies & Archives (OLA)
- Prerogative Courts of Canterbury
- Saddleworth Historical Society (SHS)
- Shaw Family Papers
- Tameside Local Studies &Archives (TLA)
- West Yorkshire Archives

b) Principal Sources

- The Ashton Reporter, Tameside Local Studies and Archives
- Ancestry.co.uk:
  'England and Wales Non-Conformist and Non-Parochial Registers': 1567-1970
  'England Census': 1841-1911

Manchester England, Church of England registers of Baptisms, Marriages and Burials 1541-1812
'West Yorkshire, England Select Land Tax records 1704-1932': Quick in Agbrigg, 1780-1832;

- Baines, Edward, *History, Directory & Gazetteer of the County of York*, Leeds, 1822;
- Bailey, William, *Bailey's British Directory, or merchant's and Trader's useful companion, for the year 1784:* Warrington, Birmingham & London, 1784
- *Beaumont of Whitley Collection*: Deeds of Properties in Saddleworth: West Yorkshire Archives, Kirklees DD/WBD/X/63-71
- 'Contrariants Roll, Pontefract Castle and Honor, Sadelworthfryth', 15-16 Edward II': TNA SC6/1145/21
- 'Extent of the Lordship of Longdendale, 1360': TNA SC11/897 transcription in Record Society of Lancashire and Cheshire, Vol.140
- *Foljambe of Osberton Deeds and Estate Papers*, Nottinghamshire Archives, DDFJ series
- *Harleian manuscripts*, The British Library
- 'Hearth Tax Returns for Saddleworth 1664-1674': TNA E179; SHS Bulletins 32.1, 33.2
- Higson C.E., 'Lees and its Neighbourhood': OLA H151
- Grace's Guide to British Industrial History, 'Cotton Mills in Ashton-under-Lyne', 1891
- 'Lay Subsidies: West Riding of Yorkshire, Agbrigg & Morley Wapentakes': TNA, E179 series
- 'Non-Conformist Registers': Dukinfield Cemetery

- Pigot, James, *Pigot and Co.'s National Commercial Directory of Yorkshire for 1828-9*, London & Manchester,
- 'Protestation Returns for Quick-cum-Sadleworth: 1641-1642': Parliamentary Archives: Cat. Ref. No. HL/P0/J0/10/1/109/11
- *Providence Chapel, Springhead: Monumental Inscriptions*: (OLA, L8533)
- Radcliffe, John, (ed.), *Records of Saddleworth Chapelry: 1613-1800*, Vols I and II, CDRom, Manchester & Lancashire Family History Society, 2009
- 'Ryecroft Church Records' (TLA: NC1)
- *Saddleworth & Lees Churchyard Burials*, Manchester & Lancashire Family History Society, CDRom 2005
- *Wentworth Woolley Collection,* Box 4, 8/4b and 8/5a: Brotherton Library Special Collections, University of Leeds
- *Worrall's Commercial and General Directory of Oldham, Royton, Shaw, Middleton, Lees, Saddleworth and adjoining districts*, 1880 (OLA L2624)
- *Yorkshire Archaeological Journal VI*, Yorkshire Archaeological and Historical Society, London, 1881

c) Secondary Sources

- Ackroyd, Peter, *The History of England Vol III*, Pan Macmillan 2015
- Anonymous, *Half a Century of Independency in Ashton-under-Lyne*, T Cunningham & sons Printers, Ashton-under-Lyne, 1867
- Barraclough, G., *Facsimilies of Early Cheshire Charters,* Oxford, Blackwell,1957 (TNA 942 Cheshire; TLA qL340)
- Barrow, Neil; Buckley, Mike; Petford, Alan; Sanders, Jean, *Saddleworth Villages*, Saddleworth Historical Society, Holmeprint, Ashton-under-Lyne, 2003

- Bateson, Hartley, *Providential Lives: A History of Providence Church, Springhead, 1807-1957*, Hirst, Kidd & Rennie Limited, Oldham, 1957

- Baxter, Richard, *The Poor Husbandman's Advocate to Rich Racking Landlords,* 1691; copied from the manuscript in Dr Williams' Library and edited by Frederick J Powicke, John Rylands Library, p.181

- Bebbington, David W., *Victorian Nonconformity,* Cascade Books, 2011

- Bowman, W.M., *England in Ashton-under-Lyne*, Ashton-under-Lyne Corporation, 1960

- Brierley, Morgan. *A Chapter from a Manuscipt History of Saddleworth,* Chronicle Printing Works, 1891

- Ed. Buckley, Mike; Harrison, David; Khadem, Victor; Petford, Alan; and Widdall, John, *Mapping Saddleworth Volume I, Printed Maps of the Parish 1771-1894;* Saddleworth Historical Society (SHS), Uppermill 2007; *Volume II, Manuscript Maps of the Parish 1625-1822*, SHS, Uppermill, 2010

- Buckley, Mike Ed., *St Chad's Church Saddleworth: Monumental Inscriptions in the Old Churchyard*, Saddleworth Historical Society, Uppermill, 2015

- Butterworth, J., *History and description of the town and parish of Ashton-under-Lyne*, Ashton, 1823

- Butterworth, James, *History and description of the Towns and parishes of Stockport, Ashton-under-Lyne, Mottram-Long-den-dale and Glossop*, Oldham 1827

- Butterworth, James, *The Parochial Chapelry of Saddleworth in the County of York*, Manchester 1828; re-published by SHS, Uppermill, 2006

- Camden, William, *Remains concerning Britain, 1605, Ed. R.D. Dunn, Toronto*, 1984,

- Christensen, Dr Penelope, 'English – Understanding Names in Genealogy', The National Institute for Genealogical Studies, 2012
- Clark, Gregory, *A Farewell to Alms: a brief history of the world*, Princeton University Press, 2007;
- Cooper, John, *The Queen's Agent*, Faber Faber, London, 2011
- Creighton, Charles, *A History of Epidemics in Britain*, Cambridge at the University Press, 1891;
- Currie, Robert, Gilbert, Alan, Horsley, Lee, *Churches and Churchgoers: Patterns of church growth in the British Isles since 1700*, Clarendon Press, Oxford, 1977
- Daniel, Thomas, *The Captain of Death*, University of Rochester Press, 1997
- Earwaker, J.P., *East Cheshire Past and Present, Vol II*, London, 1880, p.167
- Glover, William (compiled), *History of Ashton-under-Lyne, and the Surrounding District*, Ed. John Andrew, Reporter Office, Ashton-under-Lyne, 1884
- Fieldhouse, R., 'Social Structure from Tudor Lay Subsidies and Probate Inventories: a case study Richmondshire, (Yorkshire)': Local Population Studies 12, 1974
- Haynes, Ian, *Cotton in Ashton*, Tameside Metropolitan Borough, 1987Hey, David, *Family Names and Family History*, Hambledon, 2000
- Hill, Samuel, *Bygone Stalybridge*, 1907
- Historyofparliamentonline.org: 'STAVELEY, Sir Ralph (c.1362-c.1420), of Staveley, Cheshire',
- Howe, Anthony, *The Cotton Masters, 1830-1860,* Clarendon, 1984

- Hughes, Elizabeth, Ed., 'The Hampshire Hearth Tax Assessment 1665', Hampshire County Council, 1991
- Hurst, Peter. Ed., *Sadelworth: Garsomes, geld rents and gould, 1590-1630*, Taylor and Clifton, Uppermill, 2011
- Hurst, Peter, Ed., *Where Was Somtyme A Casstell: Ancient Records of Almondbury 1086-1638,* Taylor and Clifton, Uppermill, 2019
- Kenyon, Denise, *The Origins of Lancashire,* Manchester University Press, Manchester, 1991
- Loewenstein, David, and Mueller, Janel, Eds., *The Cambridge History of Early Modern English Literature*, Cambridge University Press, 2001
- Morton, Richard, MD, *Phthisiologia: or a treatise of consumptions,* 2nd edition printed for W & J Innys, London, 1720
- Nevell, Michael, *Tameside 1066-1700,*Tameside Metropolitan Borough Council, 1991
- Nevell, Michael & Walker, John, *Lands and Lordships in Tameside: Tameside in Transition: 1349-1642,* Tameside Metropolitan Borough Council, 1998
- Ormerod, G*., History of the County Palatine and City of Chester, Vol 3*, London, 1819
- Pincus, Steven C.A., *Protestantism and Patriotism*, Cambridge University Press, 1996,
- Reaney, P.H. & Wilson R.M., *Oxford Dictionary of English Surnames*, Oxford, 2005.
- Redmonds, George, *Yorkshire West Riding*, Phillimore, Chichester,1973
- Redmonds, George, *Christian Names in Local and Family History*, Toronto, 1935

- Roskell, J.S. Ed., Clark, L, & Rawcliffe, C, *The History of Parliament: The House of Commons 1386-1421*, 1993
- Saddleworth Historical Society Bulletins: 1971-2024
- Shaw, R. Cunliffe, *The Records of a Lancashire Family from the XIIth to the XXth century*, Preston, 1940
- Shaw, R. Cunliffe, 'Two Fifteenth Century Kinsmen, John Shaw of Duckinfield Mercer, and William Shaw of Heath Charnock', Transactions of the Historic Society of Lancashire and Cheshire, 1958, Vol.110
- Ed. Smith, Nigel, *History in the South Pennines*, Hebden Bridge Local History Society, Hebden Bridge, 2017
- Waugh, Edwin, *Home-Life of the Lancashire Factory Folk during the Cotton Famine*, reprinted from the Manchester Examiner and Times of 1862, a Public Domain Book, 2012.

NOTES

I : WHAT'S IN A NAME? (1200-1545)

1 : SURNAMES

1. William Camden, *Remains concerning Britain, 1605, Ed. R.D. Dunn, Toro*nto, 1984, p. 117
2. Ibid, pp. 115-116.
3. Lay Subsidy, Richard II, 1378/9, Qwyk: The National Archives (TNA), E 179/206/49. For transcripts of the Poll Tax returns of 1379 covering Agbrigg and Morlay Wapentakes of the West Riding, see Yorkshire Archaeological and Topographical Journal, Vol VI
4. For Sheffield see David Hey, *Family Names and Family History*, Hambledon, 2000: pp. 54-55; quotation from Henry de Huntingdon, p. 35.
5. George Redmonds, *Christian Names in Local and Family History,* Toronto, 1935, p. 178
6. Reaney & Wilson, *Oxford Dictionary of English Surnames*, Oxford, 2005.
7. List of the 50 most common surnames compiled by the Registrar General, 1853: contained in David Hey, pp. 189-192.
8. Britishsurnames.co.uk provides data on current surname numbers and analysis of the 1881 survey.
9. R Cunliffe Shaw, *The Records of a Lancashire Family from the XIIth to the XXth century*, Preston, 1940

2: STALEY MANOR

1. G. Barraclough, *Facsimilies of Early Cheshire Charters,* Oxford, Blackwell,1957, pp. 42-43
2. For the pedigree of the Staveleys of Staley Manor see: *Harleian Manuscripts*, no. 2142, The British Library; also J P Earwaker, *East Cheshire Past and Present, Vol II*, London, 1880, p. 167

3. Denise Kenyon, *The Origins of Lancashire*, Manchester University Press, Manchester, 1991 p. 104
4. For the history of Longdendale and the manor of Staley see: Michael Nevell, *Tameside 1066-1700*, Tameside Metropolitan Borough Council,1991; also M Nevell and John Walker, *Lands and Lordships in Tameside*, Metropolitan Borough Council,1998.
5. M Nevell, *Tameside: 1066-1700*, pp. 11-13
6. J P Earwaker, p. 167
7. 'The Rent Roll of John de Assheton, Tempus, first of Henry the Sixth. A.D. 1422'. Transcribed in J Butterworth, *History and description of the town and parish of Ashton-under-Lyne*, Ashton, 1823, p. 133. The italics are mine for emphasis.
8. Quoted in: John Cooper, *The Queen's Agent*, Faber Faber, London, 2011, p. 182. 'Seven feet of inheritance': ie the length of a grave; 'hic et ubique': Latin for 'here and everywhere'
9. W M Bowman, *England in Ashton-under-Lyne*, Ashton-under-Lyne Corporation, 1960, p. 90
10. Quoted from Canon Raines by: Victor Khadem, 'Early Saddleworth Records – 4, Miscellaneous Charters in the Raines MSS', *Saddleworth Historical Society (SHS) Bulletin 40.3*, 2010, p. 73
11. M. Nevell, *Tameside*, p. 42, fig.3.26; also M.Nevell & J Walker, *Lands and Lordships in Tameside*, p. 10, fig.1.2
12. See chapter 3, Note 7.
13. M. Nevell, *Tameside*, p. 128
14. V.M. Bowman, p. 90
15. G.Ormerod, *History of the County Palatine and City of Chester, Vol 3*, London, 1819, p. 416; also J P Earwaker, p. 165
16. M.Nevell, *Tameside*, p. 112
17. J. Butterworth, *History and Description of the Town and Parish of Ashton-under-Lyne*, Ashton, 1823, p. 126
18. 'Extent of the Lordship of Longdendale, 1360', TNA: SC11/897 (M3); transcribed in: *Record Society of Lancashire and Cheshire, Vol.140*, 2005
19. 'Trial by Combat': Tameside Local Studies and Archives, DDSW/ Med/3
20. For an account of the life of Sir Ralph Staveley see: 'STAVELEY, Sir Ralph (c.1362-c.1420), of Staveley, Cheshire',

historyofparliamentonline.org; also published in *The History of Parliament: The House of Commons 1386-1421.* J S Roskell (Ed.), L Clark, C Rawcliffe, 1993

21. V M Bowman, pp. 48, 50: cited by J M Hunt, 'The Staley Rental', *SHS Bulletin 16.3*, 1986, pp. 38-42

22. V.M.Bowman pp. 48, 50; See also Mike Buckley, 'The origins and evolution of a Pennine township: medieval and early modern settlement in Saddleworth'; in Nigel Smith (Ed.), *History in the South Pennines*, Hebden Bridge Local History Society, Hebden Bridge, pp. 250 & 255-256. Also *SHS Bulletin 16.3, 1986,* p. 40

23. G. Ormerod, p. 415

24. James Butterworth, *A History and Description of the Town and Parish of Ashton-under-Lyne,* pp. 144, 146

25. Various accounts of the legend can be found, for example: James Butterworth, *History and description of the Towns and parishes of Stockport, Ashton-under-Lyne, Mottram, Longdendale and Glossop*, Oldham 1827; Samuel Hill, *Bygone Stalybridge*, 1907; also V M Bowman p. 90.

3: THE MANOR DEL SCHAGHE

1. For an account of the Stapleton family and the early history of Saddleworth see M.Buckley, 'Seeing through a glass darkly', *SHS Bulletin 39.2*, 2009, pp. 29ff

2. For a study of enclosures and estate sub-divisions in early Saddleworth, see: Mike Buckley, 'The origins and evolution of a Pennine township', Ed. Nigel Smith, *History in the South Pennines,* Hebden Bridge, 2017, pp. 231-282

3. See Note 1 above. 'Staveley Charters': *Wentworth Woolley Collection*, University of Leeds, Brotherton Library Special Collections, MS 1946/1 Box 4.

4. See M. Buckley, 'The Schagh Halmote Court Roll, 1401', *SHS Bulletin 48.2*, 2018, p. 36 and FN 32.

5. Mike Buckley, 'Seeing Through a Glass Darkly', *SHS Bulletin 39.2, 2009,* p. 36

6. 'Feoffment of land in Saddleworth, 1293': *Beaumont of Whitley Collection*, West Yorkshire Archives, Kirklees: WBD/X/63; transcribed in Michael Buckley, 'Saddleworth Records Part 4', *SHS Bulletin 11.2, 1981*, pp. 29-30

7. 'Feet of Fines Octave of Martinmas, 33 Edward I', The National Archives (TNA) CP25/1/269/81; quoted by Mike Buckley, 'Seeing Through a Glass Darkly', *SHS Bulletin 39.2*, p. 37. Documents at this time often refer to Saddleworth as Quick.

8. 'Contrariants Roll, Pontefract Castle and Honor, Sadelworthfryth, 15-16 Edward II, 1322/3': TNA SC6/1145/2. Transcription in: Ed. Peter Hurst, *Where Was Somtyme A Casstell: Ancient Records of Almondbury 1086-1638,* Uppermill, 2019, pp. 36-38

9. R. Cunliffe Shaw, *The Records of a Lancashire Family, Preston, 1940, p. vii*

10. 'Ricus fil Robert de Staveley de Sadelworth'; TNA: C241/55/75, 14 May 1307; C241/53/68: 15 June 1307. 'Ricus fil Robert de Stavelay del Schaghe'; TNA: C241/55/1, 10 January 1307/8 (3 Marks = £2)

11. TNA, KB27/173/m34

12. The charter recording the lease of land by William del Schaghe to John de Radclyffe dated 10 December 1351 is referred to as evidence in later court cases, including: TNA, KB/27/526 and TNA, JUST1/1517 m17; for a detailed account of the legal dispute see M.Buckley, 'The Schage Helmote Court Roll, 1401', *SHS Bulletin 48.2*, 2018, pp. 31-39

13. Recorded in M.Buckley, 'The Schage Helmote Court Roll, 1401', pp. 33-34, FM17, 19 and 20. Also R. Cunliffe Shaw, *The Records of a Lancashire Family, Preston, 1940, p. 15, FN1*

14. V M Bowman pp. 48, 50: cited by J M Hunt, 'The Staley Rental', *SHS Bulletin 16.3,* 1986, pp. 38-42

15. 'Rolls of the Collectors in the West Riding of Yorkshire of the Lay Subsidy, 2 Richard II, Wapentake of Morlay, 1379'; TNA E179/270/21; transcribed in *Yorkshire Archaeological Journal VI*, p. 279: Yorkshire Archaeological and Historical Society, London, 1881

16. 'Grant: Manor of Schaghe in Qwyke: 1. Robert son of William del Schaghe; 2. John de Assheton Knight; 2 Henry IV, 14 August 1401'; *Foljambe of Osberton, Deeds and estate papers*: Nottinghamshire Archives, DD/FJ/1/265/4

17. 'Robert son of William del Schaghe: grant of manor of the Schaghe'; Nottinghamshire Archives: DD/FJ/1/265/6

18. 'Agreement: 1) John de Assheton kt, 2) Rob s. of Wm. Del Schaghe, 11 Henry IV, 19 April 1410': Nottinghamshire Archives: DD/FJ/1/265/7

19. R. Cunliffe Shaw, 'Two Fifteenth Century Kinsmen, John Shaw of Duckinfield Mercer, and William Shaw of Heath Charnock', *Transactions of the Historic Society of Lancashire and Cheshire*, 1958, Vol.110

4: RAMIFICATION

1. 'Court Roll of Manor of the Schaghe for Halmote:' Nottinghamshire Archives: DD/FJ/6/6/20

2. TNA, Assize at York, 3 Henry IV, JUST 1/1517 m17; see also Mike Buckley, 'The Schagh Halmote Court Roll, 1401', *SHS Bulletin 48.2, 2018,* p. 32, FN 9

3. R.Fieldhouse: 'Social Structure from Tudor Lay Subsidies and Probate Inventories: a case study Richmondshire, (Yorkshire)': *Local Population Studies 12, 1974*, pp. 9-24. Fieldhouse calculates that about 55% of households in Richmond were required to pay the lay subsidy, while 45% were exempt because the value of their goods fell below the threshold for payment.

4. 'Lay Subsidy granted by Parliament 1545, Agbrigg and Morlay Wapentakes': TNA, E179/207/186; Thoresby Society Publications, Vol XI pp. 349-350

5. 'Deed of Feoffment from John Fernele', *Beaumont of Whitley Collection*: WBD/X/65; West Yorkshire Archives, Kirklees. Also *SHS Bulletin 11.2, 1981*, p. 30

6. Contrariants Roll 1322, TNA SC6/1145/2. See Note 8, Chapter 3

7. 'Ramsden Account Book': West Yorkshire Archives Service, Kirklees, DD/RA/F/4a. Transcribed in Peter Hurst (Ed.), *Sadelworth: Garsomes, Geld Rents and Gould*, Taylor and Clifton, Uppermill, 2011

8. 1322: Contrariants Roll; 1379: Poll Tax; 1397/8: Staley Rental; 1401/10: Helmote del Schaghe; 1545: Lay Subsidy; 1590: Saddleworth Manor Rentals

9. George Redmonds, *Christian Names in Local and Family History*, Toronto, 1935, pp. 173-177

10. Author's survey of twelve settlements in 1379 and 1545: Qwyk, Slaithwaite, Huddersfield, Eland, Crosland, Meltham, Holmfirth,

Honlay, Fernlay Tyas, Thurstonland, Almondbury and Wharmby. There are no separate records for Marsden in 1379, but records are included in this survey for 1545.

11. Own 'country': indicating a local area beyond which migration rarely took place. See David Hey, *Family Names and Family History,* Hambledon, 2000, p. 126; also George Edmonds, *Yorkshire West Riding,* London 1973, p. 214.

12. Carolyn C Fenwick, 'Salford Wapentake, 1379'; 'Taxation in Salford Hundred', 1524-1802', Chetham Society Vol 83

13. 'Yorkshire Lay Subsidies, 1545, Agbrigg and Morley Wapentakes', Thoresby Society Publications, Vol IX pp. 313-316, and Vol XI pp. 101-129 and pp. 338-368

14. Ed. Carolyn C. Fenwick, 'Salford Wapentake 1379', *The Poll Taxes of 1377, 1379 and 1382,* Part I, OUP, 1997, pp. 461-469.

15. 'Protestation Returns, York' and 'Protestation Returns, Lancaster', Parliamentary Archives

16. See Peter Hurst, Ed, *Almondbury: Where was Somtyme a Castell,* Taylor and Clifton, Uppermill, 2019

17. See Chapter 9: 'Will of Marie Whewall, 8 July 1658', PROB11/283

II : SADDLEWORTH

5 : TENANTS AT WILL

1. Denise Kenyon, pp. 107, 137. See also M.Buckley, 'Seeing through a glass darkly', pp. 26, 27; and 'The origins and evolution of a Pennine Township', p. 233.

2. James Butterworth, *The Parochial Chapelry of Saddleworth in the County of York,* Manchester 1828; re-published by The Saddleworth Historical Society, Uppermill 2006, p. 13

3. Yorkshire Lay Subsidies, 1545, Thoresby Society Publications, Vol XI

4. Peter Hurst, Ed., *Sadelworth: Garsomes, geld rents and gould, 1590-1630,* Taylor and Clifton, Uppermill, 2011pp. 1-9

5. See Michael Buckley, 'Saddleworth Hearth Tax Returns': 1664: *SHS Bulletin 31.3,* 2001, pp. 13-15; TNA E179/210/393.

6. Edward Baines, *History, Directory & Gazetteer of the County of York*, Leeds, 1822; James Pigot, *Directory of Yorkshire*, 1818, 1829 and 1834

7. When the future King Charles II was on the run from Cromwell's forces in 1651, one of the disguises he adopted was that of a tenant farmer's son.

8. Various forms of lease were introduced in the 17th and early 18th centuries and become important to our family story then – see chapter 13.

9. 'Court of Chancery, Shawe v Shawe: 1666', TNA, C 8/183/156.

10. Peter Hurst, Ed., *Sadelworth,* p.xix

11. Provided by Mike Buckley. Transcribed from the original now in the possession of the landlord of the Farrers Arms Public House, Grasscroft

12. Lease to James Whewall of Ballgreave, 1612: *Beaumont of Whitley Collection*: WBD/X/68; West Yorkshire Archives, Kirklees.

13. 'Edmund Shawe of Overmylne, leasee': Saddleworth Archives, H/HOW/GS pp. 136ff.

14. Lease to Robert Shay of Saddleworth husbandman, 1648/9, WBD/X/71; *recorded in SHS Bulletin 11.2.*

6 : EVEN SUCH IS TIME

1. Will of Joseph Scolefeild of Arthurs, 1713, LRO: WCW/Supra/ C304B/6; Will of Gyles Shawe of Boarshurst, 1634, LRO, WCW/ Supra/C113a/10; Will of John Whewall of Tunstead, 1641: LRO WCW/Supra/C1338/27; Will of Thomas Shaw Senior of Uppermill,1727, LRO:WCW/Supra/C340B/34.

2. Gregory Clark, *A Farewell to Alms: a brief history of the world*, Princeton University Press, 2007, pp. 111-120. See also Statista. com

3. Charles Creighton, *A History of Epidemics in Britain,* Cambridge at the University Press, 1891; Willis p. 570; Holland p. 505; stupor p. 572; plague pp. 542-543

4. Gregory Clark, p. 116

5. ibid, p. 122

6. Charles Creighton, quoting from Thomas Willis, *Diatribae Duae, 1659*: 'some blast of the stars': p. 570; fever epidemic and Cromwell: p. 574

7. Richard Morton MD, *Phthisiologia: or a treatise of consumptions*, 2nd edition printed for W & J Innys, London, 1720

8. Thomas Daniel, *The Captain of Death,* University of Rochester Press, 1997

9. Ed. Mike Buckley, *St Chad's Church Saddleworth: Monumental Inscriptions in the Old Churchyard*, Saddleworth Historical Society, Uppermill, 2015, No.470, p. 83

10. Ibid, No.171, p. 37

11. Unless otherwise stated, parish records are found in: John Radcliffe (ed.), *Records of Saddleworth Chapelry: 1613-1800, Vol. I*, CD-Rom, Manchester & Lancashire Family History Society; for images of the original entries see *Ancestry.co.uk: Manchester England Church of England Baptisms, Marriages and Burials 1541-1812;*

12. John Radcliffe (ed.), *Vol I*, p. 423 and Vol II pp. 534-539.

7 : THE OLD ORDER CHANGETH

1. 'Protestation Returns for Quick-cum-Sadleworth, Agbrigg Wapentake*: 1641-1642*', Parliamentary Archives: HL/P0/J0/10/1/109/11;

2. See 'A Godly Preaching Minister: John Wild, minister of Saddleworth 1583-1592', *SHS Bulletin 18.1*, 1988, pp. 6-7

3. Richard Baxter, *The Poor Husbandman's Advocate to Rich Racking Landlords,* 1691, p. 190

4. Lord Fauconberg, quoted by Steven C.A.Pincus, *Protestantism and Patriotism*, Cambridge University Press, 1996, p. 215

5. James Butterworth, *The Parochial Chapelry of Saddleworth*, p. 36.

6. Population estimate for 1379 is derived from poll tax returns, allowing for households of five, plus single individuals, plus 10% non-enumeration, and rounded. Figures for 1545 make similar assumptions plus 10%/45% non-enumeration. National calculations indicate a 13% population growth in 1379-1545. For other population estimates see: B. Barnes, 'Early Woollen Mills

in a Pennine Parish', *SHS Bulletin 13.2, 1983,* p. 26; William White (ed.), *Directory and Topography of the Borough of Leeds and the Whole of the Clothing District of the West Riding of Yorkshire,* Sheffield, 1842, p. 496; M. Fox, 'Saddleworth in 1841 – a view through the census', *SHS Bulletin 26.3*, 1996, p. 9.

7. 'Indenture, 2 Feb 1713 between Jo: Farrer of Ewood, Yorkshire, Esq. of the one part & Thos Shaw of Lowerhouse in Saddleworth, Clothmaker of the other part', Manchester Libraries Archives, Owen MSS, Book 44. P.229; GB127.M740/8/21/1/4/9; copy on microfilm MF573; provided by Mike Buckley

8. John Goodchild, 'John Radcliffe: 1756-1840', *SHS Bulletin 29.2,* 1999, p. 3

9. Edward Baines, p. 263

10. James Butterworth, *The Parochial Chapelry of Saddleworth,* pp. 5-8

11. James Pigot, P*igot and Co.'s National Commercial Directory for 1828-9,* London & Manchester, pp. 1057-1058

12. G Woodhead, 'The Peterloo Massacre and the Saddleworth Connection', *SHS Bulletin 32.1*, 2001, p. 3

13. David Cressy, *'Levels of Illiteracy in England, 1530-1730'*, The Historical Journal 20.1, 1977; *'Literacy and the Social Order'*, Cambridge, 1980

14. Quoted in Ed. David Loewenstein and Janel Mueller, *The Cambridge History of Early Modern English Literature*, CUP, 2001, p. 288

15. Richard Baxter, *The Poor Husbandman's Advocate to Rich Racking Landlords,* 1691; Ed. Frederick J Powicke, 'copied from the manuscript in Dr Williams' Library', p. 181. Baxter also comments a few lines later, however: 'Yea, abundance, bred in toil and poverty, cannot read, nor cannot have their children taught to read.'

16. Will of Marie Whewall, 8 July 1658, PROB11/283; LRO Wills: Michael Shaw of Ryetop, 1703, WCW/Supra/C2771/67; Michael Shaw of Ryetop. 1759, WCW/Supra/435A/63

17. 'Shawe v Broadbent, Hearings of the Commission of the Court of Chancery', 1666, TNA: C 22/912/11

18. John Shawe and his wife Margaret v William Broadbent, 1679-1680: TNA: E 134/31/Chas2/Mich14

19. Will of Henry Shaw of Lane, 1689: LRO: WCW/Supra/C255B/5; Will of Joseph Scolefeild of Arthurs, 1713, LRO: WCW/Supra/ C304B/6; Inventory of Henry Shaw husbandman, prized 1702, LRO: WCW/Infra/C1383/57

20. 'Will of William Shaw of Boarshurst, 1701', LRO, WCW/Supra/ C275B/14. 'Indenture of Apprenticeship 1674', SHS Bulletin 2.3, 1972, p. 41. 'Will of John Shaw of Boorshurst, 1697': LRO, WCW/Infra/C1370/94; 'Will of Thomas Hawkyard of Thamewater, 1731', LRO: WCW/Supra/C358/17.

21. 'Will of William Shaw of Grottonhead, 1782', LRO, WCW/ Supra/C511A/54

22. Morgan Brierley, *A Chapter from a Manuscipt History of Saddleworth,* Chronicle Printing Works, 1891, pp. 8-11. The curate John Lees is thought to have carried out some teaching in St Chad's from 1655.

23. 'Will of Ralph Hawkyard, 1729': LRO, WCW/Supra/C350/67

24. Morgan Brierley, ibid, pp. 18, 40, 62

III : BOARSHURST (1590-1770)

8 : WILLIAM AND KATRINE

1. For garsome payments, see Peter Hurst, *Sadelworth*; also West Yorkshire Archives, Kirklees: DD/RA/F/4a and 4b.

2. James Butterworth, 'The Parochial Chapelry of Saddleworth', p. 57

3. See Chapter 8, FN 18

4. 'Lay Subsidy granted by Parliament 1545, Agbrigg and Morlay Wapentakes': TNA, E179/207/186. 'uxor John Whewall' = wife of John Whewall.

5. Peter Hurst, *Sadelworth,* pp. 2-4.

6. ibid, pp. 7 & 9; 18 & 20; 14 & 17. vijs = 7 shillings; 4li = £4; ijs viijd = 2 shillings and 8 pence

7. ibid pp. 18 and 20: Manorial record of 13 April 1612: 'Rec. of Edmunde Shawe new house in pte of his garsome £5.16s.3d. – and 40s before for his admittance'; followed by on 2 February 1612: 'Rec. of Edmund Shaw of Boarshurst in full payment £5. 16s. 3d'.

8. According to evidence given to a court of Chancery dispute, Gyles held two tenancies at the time of his death, one of 20 acres and the other of 10 acres. 'Shawe v Shawe', 1666: TNA, C 8/186/156. See chapter 10.

9. Peter Hurst, Sadelworth, p. 4: undated Manorial record, probably of 1591: 'William Shawe & Gyles ijs viijd 3° and they to bulde the howse … & William Shawe & Gyles muste paye after the rate of 3° for 6 yeares. The house built jointly by William and Giles may have been the 'new house' or workshop that became part of a legal dispute amongst Giles's descendants 32 years after his death: see chapter 10.

10. 'Will of William Shawe of the Borshurst, 23 October 1623', Lancashire Record Office (LRO): WCW/Supra/C90B/5

11. Nationalarchives.gov.uk/currency converter. The sum of £47. 17s. 04d in 1620 is calculated to be equivalent to 957 days' work by a skilled tradesman in 2017.

12. Four year's later, the reversion of the lease for William's widow Katrine, who had inherited ¾ of the tenancy, was 55 shillings. This too is consistent with these calculations for a 21 year lease.

13. 'Will of Katrine/Katterene Shawe, late wife of William Shaw, 25 December 1627', LRO: WCW/Infra/C1330A/78. Ralph Shawe was Katrine's brother-in-law, the brother of her husband William. John Shaw of Boarshurst was the eldest son of William's cousin Giles Shaw. Francis Whewall was the husband of William and Katrine Shaw's daughter Marie. William Cartwright was a neighbour whose freehold land at Greenfield Stye became the subject of a legal dispute after his death (see chapter 11).

14. The payments by the under-tenants amounted to 20 shillings a year. By way of comparison, William Shawe, who held the manorial tenancy, paid an annual rent of 11s.4d. in 1590. Although garsome payments on the manorial estate tended to increase each time a lease was renewed, typically after 21 years, rental payments customarily remained relatively static.

15. 'Will of George Shawe of Sadleworth', 28 January 1600/1', LRO, WCW/Infra/1600.

16. Ralph's tenancy passed through his son Richard to a Henry Shaw who died in 1703. Henry's son, John Shaw of Boarshurst (1686-1744), paid rent of 4s. 0d. In 1719. This John's widow Elizabeth

Shaw occupied tenancy 137 at Boarshurst in 1770, with 'about 4 or 5 bays of very old Thatched Housing in length about 23 yards'. In 1789 John and Elizabeth's children, Henry and James Shaw, were the occupants. See: 'Will of Henry Shaw of Saddleworth, 10 January 1710': LRO: WCW/Infra/ C1383/57; 'Rental Records', *Wentworth Woolley Collection* Box 8/5; Ed. M.Buckley etc, *Mapping Saddleworth Vol II*, p. 89.

17. Peter Hurst, *Sadelworth*, pp. 2, 8 and 10
18. 'Will of Edmunde Shawe of the Boarshurst, husbandman, 3 October 1623', LRO WCW/1624
19. 'Will of Marie Whewall, 8 July 1658', PROB11/283;
20. 'Proceedings of the Court Baron of the Manor of Quick in the year 1636', Saddleworth Historical Society Archives. John Whewall would die in 1641 – see his will at: LRO, WCW/Supra/ C1338/27

9 : FIVE CHILDREN

1. 'Will of Edmunde Shawe of the Boarshurst, husbandman: 1623', LRO, WCW/Supra/C90B/6
2. 'Will of Marie Whewall, 8 July 1658', PROB11/283; 'Will of Francis Whewall husbandman of Boegreave in the parish of Sadleworth, 29 March 1650': PROB11/269
3. Charles Creighton, p. 372; quoting H. Whitmore MD, *'Febris Anomala'*, London, 1659.: p. 572
4. For a study of the cultivation of flax and the production of linen in Saddleworth, see: Elizabeth Paget, 'No longer a singularity: linen production in Saddleworth in the seventeenth century': Nigel Smith (Ed.), *History in the South Pennines*, Hebden Bridge, 2017
5. The child Robert is named in Edmund's will, but not in William's two weeks later. Joane is named in William's will but not in Edmund's.
6. David Pedgley, in his valuable research into the Shaws of Boarshurst (SHS Bulletins 25.3 and 25.4), takes it that Robert was the father of Thomas Shaw, born in about 1628; but I find no evidence for this and think it unlikely.
7. Francis Whewall named 'George Shaw of Boarshurst' as an overseer of his will in 1650. This George was the son of Gyles

Shawe, now a relatively wealthy yeoman farmer at Boarshurst (see chapter 10). William Shawe's son George held lands at Lower House, Boarshurst and is presumed to have died earlier in 1638 or 1642. We can note that Marie Whewall's will refers to her 'kinsman John Shaw of Lower House' to distinguish him from Gyles's son, 'John Shaw of Boarshurst'.

10 : THE GYLES SHAWE INHERITANCE

1. 'Will of Adam Shaw of Saddleworth, 27 November 1583', SHS Archives
2. 'Inventory of Alice Shaw of Saddleworth, widdowwoman, 2 May 1609', LRO WCW/Infra/C1326B/100
3. 'Henry Shawe Bill of Complaint: Shawe v Shawe in the Court of Chancery, 1666': TNA C8/186/156.
4. 'Will of Gyles Shawe of Boarshurst, 1634', LRO: WCW/Supra/C113a/10
5. 'Will of Gyles Shawe of Boarshurst, husbandman, 19 September 1634', LRO WCW/Supra/C113a/110
6. An account of Gyles and his sons is given by David Pedgely, 'The Shaw Family of Boarshurst, Part One', *SHS Bulletin 25.3*, 1995, pp. 6-9.
7. 'Inventory of John Shawe of Boarshurst Yeoman, 1665': LRO, WCW/Supra/C167A/14
8. 'Feet of fines': TNA, CP,25/2/523. The record mentions John Shaw senior and a John Shaw junior: the latter must have been a son who did not live long. 'Will of John Shaw of Boarshurst, Yeoman, 7 August 1665': LRO WCW/Supra/C167A/14
9. 'Will of George Shaw of Boarshurst, Yeoman, 22 April 1653': LRO Supra/C167A/13. The will is dated 22 April 1653 but was not proved until 27 January 1665: The testimony to the Court of Chancery given by Mary Shaw, Ralph Andrew and Sarah Andrew in 1666 clarifies that George Shaw died 'about thirteene yeares since' – ie in 1653. They also give testimony that he lived with John Shaw later in his life. TNA C8/183/156
10. 'Will of Thomas Shaw of Saddleworth, 7 October 1650': Prerogative Courts of Canterbury, PROB11/215. For the purchase of lands, see 'Old Saddleworth', *SHS Bulletin 7.4*, 1977, p. 81;

and David Pedgeley, 'The Shaw Family of Boarshurst, Part One', *SHS Bulletin 25.3, 1995, p. 8*

11. See 'Shaw Hall As It Was', *SHS Bulletin 6.3, 1976, p. 34.* Ed.Mike Buckey et al, *'Mapping Saddleworth Volumes I and II'*, SHS Uppermill, 2007 and 2020, show plantation woodland covering the hillside in 1822 (Vol II), 1854 and 1892 (Vol I).

12. Datestone, *SHS Bulletin, 6.4, 1976,* p. 53. 'Conveyance of land at Grotton', *SHS Bulletin 7.4, 1977*, p. 81. 'Will of Henry Shaw of Lane, Yeoman, 26 October 1689', LRO WCW/Supra/C255B/5

13. 'Henry Shawe Bill of Complaint', 1666; 'The Joint and Severall Answeres of Mary Shawe Raph Andrew & Sarah his wife Defendants', 1666: TNA C8/186/156. 'Mary Shawe Complaint', 4 December 1668: TNA C8/183/170

14. 'Quit Claim, Henry Shaw of Lane', 1666/7, provided by Mike Buckley

11 : LOWER HOUSE

1. Charles Creighton, pp. 569-570, quoting from Thomas Willis, *Diatribae Duae, 1659.*

2. There were in fact two houses – the main house and a 'little house' – as well as a barn and outhousing. See chapters 11 and 13. If the two boys were descended from George Shaw rather than Robert Shaw, as we suggest, then Uncle John was technically their 'first cousin once removed'. However, given the close family ties and the age gap between them of almost 40 years, it is unsurprising that his is referred to as 'uncle' in an Indenture of Apprenticeship' (see Chapter 12 and Note 8) and his wife Margarett as 'aunt' in William's will of 1701 (see chapter 12 and Note 1).

3. D F E Sykes, *The History of Huddersfield*, 1906, p. 181, quoting T.B. Macaulay; Elizabeth Hughes (Ed.) 'The Hampshire Hearth Tax Assessement 1665', Hampshire County Council, 1991

4. 'Saddleworth Hearth Tax Returns': 1664: TNA E179/210/395: *SHS Bulletin 31.3, 2001,* pp. 11-15; 1670: TNA: E179/210/411: *SHS Bulletin 32.1 2002*, pp. 17-21; 1672: TNA E179/210/413; 1674: TNA: E179/262/13, SHS Bulletin *33.2 2003*, pp. 6-13.

5. J M Hunt, 'Saddleworth Corn Tithes in 1669', *SHS Bulletin 14.2 1984*

6. 'Will of John Shaw of Boorshurst 1692 and Inventory 1696/7': LRO WCW C1370/94. A sum of £27 is calculated as the equivalent of 300 days' wages for a skilled tradesman in 2017: nationalarchives.co.uk/currency converter.
7. 'Shawe v Broadbent, Hearings of the Commission of the Court of Chancery', TNA, C 10/86/72 (1662); C22/912/11 (1660-1684); C 22/826/45 (1666-1668); E 134/31/Chas2/Mich14 (1679).
8. 'Shawe v Broadbent': TNA: C 22/826/45

12 : THE LAST HUSBANDMAN

1. 'Will of William Shaw husbandman of Lower House in Boarshurst within Sadleworth, 7 June 1701', LRO WCW/Supra/C275B/14
2. Assuming a standard 21 year lease, a remaining period of 11 or 12 years valued at £22 implies an entry fine of more than £40.
3. Nationalarchives.gov.uk/currency converter: £59. 01s. 08d. in 1700 equates to 656 days' wages for a skilled tradesman in 2017. See also chapter 8, note 11, and chapter 11 note 6.
4. 'Will of John Whitehead of Kinders, 9 April 1708', OLA L24532
5. J E Wood, 'The Whitehead Family', *SHS Bulletin 1.3,* 1971, p. 6
6. 'A map of Mr Giles Shaw's Estates, to wit, Furlane Carrbarn and Upper-Mill all within Saddleworth in the West Riding of the County of York, measured by John Lees 1766': Ed. M Buckley, D Harrison, V Khadem, A Petford and J Widdall, *Mapping Saddleworth Vol II, Manuscript Maps of the Parish 1625-1822*: Saddleworth Historical Society, Uppermill 2010: pp. 16-21
7. 'Indenture of Apprenticeship', SHS Archives M/HOW/1a; reproduced by B.Barnes in *SHS Bulletin 2.3*, 1972, p. 41
8. 'Indenture of Apprenticeship: Thomas Hayes son of James Hayes Tailor of Audley in the county of Stafford': 2 February 1842, Shaw Family Papers

13 : THE LAST SHAW OF LOWER HOUSE

1. John Radcliffe, Vol. I
2. *Wentworth Woolley Collection*, Box 8/5: Brotherton Library Special Collections, University of Leeds. Several tenants held more than one tenancy on the same manorial lease, sub-letting at

a profit. But I do not cover that here. I am grateful to Mike Buckley for his advice on manorial leases.

3. *Wentworth Woolley Collection*, Box 8/5

4. John Radcliffe, Vol II, p. 425

5. Peter Hurst, *Sadelworth*, p. 87

6. Ed. M. Buckley; *St Chad's Church Saddleworth: Monumental Inscriptions in the Old Churchyard:* SHS Uppermill 2015, Entry no. 345, p. 65: 'Here was buried the body of Hugh son of John Shaw of Halls who departed this life the 27th Dec 1760 in the 14th year of his age. Also Mary his wife June 5th in the 68 year of her age. Also John Shaw of Birches, late of Halls, who departed this life March 8th 1799 in the 80 year of his age.'

7. The will of John Platt of Boarshurst in 1671 names two children: a son John who was to inherit the tenancy and a daughter Ellen, who had married Thomas Bentley. It appears that the son John died soon afterwards, leaving his sister Ellen to inherit the tenancy. LRO WCW//Infra/C1342/66.

8. 'Indenture 2 Feb 1713 between Jo: Farrer of Ewood, Yorkshire, Esq. of the one part & Thos Shaw of Lowerhouse in Saddleworth, Clothmaker of the other part'. Manchester Libraries Archives, Owen MSS, Book 44, Page 229; provided by Mike Buckley

9. *Wentworth Woolley Collection*, Box 8/5: Brotherton Library Special Collections, University of Leeds. John Bentley also paid 6 shillings pa for 7 acres at Boarshurst and 7shillings pa for a 15 acre tenancy at Saddleworth Fold (jointly numbered No. 4 in the 1770 survey)

10. ibid

11. Historicengland.org.uk: 'The Farmhouse and the Cottage, Boarshurst Lane', List Entry Number 1309759

12. *Wentworth Woolley Collection, Box 8/5*

13. 'Manor of Saddleworth or Quick, Court Papers 1743-1784': *Wentworth Woolley Collection*, Box 8/4b

14. ibid

15. Radcliffe Vol I; also Ed. Mike Buckley, *St Chad's Church Saddleworth: Monumental Inscriptions in the Old Churchyard*, Saddleworth Historical Society, Uppermill, 2015: gravestone no. 276. His son William is buried at gravestone no. 277.

IV : SHAWHOUSES

14 : WILLIAM AND THE HAWKYARDS

1. The early tenants of Shawhouses are named in manorial records for 1590-1612: see P. Hurst, *Sadelworth.* The three relevant wills are: 1. Will of George Shaw of Shawhouses, 1633, LRO Supra/C110B/18: this names Ralphe Shawe as his father, to whom he bequeathed £2; also his son George, the first of his seven children and an executor of the will; 2. Inventory of George Shaw Junior of Shawhouses, 1633: LRO Supra/C110B/19: this lists among his assets 'the halfe of the lease'; 3. Will of John Shaw of Shawhouses, 1627: LRO Supra/C96B/21: this names his brother Bernard and Bernard's daughter Ellen but no sons; it also bequeaths 12d to 'John Shawe sonne of George Shawe', a probable godson who appears to have inherited his father George's tenancy. The inventories of all three wills were prized, among others, by Francis Whewall, whose wife Marie was the daughter of William Shawe of Boarshurst, and whose niece married John Shaw of Shawhouses.

2. This is not the same Ralphe Shawe as William Shawe's brother, Ralphe of Boarshurst. See also the will of Bryan Haselgreauffe of Knarr, 1618 which records that 'Raphe Shawe and George Shaw his sonne de shawe houses' owe £5.13s.4d. payable on Swithins day. LRO: WCW/Supra/C70B/5

3. Baxter, Reverend Richard, pp. 179-180

4. Peter Hurst, *Sadelworth,* pp. 81-83.

5. *Wentworth Woolley Collection*, Box 8/5: 1739: 'Widow Hawkyard & Executors of Thomas Hawkyard for Tamewater: £1. 15s. part ffine part racke; also for Third part of Wadhill: 1s.8d.'; Will of Thomas Hawkyard of Thamewater, 1731: LRO:WCW/Supra/C358/17

6. Will of Thomas Hawkyard of Thamewater, 1743: LRO: WCW/Supra/C388/12. His legacies included £50 from his half-brother Ralph Hawkyard, who had died in 1729 aged 39. However the legacy from Ralph was conditional on him reaching the age of 21; it would otherwise be used to increase the endowment of a school in Saddleworth.

7. Will of Ralph Hawkyard of Thamewater, 1729, LRO: WCW/ Supra/C350/67
8. Neil Barrow et al, *Saddleworth Villages,* SHS, 2003, p. 67

15 : SHAWHOUSES DIVIDED

1. LRO: WCW/Supra/C352/107. Jonathan's land at Barn was near Saddleworth Fold – not the manorial tenancy of Barn in Shaw Mere, adjacent to Gibbs, Wellihole and Lanehead, all of which farms were also occupied by families named Shaw. A list of people owing money to Jonathan includes William Shaw of Shawhouses, who owed £2. Jonathan's assets were valued at £166.
2. See chapter 13. Thomas Shaw Senior (1682-1747/8) had inherited the Lower House tenancy in 1701. On his death, his eldest son, William (1701-1772), born to his first wife, inherited the tenancy, but died in Grottonhead in 1772. His second son, by his second wife, was Thomas Shaw Junior, who married Jane Buckley in 1730.
3. *Wentworth Woolley Collection,* Box 8/5
4. John Radcliffe, Vol 2, p. 546
5. Admon John Shaw of Gowburnclough, 1789, LRO WCW/Supra/ C536A/37; nationalarchives.gov.uk/currency converter: £339 in 1790 = 2,260 days wages for a skilled tradesman

16 : GOLBURNCLOUGH

1. See Chapter 14. 'to my cousin William Shaw': 'Will of Thomas Hawkyard, 1743,'LRO: WCW/Supra/C388/12
2. Ed. M.Buckley et al, 'Mapping Saddleworth Vol II', pp. 16-22
3. 'West Yorkshire England Select Land Tax Records, Agbrigg Division'
4. Ed. M Buckley et al, *Mapping Saddleworth Vol II,* p. 90
5. 'West Yorkshire England Select Land Tax Records', Agbrigg Division, 1782
6. *Wentworth Woolley Collection*, Box 8/4b
7. Historicengland.org.uk, 'Golburn Cottage, Higher Golburn', List Entry Number 1067424

V : QUICK MERE (1764-1881)

17 : THORNLEE

1. From 1800 onwards, unless stated otherwise, Church records are sourced from the 'Manchester, England, Church of England' records at Ancestry.co.uk .

2. 'Will of Henry Shaw Yeoman of Lane', 1688, LRO: Supra/ C255B/5; 'Will of James Shaw Yeoman of Lane', 1733, LRO: Supra/C363A/31. See also the gravestone of James Shaw: *St Chad's Church Saddleworth, Monumental Inscriptions in the Old Churchyard*, SHS, Uppermill, 2015, No.74, p. 23

3. 'Will of Thomas Shaw, Yeoman, of Lane', 1776, LRO: Supra/ C493B/3

4. Thomas's children: Mary, 1736, in 7th year; John, Yeoman of Loadhill Platting, 1748, aged 23; Mary, wife of John Stuart of Manchester, 1774 aged 36; also her daughter Jane, 1778, in 4th year: see also Ed. M.Buckley, *St Chad's Church Saddleworth, Monumental Inscriptions in the Old Churchyard*, No.81, p. 24

5. 'Will of Thomas Shaw, Clothier, of Brownhill', 1785, LRO: Supra/C524A/47

6. Ed. Mike Buckley, *St Chad's Church Saddleworth, Monumental Inscriptions in the Old Churchyard*, p. 24

7. Mike Buckley et al, *Mapping Saddleworth Vol II*: pp. 96-127

8. Records relating to the Shaws of Grottonhead are drawn from: 'West Yorkshire England Select Land Tax Records 1704-1932, Agbrigg Division', Ancestry.co.uk; and from 'Manchester, England, Church of England' records at Ancestry.co.uk.

9. Ed. Mike Buckley, S*t Chad's Church Saddleworth, Monumental Inscriptions*: p. 54: No. 276 William Shaw of Grottonhead, 1776 and Esther his widow, 1779; No. 277 'Alice, the wife of William Shaw of Grottonhead, she died Sep 8th 1767 in the 35th year of her age. Also the said William Shaw died June 8 1782 in the 53 Year of his Age'.

10. *Bailey's British Directory, or Merchant's and Trader's useful companion, for the year 1784*: Bailey, William, printer in Warrington, Birmingham & London

11. James Butterworth, The *Parochial Chapelry of Saddleworth*, p. 46

12. 'West Yorkshire England Select Land Tax Records 1704-1932, Agbrigg Division'
13. 'Estates in the Several Counties of York and Lancaster and Chester belonging to John Buckley Esq., 1779': M. Buckley et al, 'Mapping Saddleworth Vol II': pp. 96-127, in particular pp. 114-115. An informative account of the Buckley family is at pp. 97-99
14. *C.E.Higson papers, Lees and its Neighbourhood*: Oldham Local Studies and Archives, H151.
15. *Saddleworth & Lees Churchyard Burials*, Manchester & Lancashire Family History Society, CDRom 2005; also 'Manchester England, Church of England: Deaths and Burials 1813-1985', Ancestry.co.uk
16. 'England and Wales Non-Conformist and Non-Parochial Registers, 1567-1970', Ancestry.co.uk
17. 'England Census 1841', Ancestry.co.uk. All subsequent data from census returns is sourced at Ancestry.co.uk
18. The National Archives (TNA), WO/12/522-525: 'General Muster Books and Pay Lists: 2nd Dragoons (Royal Scots Greys)'
19. 'Marriage certificate' in Shaw family papers: Samuel, Sarah Jane and Thomas Hayes all signed their own names confidently. Thomas Hayes had served a seven year apprenticeship as an engraver in Staffordshire from 1842-1849, starting at the age of 13. A record of his indenture of apprenticeship has survived in family papers; the principal conditions are almost identical to those of John Shaw in 1674 who trained as a weaver in Saddleworth – see chapter 12.
20. 'Will of Samuel Shaw formerly of the city of Manchester', 1868, District Probate Registry

18 : A PROVIDENTIAL LIFE

1. Marriage certificate, St Michael & All Angels, Ashton-under-Lyne
2. Baptism Register, Providence Chapel, 1807-1837; 'England and Wales Non-Conformist and Non-Parochial Registers: 1567-1970', Ancestry.co.uk
3. Edward Baines, p. 264

4. Ibid, pp. 262-269. The population of Woodbrook and employment details: 'England Census', 1841 and 1851.

5. Bernard Barnes, 'The Early Cotton Industry in Saddleworth', *SHS Bulletin 10.1*, 1980, p. 11

6. Anthony Howe, *The Cotton Masters, 1830-1860,* Clarendon Press, 1984, p. 62

7. David W Bebbington, *Victorian Nonconformity,* Cascade Books, 2011, p. 23

8. See Edwin Waugh: Home-Life of the Lancashire Factory Folk during the Cotton Famine, reprinted from the Manchester Examiner and Times of 1862, a Public Domain Book, 2012.

9. 'Lincoln's Letter to the Working-Men of Manchester, 19 January 1863', American Civil War Society (UK), Archives

10. *Worrall's Commercial and General Directory of Oldham, Royton, Shaw, Middleton, Lees, Saddleworth and adjoining districts,* 1880, Oldham Local Studies and Archives, L2624 F7: Coal Dealers listed in Lees in 1875 and 1880 include: Stephen Shaw, Spring Lane; also Winterbottom Brothers & Co Limited, Lees, Mossley, Grotton, Gorton, Openshaw, Delph, Saddleworth & Oldham Stations and at Royle Street Wharf Manchester.

11. See: Hartley Bateson: *Providential Lives, A History of Providence Church Springhead: 1807-1957*, Oldham, 1957

12. M A Smith, 'Saddleworth and the Religious Census of 1851', *SHS Bulletin 13.3*, 1983, p. 72

13. Ed. C.E. Higson, *Providence Chapel, Springhead: Monumental Inscriptions*, No.104, OLA: L8533. The same grave contains Stephen's grandson Harry Wilde (Mary Emma's son, a builder's merchant) who died in 1939, and Harry's wife Esther, who died in 1953.

14. 'Manchester England Non-Conformist Marriages: 1758-1937', Ancestry.co.uk

15. Ed. C.E. Higson, *Providence Chapel Springhead: Monumental Inscriptions*, No. 103

16. 'England Census': 1881: Hugh and Hannah are recorded living with Stephen's widow Mary, who is a "coal dealer". Hugh's occupation is "coal salesman".

17. 'Will of Hugh Winterbottom', proved 1921': District Probate Registry

18. 'Company No. 9752, Winterbottom Brothers and Co. Ltd.', incorporated 1875; reconstituted as Hugh Winterbottom & Sons 1933; dissolved by 1948; TNA BT31/30870/9752
19. 'Matilda Standring death certificate, 1859', General Register Office
20. 'England and Wales FreeBMD Marriage Index: 1837-1915', Ancestry.co.uk. Sarah Jane Edwards death certificate: General Register Office
21. Administration of the estates of Robert Wilde, 1914, and Mary Emma Wilde, 1917: District Probate Registry

VI : ASHTON-UNDER-LYNE (1839-1960)

19 : 'A CONSCIENTIOUS AND HIGH PRINCIPLED MAN'

1. William Glover, *History of Ashton-under-Lyne and the Surrounding District,* Reporter Office, Ashton, 1884, p. 30
2. 'Letters patent of Henry VI': Tameside Archives and Local Studies (TLA): DDSW/MED; also John Rylands University Library Special Collections (Deansgate): EGR1/5/1/1
3. Family record entries in: *A Practical & Explanatory Commentary of the Holy Bible*, published by J S Virtue, London,1864, Shaw Family Papers
4. Robert Currie, Alan Gilbert, Lee Horsley, *Churches and Churchgoers: Patterns of church growth in the British Isles since 1700,* Clarendon Press, Oxford, 1977, pp. 86-89
5. Hartley Bateson, p. 10
6. 'Prospectus, Zion British School Lees'; 'Public Examination of the British School at Lees', Oldham Chronicle April 7 1860: Oldham Local Studies and Archives, L32232
7. This and several other details of Eli's life and funeral are drawn from his detailed obituary: 'Sudden Death of Mr Eli Shaw', Ashton Reporter, Saturday July 16 1898, TLA
8. 'Ryecroft Church Member Rolls 1865-1883': TLA, NC1/10/3/2
9. Anon, *Half a Century of Independency in Ashton-under-Lyne*, Ashton-under-Lyne, 1867: pp. 27 and 59-60; William Glover pp. 269-271
10. William Glover, pp. 269-273

11. 'Ryecroft Sunday Schools', Church Meeting Book 1865-1885, p. 22: TLA: NC1/10/3/2
12. *The Ryecroft Congregational Magazine*, March 1891: TLA: NC1/8/8. The Parallel Bible is in the Shaw family papers. Published in 1890, it contains parallel texts of the Authorsied and Revised translations of the Bible.
13. Ian Haynes, *Cotton in Ashton*, Tameside Metropolitan Borough, 1987, p. 41
14. ibid, pp. 37-38
15. William Glover, p. 270
16. *Eli Shaw Photograph Album*, c. 1898, Shaw Family Papers, p. 38
17. William Glover, p. 272
18. Shaw family papers
19. 'Will of Thomas Hulme, Shopkeeper, of Lees', 1828, LRO: WCW/Supra/C847/41
20. 'Will of Richard Hulme, Provision Dealer of Lees', 1863: District Probate Registry
21. George Shaw's account book, and Charles Shaw's letter to his children, 1931: Shaw family papers.
22. 'Will of Mary Hulme', 1866, District Probate Registry
23. See Hartley Bateson, pp. 41-44.
24. 'Will of Richard Henry Shaw', 27 July 1898, District Probate Registry. For Richard Shaw's life, see chapter 20.
25. 'New York Passenger and Crew Lists, 1820-1957'; Ancestry.co.uk; Joseph Ogden Lees arrived in New York from Liverpool on 28 September 1907;
26. 'Will of Joseph Ogden Lees, 1919' and 'Will of Sarah Ogden Lees, 1924', District Probate Registry

20 : THINGS FALL APART

1. *'Sudden Death of Councillor Eli Shaw of Ashton',The Ashton Reporter*, 16 July 1898, TLA
2. 'Will of Eli Shaw, 1898', District Probate Registry. The valuation of his estate at £2,631. 17s. 11d equates to 7,975 days' wages in 2017 for a skilled tradesman according to nationalarchives.gov.uk/currency converter. This compares to 957 days for William Shawe in 1623 (see chapter 8, note11)and to 656 days for William Shaw in 1701 (see chapter 12, note 3).

3. *Eli Shaw Photograph Album*, Shaw family papers, c. 1898
4. TLA: Images: t15489
5. *Grace's Guide to British Industrial History*: Grace'sguide. co.uk/1891_Cotton_Mills-in_Ashton-under-Lyne, p. 49: 'Harper Twist Co, Limited, Mossley road; 40,968 spindles, 288/368 twist, 341/448 weft. Pay day second Wednesday. George Hy. Shaw, secretary and salesman.'
6. TNA: WO372/18/18161. See also: 'UK World War I Service Medal and Award Rolls 1914-1920'; and 'British Army World War I Medal Rolls Index Cards, 1914-1920'; Memorial Plaque, TLA: images: t16716
7. 'Will of George Hervey Shaw, 1923', District Probate Registry
8. 'Will of Herbert Eli Shaw, 1956', District Probate Registry
9. 'Ryecroft Church Minute Book pp. 245-247', TLA: NC1/10/3/7
10. 'Ryecroft Church Meeting Book, p. 160; TLA NC1/10/3/2
11. Death Certificate in Shaw family papers. Grave of Richard Shaw: Dukinfield Cemetery B4- ASH812
12. 'Will of Richard Henry Shaw, 1898', District Probate Rewgistry
13. 'Ryecroft Church Members Roll', TLA: NC1/10/5/1
14. See 'Electoral Rolls' 1901-1925, Ancestry.co.uk; also 'England Census 1921', FindmyPast
15. Dukinfield Cemetery B3-68ASH. Records for Alfred, Edward and Frank are in the Shaw family papers
16. 'Probate of Frank Hayes, 1878', District Probate Registry

21 : A MODERN MAN

1. Record entries in family bible, Shaw family papers
2. Manchester City Football Club (previously known as St Mark's in 1880, and Ardwick in 1887) was founded and adopted its current name in 1894, the same year that the Manchester Ship Canal opened. The club badge has always shown a ship in full sail, representing the Ship Canal, and three diagonal stripes below, representing the three rivers of Manchester: the Irwell, Irk and Medlock.
3. This and other quotations, unless stated, are taken from his obituary: 'Death of Mr Charles Shaw, Prominent Liberal and Sunday School Worker': The Ashton Reporter, July 16 1937, Tameside Local Studies and Archives

4. Ashton Golf Club: the first hundred years: 1913-2013: TLA qL796.352
5. 'Ryecroft Church Records: Members Roll', TLA, NC1/10/5/1; 'Deacons Minute Book', NC1/10/4/5; 'Church Meeting Book', NC1/10/3/4
6. 'Ryecroft Temporary Council School – former British School', TNA: ED 21/8894 (1891-1911); ED 49/3569 (1911-1913); ED 21/31977 (1929-1933)
7. ' Note to Donald & Madge and my Wife', 1931, Shaw family papers
8. 'Ryecroft Church Meeting Book', TLA NC1/10/3/4
9. Shaw family papers
10. 'Manchester Grammar School Dinners': March 25th 1918. Shaw family papers
11. *Ashton Lacrosse Club Centenary Brochure: 1896-1996*, Stalybridge, 1996, Shaw Family Papers. The front page displays a photograph of the 1896 team, which includes Charles Shaw. A framed copy of the photograph is at TLA: DD380/4/3. The English Lacrosse Union (1892 -) merged with the Ladies' Lacrosse Association (1912 -) to form the English Lacrosse Association in 1996.
12. 'Fashionable Wedding in Ashton', Ashton Reporter, September 1933
13. See chapter 1, Note 8. The 1881 census records Staffordshire as the county with the third highest number of Shaws in England, albeit many fewer than Yorkshire or Lancashire.
14. For a photograph of the Hewitt pharmacy, see TLA Images, t48094
15. 'Diploma of Honour', Shaw family papers
16. A1-ASH 560/1: Shaw family papers

INDEX

Entries are in alphabetical order, except for the last two sections, where they are grouped by generation, in broadly chronological sequence

Albion Chapel, Ashton 189, 195, 205, 223
Almondbury 37, 38, 46
Andrew family 96-103, 119
Apprenticeship 121-2
Arthurs ix, 49, 65, 73, 106, 120, 126
Ashton 24, 27, 36-7, 43, 56, 59, 61, 123, 142, 155, 162-3, 170-1, 178, 187-228
Ashton, Manor of 13, 15, 18, 26
Ashton Reporter 208, 222
de Assheton family 12, 18, 26, 187
Austerlands 17, 43, 170-174, 190

Barn 141
Baxter, Rev. Richard 57, 63, 136, 143
Bees 50
Bentley, John 54, 65, 118, 127-8
Boarshurst 20, 31, 39, 44-6, 50, 53, 56, 58, 69-83, 87-9, 94-7, 104-8, 129-30, 156
Booth, of Dunham Massey 8, 95, 187
Broadbent, William 111-4
Brown, Jane Ellen w/o Richard Shaw, d.1966, & Annie, Alice 212-4, 223
Buckden Castle 13
Buckley, name 36
Buckley, Abel of Ashton 195-6
Buckley, of Grottonhead 158-9, 162-4
Burgh, Thomas de 9-10
Butterworth, James 19, 42, 60, 70, 162

Carr Barn 44, 97, 120, 148
Cartwright of Boarshurst & Fur Lane

76, 77, 88, 110-114, 127
St Chad, Church of 53-5, 57-8, 67, 84, 131, 137-142, 145-8, 151, 165-6
Charles I, King 48
Charles II, King 107
Civil War, The English 48, 57; The American 175
Clothiers 56, 59, 64, 123, 142, 147
Coal 176, 178, 185
Contrariants Roll (1322) 22, 24, 28, 31
Cotton 59, 171-2, 174-8, 185, 196, 210 218, 226, 230
Courts Baron & Leet 46, 79-80, 130, 149
Court of Chancery 64, 98-103, 110-114, 156
Cromwell, Oliver 52, 85

Disease 22, 28, 34, 51-4, 58, 86, 105, 131
Domesday Book 6, 10, 11

Eastwood, Mary & family of Lees 170-180
Edward VI, King 63

Fur Lane (Greenfield Stye) 23, 28, 31, 44, 97, 106, 120, 148, 161, 165
Friarmere 43, 154
Farrer, of Saddleworth Manor, 43, 96, 150

Garsome 45-6, 70-2, 76-8, 81, 94, 123-4, 135, 143

Gartside, name 36
Gaunt, John of 16
Glossop 123, 148
Godley, Manor of, 9, 10, 13
God-parents xix, 75, 83, 86, 104
Golburn Clough xxi, 44, 145-52,
    154-5, 161
Green, Rev Thomas of
    Ryecroft 199-203, 207
Greenfield River (Chew Brook) 70,
    71, 128
Grotton 17, 34, 43, 160, 164
Grottonhead 56, 66, 130, 158-161
Grotton Hollow 176, 178

Halls ix, 125-6, 142, 181
Hayes, Frank, Sarah Jane &
    Thomas 122, 169, 215-16
Halmote del Schagh (1401) 29-30
Harper Twist Mill, Ashton 200-1, 210
Harrop, of Shawhouses 143
Hawkyard, of Tamewater 32, 137-142,
    148, 215
Hearth Tax 35, 38, 44,107, 135, 156
Henry IV, King 12, 17
Henry V, King 17
Henry VIII, King 30, 63
Hewitt, Silas, Clarissa, Marion of
    Dukinfield & Ashton 227-230
Hirst, of Springhead 206, 223, 226
Huddersfield 36, 37, 70, 111
Hulme, of Lees 194, 204-7, 211,
    215, 226,
Husbandmen 44, 56, 63-4, 87, 94,
    98, 112, 123, 136
Husbandry gear xxi, 49-50, 83, 109

James I, King 74
John, King xx, 9
Julian Calendar xxi-xxii

Kenworthy, of Lower House &
    Thornlee 109, 115, 118-9,
    154, 165

Kinders, John Whitehead of 65, 97,
    117-8, 121, 126-7

Land Tax 149-152, 162, 165
Lane 43, 156-7, 160, 164
Lay Subsidy (1543/5) 30-35, 44
Leases 45-8, 70, 75-77, 81, 123-8, 130,
    135-7
Lees 43, 61, 167, 170-1, 174, 176, 205,
    207, 217-8, 225
Liberal party 219
Lincoln, Abraham 175
Literacy 62-3, 66
Longdendale 9-10, 15-16, 25
Lordsmere 28, 31, 41, 70, 95, 154-5
Lower House 44, 58, 65, 71, 73, 76, 81,
    89, 92-3, 97, 104-10, 117-8, 121,
    123-131, 136, 142, 150, 158, 215
Lydgate 43, 119, 161. 167, 170
Lytham St Anne's 211, 213-4

Manchester 56, 61, 111, 155, 168,
    175-8, 187, 194, 228
Manchester Ship Canal 218, 222-3
Manchester Grammar School 225
Marsden 36, 38-9, 88, 111
Mason, Hugh 188, 196, 201
Mossley 56, 61, 123, 212
Mottram 18, 56, 50

Names 2-8, 32-5
Neville, William de 10, 11, 13
Non-conformism 57-8, 62, 67, 165,
    170-2, 178, 189-90, 194-6

Oldham 36-7, 43, 56, 59, 61, 67, 123,
    155, 171, 178
Oldham Chronicle 193, 203, 226

Peterloo Massacre 61-2, 166
Platt 32, 73, 75, 77-8, 83, 89
Poll Tax (1379) 4, 5, 26, 28, 33-5
Population: of Saddleworth 34, 44,
    51-4, 58-9, 123; of Ashton 188

Primogeniture xx, 9, 13, 20, 22, 23
Protestation Returns (1641) 35, 37, 38, 57, 60
Providence Chapel & Sabbath School 62, 67, 165-6, 170, 172-8, 190, 196, 206

Quick Mere 18, 43, 56, 95, 97, 111, 130-1, 153, 155-161

Radclyffes of Shaw Hall & Ballgreave 25, 29, 43, 85, 88, 93
Ramsdens of Saddleworth Manor 31, 37, 43, 47-8, 57, 70, 95
Richard I, King 18
Richard II, King 16
Richard III 27
Rochdale 7, 36-7, 43, 67, 174, 194
Ryecroft church & schools 62, 177, 194-200, 207-8, 211-2, 220-1, 223
Ryetop, 44, 64, 88, 147, 155

Scolefield, of Arthurs 36, 50, 65, 73, 82, 89, 94, 106, 121-2
Schaghe, William del 22, 24-6, 30
Schaghe, Robert del 26-28-30, 34
Shawhouses 44, 87, 133-8, 141-5, 150
Shaw Hall 7, 20-1, 43, 85
Shaw, Herbert, of Staffordshire & Ashton, d.1923: 228
Shaw Mere 7, 17, 21, 42, 130
Shaw, R Cunliffe 7, 23, 27, 36
Shaw, Gyles of Boarshurst d.1634: 46, 50, 72-8, 87-9, 94-103, 148, 156
Shaw, Henry of Lane s/o Gyles, d.1688: 65, 87, 95, 98-103, 115, 123, 156-7
Shaw, John of Boarshurst s/o Gyles, d.1665: 76, 79, 96, 98-103
Shaw, Thomas of Uppermill s/o Gyles, d.1650/1: 95-6
Shaw, Ralphe of Boarshurst d.1637: 52, 65, 71-3, 75-80, 87, 89, 94-6, 104
Shaw, Richard of Boarshurst s/o Ralphe, living 1658: 78, 79, 87
Shay (1545) xxi, 31, 32

Slaithwaite, 37-9, 87
Smethurst, Helen of Oldham & Ashton: 218, 222-3
Sport 212, 219-20, 227
Springhead 43, 62, 67, 170, 190, 206, 225
Staley Rental 16, 25-6
Stalybridge 10, 106, 188, 211
Staveley, of Staley Manor 8-21, 25, 28, 43, 187-8
Staveley, de Saddleworth 9, 17, 20-8, 32-3
Sunday Schools 67, 171, 176, 189-90, 196

Tame, The River 44, 70, 187
Tamewater 66, 137-8
Thornlee 17, 43, 61, 154-7, 160-8, 170
Tithes, Corn 108
Trial by Combat xix, 16
Tunstead 28, 31, 50, 85, 94, 107, 126

Uppermill 44, 48, 50, 53, 56, 97, 120, 134, 142, 167, 174

Vick, Madge, Helen, Dorothy 224
Victoria, Queen 218

Wellihole 56, 130
Whewall, Marie & Francis 39, 45, 52, 64-5, 74-80, 85-9, 92-3, 105
Whewall, of Tunstead & Lane 31, 33, 50, 77, 87-90
Wilde, of Springhead 184-5, 207
William, King and Mary, Queen 107
Windows Tax 107
Winterbottom, Johnson & Edna of Miles Platting 174, 176-8, 180-2, 205
Winterbottom, Hugh & Hannah of Lees 176, 181-3, 205, 207
Woodbrook 171-4, 189
Wool, 23, 50, 59, 95-8, 110, 115-7, 123, 127, 129, 141-5, 155, 166, 174, 178

Zion, Chapel & School, Lees 62, 167, 174, 191-3, 196, 215

SHAWS OF LOWER HOUSE & ASHTON (Table 1: x-xii)
William of Boarshurst d.1623: 39, 45, 52, 65, 70-80, 92-3, 94, 98, 104, 156
Katrine, w/o William, d.1627/8: xix, xxi, 76-7, 81, 89-92, 110
Edmund s/o William, d. 1623: 72-4, 78, 81-3
Agnes d/o William, d.1633: 76-7, 83-4, 91-2
Robert s/o William, d.1623: 82, 89- 93
George s/o William, d.1638/42: 82, 91-3, 104
John of Lower House s/o Robert, d.1697/8: 66, 88-9, 92-3, 106-114
Thomas s/o George, d.1657: 89, 91, 93, 104-5
William s/o Thomas, d.1701: 65, 74, 77, 89, 93, 104-5, 109, 115-20, 125
John of Fur Lane s/o Thomas, b. 1655: 89, 104-8, 120-22, 215
William of Shawhouses s/o William, d.1737: 115, 134-9
John of Golburnclough s/o William, d.1789: 141-152
William of Golburnclough s/o John, d.1798: 147-151
John of Thornlee s/o William, d.1821: 148, 152, 154-5, 160-2, 164-6, 170
Samuel of Manchester s/o John, d.1868: 168-9, 215-6
Stephen of Lees s/o John, d.1881: 61, 166, 169-185, 231; children 170-185
Eli of Ashton s/o Stephen, d.1898: 62, 106, 169, 171, 174, 185, 189-203, 207-216, 218
George of Ashton, s/o Eli, d.1923: 201, 209-211
Herbert Eli s/o George, d.1956: 210-11
Richard of Ashton s/o Eli, d.1898: 198-9, 202-3, 209-214
Alfred of Bristol, s/o Richard, d.1972: 212-14
Charles of Ashton s/o Eli, d.1937: 205, 208-9, 217-224
Donald of Ashton s/o Charles, d.1982: 224-231

SHAWS OF LOWER HOUSE & GROTTONHEAD (Table 7: xviii)
Thomas Senior of Lower House s/o William, d.1748: 125-129, 142, 158
William of Grottonhead s/o Thomas, d.1772: 129-131, 158
William of Grottonhead s/o William, d.1782: 158-9
Hugh the Younger of Grottonhead s/o William, d.1831: 159
Hugh the Elder of Grottonhead, s/o Thomas, d.1814: 158-162, 165
William of Thornlee & Grotton s/o Hugh the Elder, d. 1797: 160-162
John of Lane & Knowles Lane s/o Hugh the Elder, d.1838: 160-2, 165
Thomas of Grottonhead & Springhead s/o Hugh the Elder, d.1853: 161